# CHAMPAGNE CHARLIE

# CHAMPAGNE CHARLIE

## THE FRENCHMAN WHO TAUGHT
## AMERICANS TO LOVE CHAMPAGNE

DON & PETIE KLADSTRUP

Potomac Books

AN IMPRINT OF THE UNIVERSITY OF NEBRASKA PRESS

© 2021 by Don and Petie Kladstrup

All rights reserved. Potomac Books is an imprint of the
University of Nebraska Press.
Manufactured in the United States of America.

Library of Congress Cataloging-in-Publication Data
Names: Kladstrup, Don, author. | Kladstrup, Petie, author.
Title: Champagne Charlie: the Frenchman who taught
Americans to love champagne / Don and Petie Kladstrup.
Description: Lincoln: Potomac Books, an imprint of the
University of Nebraska Press, [2021] | Includes bibliographical
references and index.
Identifiers: LCCN 2021015716
ISBN 9781640123946 (hardback)
ISBN 9781640125025 (epub)
ISBN 9781640125032 (pdf)
Subjects: LCSH: Champagne (Wine)—History.
Classification: LCC TP555 .K59 2021 | DDC 663/.224—dc23
LC record available at https://lccn.loc.gov/2021015716

Set in Arno Pro by Laura Buis.

# CONTENTS

# ILLUSTRATIONS

# INTRODUCTION

Charles Heidsieck felt his knees buckle and the blood drain from his face as Union soldiers hauled him away to prison. Snarls of the man in charge, General Benjamin Butler, a figure nicknamed "the Beast," rang in his ears: "You are a spy! You're nothing but a French dog and deserve to be hanged!"

For the better part of a year, the man widely known as "Champagne Charlie" had been roaming the South, shuttling between the ports of Mobile and New Orleans, then parts of the Confederacy, in an effort to collect money for champagne that had been shipped there, money his sales agent had cheated him out of.

But with the Civil War intensifying and a Union blockade of Southern ports tightening, Heidsieck decided it would be better to leave the country and return to France. His plan—get to New Orleans and make his way to Mexico or Cuba, where he'd try to make connections to Europe.

New Orleans, however, had fallen to Union forces. Nevertheless, as a citizen of France—a country officially neutral though sympathetic to the Confederacy—Heidsieck still thought he was safe, that his French passport would protect him. He was wrong. When soldiers discovered he was carrying a diplomatic pouch containing secret dispatches offering help to the Confederates, he was arrested as a spy and thrown into prison.

Was Heidsieck a spy, an agent of the French government bent on helping the South? Or was he merely an innocent business-man, as he claimed, trying to make a name for himself by selling champagne?

Heidsieck had gambled everything to go to America and do business there. He was convinced it was the "land of opportunity," a place where he could make a name for himself and his champagne house. He would succeed beyond his wildest dreams, his name becoming synonymous with celebration and good times.

But now, languishing in a federal prison with a hangman's noose awaiting him, he was about to experience the worst of times.

||||||||

The only thing on our minds was a good time.

It was Christmas 1989. We were living in South Africa and about to host a party for some of our colleagues in the news business. At the time the country was still ruled by the repressive system of apartheid, but there were increasing rumors that Nelson Mandela would soon be freed from Robben Island after twenty-seven years of imprisonment.

News media from around the world rushed to step up their presence in the country to be ready for the historic event, many of them headquartered in the same building where Don's office at ABC Television News was based. We invited all of them to our party.

One of our guests was a woman from Soweto, the sprawling Black township outside Johannesburg. Her name was Mpho, which means "gift" in Zulu. She was the wife of the man who ran the front desk at ABC. Although he spent his days working with a multinational group of journalists who were nearly all white, *her* life was centered in Soweto. Johannesburg was like a foreign country to her, as it was to most of Soweto's residents, all of whom needed a government pass to enter the city. We made the necessary arrangements to get the couple to our home for the evening.

We'd recently returned from France with several bottles of champagne for the party but were hoping at least one of them would "survive" so we could have it all to ourselves. Nonetheless, all the bottles were well chilled by the time the first guests came through the door, and Don had uncorked the first of them.

Mpho was visibly nervous when she and her husband arrived. She had never been a guest in the home of a white person before.

It was midsummer in the Southern Hemisphere, and we had tables and chairs outside. Don ushered her to one and asked her if she would like a glass of champagne. She said she had heard of champagne but never tasted it. She wasn't sure if she would like it; it sounded strange. But because everyone else was drinking it, she bravely agreed to try "just a little."

Don poured about half a glass and smiled. "It may tickle your nose, but don't worry," he said. "If you don't like it, we have other stuff."

Looking puzzled and wary, Mpho very cautiously lifted the glass to her mouth, barely wetting her lips.

And then a small surprised smile appeared, quickly growing into a gorgeous grin. There was a glow in her eyes and a look of pure wonder on her face.

With that look of discovery and delight still on her face, she shyly asked, "Could I have a little more, please?"

Rarely has champagne given us more pleasure than it did then, for in that brief moment, champagne did what it has done millions of times before and since: it broke down barriers, set the stage, and started the celebration.

Most importantly, it brought people together.

|||||||||

History is replete with such "champagne moments," including a famous one that never happened. Dom Pérignon, "the father of champagne" who codified the rules of good winemaking in the seventeenth century, did not, as the story goes, accidentally "invent" champagne and exclaim, "I have tasted the stars!" That comment was the creation of marketing moguls, and a brilliant one as well, for it embodies the feeling and spirit so many people have experienced upon their first taste of champagne.

Many of those moments have been associated with romance, both its beginning and its end. "You were my cup of tea," some departing lover said, "but I drink champagne now." Honoré de Balzac viewed it from a different angle: "Great love affairs start with champagne and end with tisane." Bette Davis, who knew a thing or two about romance, realized, "There comes a time in every woman's life when the only thing that helps is a glass of champagne." Casanova certainly agreed. He considered it "essential equipment for seduction."

Weddings, baptisms, the launching of ships, spraying crowds at car rallies, ringing in the New Year . . . champagne is linked to so many things, but not all of them are happy occasions.

On June 22, 1911, for example, British explorer Robert Falcon Scott and his team sat down in their base camp in Antarctica to celebrate Midwinter Day, the midpoint of the long winter night. They were on their way to the South Pole, hoping to be the first people there. Dinner featured seal soup, roast beef, plum pudding, minced pies, fish, fruits, nuts, chocolates, and, as Scott said, "an unstinted supply of champagne." The champagne was Champagne Charles Heidsieck. "We drank to the success of the mission and woke up with a few bad heads in the morning," Scott said.

He and four companions arrived at the South Pole on January 17, 1912, only to discover that they had been beaten by a Norwegian team led by Roald Amundsen. They perished in the subzero cold as they tried to make it back to their base camp.[1]

Champagne has also been linked to war.

In World War II, Prime Minister Winston Churchill admonished his commanders, "Remember gentlemen, it's not just France we're fighting for; it's champagne!" Foreseeing the conflict to come, Paul Claudel, a French diplomat and poet, consoled fellow government officials, "Gentleman, in the little moment that remains to us between the crisis and the catastrophe, we may as well drink a glass of champagne."

Even Napoléon Bonaparte, for whom war was a regular occurrence, famously opined about champagne, "In victory you deserve it; in defeat you need it."

That this universal symbol of friendship and celebration is so closely associated with war is not really surprising. The region itself

1. Robert Falcon Scott team after one too many bottles of Charles Heidsieck champagne. Courtesy of Champagne Charles Heidsieck.

has been drenched with more blood than perhaps any other place on Earth. Throughout the centuries, nearly every European conflict, including both world wars, took place primarily or at least partly in Champagne.

World War I inflicted so much destruction that whole towns and villages disappeared for good. Vineyards were infused with so much poison gas that some remain too dangerous to cultivate even today.[2]

War, however, did nothing to stop the growth of champagne's popularity. Throughout the first half of the eighteenth century, champagne makers produced about three hundred thousand bottles a year. Today that figure is more than three hundred million. Those bottles make their way to nearly every country on the planet, with the United States ranked second, just behind Great Britain.[3] This came to be due largely to the exploits of a dashing, young Frenchman named Charles-Camille Heidsieck, a.k.a. "Champagne Charlie." More than anyone else, it was he who introduced champagne to America. He was the one who captured its heart and taste buds and sparked the love affair between a country and a wine that still exists today.

Heidsieck was a nineteenth-century figure, but in at least one place he is still vibrantly alive—the offices of Champagne Charles Heidsieck. There his spirit roams the halls and *crayères*; there his name is still invoked as though he is listening in and directing operations in person.

His name is not invoked lightly. That is a lesson we learned when we were invited to lunch at the company's headquarters in Reims. Among those present that day were Stephen Leroux, director-general of the company, and Marie-France Beck, who worked at the champagne house in public relations and as historian and archivist for many years.

The food at our lunch was wonderful, but the champagne was even better, beginning with a Charles Heidsieck Brut Réserve and followed by a Blanc de Blanc and a 2006 Brut Millésimé. But then came a champagne that one connoisseur described as "a sinful delight to the senses." He wasn't exaggerating. It was the company's luxury cuvée, the Blanc des Millénaires, a champagne produced only under the most perfect conditions. Only seven vintages of this extraordinary champagne had ever seen the light of day: 1983, 1985, 1990, 1995, 2004, 2005, and 2006. We were savoring the latest, and Don, like the rest of us, was in seventh heaven.

"This reminds me of another Heidsieck I once tasted," he said. "It was . . ." but before he could finish, Marie-France abruptly cut him off.

"Not '*Heidsieck*'!" she said. "You can say you bought a bottle of 'Charles' or a bottle of 'Charles Heidsieck' but not 'Heidsieck.' Never just 'Heidsieck'!" There was twinkle in her eye, but she meant every word.

It was a telling moment, for it underscored the close connection that those like Marie-France have for the champagne house and its founder. It also helps explain the spell the man known as Champagne Charlie continues to weave nearly a century and a half after his death.

We first "met" him several years ago while working on another book about champagne and the devastation that occurred in the region during World War I. He was little more than a footnote and reduced to a half-dozen pages, but it prompted one reader to ask,

"Isn't there more to his story?" *Well, yes*, we thought, and we always hoped the day would come when we could tell it, but information was hard to come by. Many records were lost when Reims was mercilessly bombarded in World War I and, later, when the Heidsieck champagne house underwent a change in ownership in 2011.

It was Marie-France who saved us. "Let me talk to some people," she said. She was referring to Heidsieck's descendants. It turned out that the family had archives of their own, boxes and boxes filled with hundreds of original letters, legal documents, and other papers that had never been made public. Given her close relationship with the family, Marie-France persuaded them to let us see what was there.

Much of it was private correspondence between Charles and his wife, Amélie. The letters, composed in the most delicate handwriting imaginable, were now so old and fragile that we feared they might crumble when we picked them up to read. But they provided an intimate portrait of two people who loved each other dearly and were so charged with emotion that there were times we almost felt like voyeurs as we went through them.

The letters also offered a tantalizing glimpse of America in the mid-nineteenth century as Charles traveled the country to introduce his champagne to Americans . . . and as the nation hurtled toward civil war.

For someone as famous as Champagne Charlie, for someone whose life was filled with as much adventure as his was, it's surprising that so little has been written about him. One of the first efforts was by his eldest daughter, Marie, who wrote an article for a French magazine in 1920. It was never published.

In 1957, two of Heidsieck's grandsons dipped into the family archives and compiled a lengthy memoir under the cumbersome title "The Adventures of a Citizen of Rheims in the United States in 1857, 1860, and 1861, during the American War of Secession." The title did not get in the way of the colorful stories that were there. "Friends have expressed their opinion that this story merited attention outside the family," they said. "We shall therefore endeavor to take you with us to the America of the last century."

How could we resist jumping aboard! Especially after they went on to say that they hoped their account would "serve to strengthen the ties that join France, and Rheims in particular, to the destiny of her American friends." Their family memoir was expanded in 1962 to include more material from the family archives. There was also a slim volume published in 1995 by two French historians as part of series of books aimed at promoting the champagne industry.

But that's about it, aside from a 1989 Canadian film starring Hugh Grant as Champagne Charlie. It bore little resemblance to reality and was roundly trashed by critics.

Our hope is that readers of this book will become better acquainted with the man who helped transform America from a beer-swilling, whiskey-guzzling country into one that fell in love with champagne. What struck us when we began our research was how different Heidsieck was from the carefree, party-hopping dandy his nickname implies and as he is often perceived. He was, in fact, a savvy, sophisticated businessman, a man far ahead of his time. Long before the days of advertising and mass marketing, Heidsieck understood the value of publicity and knew how to use his celebrity status.

But he could also be reckless, take too many chances . . . and it nearly cost him his life.

# CHAMPAGNE CHARLIE

# 1

|||||||||||

# The First Sip

It began with a giggle.

The year was 1791. The place, Philadelphia, then the capital of the United States, where the elegant, sophisticated but reserved Martha Washington had just had her first sip of sparkling wine. She could not stop giggling.

According to official records, her husband, the president, had broken with tradition that evening to serve "several glasses of sparkling champagne" at the end of the meal. Everyone present at the dinner, which included close friends and government dignitaries, lingered nearly an hour over the "new" beverage until finally, following the custom of the day, the men withdrew to another room, "leaving the ladies in high glee."

The bubbly they so enjoyed was some of the first to trickle into America. It was so good, in fact, that Washington promptly instructed his wine adviser to order more. The adviser's name was Thomas Jefferson, who, at that time, was also Washington's secretary of state. It would be he who would raise America's appreciation for fine wine, including champagne, even higher when he became president.

The champagne that Washington wanted more of was Dorsay, one of Jefferson's favorites. It was something Jefferson discovered during his sojourn in France as the fledgling country's plenipotentiary. Wasting no time, he wrote a letter to William Short, the American chargé

2. Martha Washington, ca. 1800. Smithsonian National Portrait Gallery.

d'affaires in Paris. "Being just now informed that a vessel sails this afternoon for a port in Normandy, and knowing that the President wished to have some champagne, I have been to him, and he desires forty dozen bottles." Jefferson asked Short to "procure it of the growth of Monsieur Dorsay's vineyard at Aÿ opposite Epernay in Champagne, and of the best year he has, for present drinking." It was clear the president planned to serve the "new" wine again soon and often.[1]

Washington's account books show he was a regular customer even before he became president, something that would continue throughout his life. On one occasion he paid sixty-six pence to have "six baskets of champagne" delivered from a boat to his residence, and each basket, or *panier*, contained about seventy-five bottles. According to records at Mount Vernon, "In 1793, as president, Washington purchased four hundred eighty five bottles of champagne and burgundy, which cost him $355.67 [about $9,500 in today's money]. Six bottles were 'got as a sample' in May of 1794 and another twelve found their way to the executive mansion in November of the same year." Washington would have paid around $1.00 per bottle for his champagne.

His first exposure to champagne may have occurred in Williamsburg, Virginia, thirty years earlier when he was a young and successful officer in the colonial militia. He and Martha spent their honeymoon there. The champagne they enjoyed, however, was probably still, that is, devoid of bubbles, for that was the fashion of the day, and it apparently came from the cellar of the colony's royal governor, who referred to his cellar as "the Vault."

Years later, with Jefferson continuing to buy and select wine for Washington, champagne flowed at presidential and personal dinners. Senator Samuel Johnson of North Carolina wrote that he attended one where "the President and Mrs. Washington served some excellent champagne."

Soon after the American Revolution, a young businessman named Robert Hunter Jr. paid a visit to Washington at Mount Vernon. He was a friend of Washington's secretary, William Shaw, and had been introduced to the general by him.

Hunter recorded he enjoyed "a very elegant supper" about nine o'clock one night, an exceedingly late hour for a meal at the Washingtons' home. Also present that evening was an old friend of Washington's, Richard Henry Lee, president of the Continental Congress. Washington was "anxious to hear the news of Congress," so he postponed his usual early bedtime in order that they could talk.

And apparently drink. "The General sent the bottle about pretty freely after dinner," said Hunter, who also noted that "the General with a few glasses of champagne got quite merry, and being with his intimate friends laughed and talked a good deal." This was a rare and special event, Hunter knew, because "before strangers, [Washington] is generally very reserved and seldom says a word. I was fortunate in being in his company with his particular acquaintances. I'm told that during the war he was never seen to smile."

The next morning after breakfast, Secretary Shaw took Hunter for a walk around the grounds and then to the stables where he saw Washington's famous racehorse Magnolia. "I also saw old *Nelson*, now twenty-two years of age, that carried the General almost always during the war. *Blueskin*, another fine old horse next to him, now and then had that honor . . . [but he] was not the favorite, on account of him not standing fire so well as venerable old *Nelson*. The General makes no manner of use of them now; he keeps them in a nice stable, where they feed away at their ease for their past services."

A nice stable was one thing; a nice table was quite another, and that was one of the things Washington made sure of for the rest of his life, according to Hunter: "Always keeping a genteel table for strangers that almost daily visit him, as a thing of course."[2]

‖‖‖‖‖‖

But no champagne would have made it to Washington's table, or anywhere else for that matter, if it hadn't been for France's King Louis XV.

It was he who, just half a century earlier, had freed champagne from a myriad of shipping restrictions and set the standards for the sparkling wine. Bottles that once came in all shapes and sizes now had to be uniform and contain the same amount of champagne. Instead of stuffing in rags or wooden plugs to seal the bottles, corks had to be used, then tied down with a "three-headed string, well-twisted and knotted in the form of a cross over the cork."[3]

The king's most important contribution, however, was allowing champagne to be shipped in bottles. Prior to 1735, all wine, including champagne, had to be transported in wooden casks because that was how it was taxed. For non-sparkling wines this was not a problem, but for champagne it was disastrous. Wood destroyed the effervescence. Its porous nature allowed the gas to escape, killing the bubbles and resulting in champagne that was flat.

Champagne makers petitioned the king, saying they would soon be out of business unless the laws were changed. Louis was reluctant, but producers had an important ally: Louis's mistress, Madame de Pompadour. She was from the Champagne region and adored its signature drink, famously proclaiming, "Champagne is the only wine that leaves a woman beautiful after drinking it."

After further deliberation, and perhaps a bit of pillow talk, the king said he would permit champagne—but *only* champagne—to be shipped in bottles.

Shipping in bottles, however, accented another problem: the bottles were too fragile and often broke during transport. It was another king, an English one, who came to the rescue.

For several years, King James had watched with growing dismay as the forests of his domain began to shrink. This was because more and more people were cutting down trees for fuel, both for heating and cooking. To help save the woodlands, the king issued a royal edict in 1615 forbidding the burning of wood in glassmaking furnaces. It was a small step from a conservation standpoint but a giant one for champagne makers, since glassmakers now turned to coal to run their furnaces. Coal provided a hotter and more reliable source of heat which resulted in much thicker glass and stronger bottles. In the end, breakage was sharply reduced.

Now, for the first time, producers could begin exploiting champagne's commercial opportunities in earnest and ship bubbly to other countries instead of selling it only for local consumption.[4]

Unfortunately, heavier-duty glass could not solve one problem, and it was an explosive one. No one understood fermentation or how to control it. No one had heard of carbon dioxide, which gives champagne its sparkle but whose buildup in pressure can cause bottles to explode. And 1776, the year of American independence—that great explosion from across the sea—was the worst ever. So much champagne was lost—up to 90 percent—that cellars resembled foamy swamps. Often, there'd be a chain reaction with one exploding bottle setting off others.

Producers were completely mystified. A wholesale wine merchant from Paris, André Jullien, writing in 1824, said, "The phenomena which cause or destroy the quality mousseux are so surprising, that they cannot be explained." Jullien visited all the major vineyards of Champagne as well as those in the rest of France. He was the first wine writer to rate wines in terms of quality, the Robert Parker of his day, using a numerical system of one to five to evaluate the wines, one being the best.

But he was thoroughly stumped when it came to explaining why bottles of champagne exploded. "The same wine drawn the same day into bottles made from the same glass, put down in the same cellar and placed in the same heap [explode in some cases but not in others]. These accidents are so varied and extraordinary that the most experienced dealers cannot foresee, nor prevent them." The worst month "for the bursting of bottles is August," Jullien said. "It is not safe to pass through cellars without being guarded by a mask of iron wire."

Even then, with shards of glass flying through the cellars, lost eyes and scarred hands marked many who labored among the bottles. For many producers, it was a financial disaster. "I started with six thousand bottles," one lamented. "By the end, only one hundred twenty were left." He was so distraught he ran through his cellar hammering the remaining bottles and screaming, "All right then, dammit. Break!"

The result was that most merchants and producers stopped making sparkling champagne. By the end of the eighteenth century, total sales amounted to less than three hundred thousand bottles, a mere 2 percent of all wine made in Champagne.

Only after champagne makers learned how to manage fermentation in the next century did production of sparkling champagne resume, and producers begin exporting their product to every country in Europe—as far east as Russia, as far north as Sweden, and to England, where the thirst for sparkling champagne seemed unquenchable.

One country nobody bothered with much was the United States. As far as most wine producers were concerned, it was too far away and too risky. Even still wines shipped in wooden casks ran into problems. Evaporation was one of them, but thirsty sailors and laborers constituted another. Whenever the spirit moved them, which was often, they would pull a plug or drill a hole in the casks, then stick a hose in and begin siphoning out the wine. Too often, casks arrived nearly empty.

||||||||

As the end of the eighteenth century approached, champagne remained a work in progress. It was like a tug-of-war with customers lined up on two different sides. Some clamored for bubbles while others preferred theirs without.

Thomas Jefferson was in the latter group. And he was in good company. Two centuries earlier, Dom Pérignon, the French monk heralded as the "father of champagne," worked strenuously to keep bubbles out of his champagne. Bubbles were considered a fault, and he prided himself on making a clean, still wine with no effervescence.

Although Jefferson could appreciate a good sparkling champagne, he much preferred it without bubbles, especially if it came from the vineyards of Dorsay. He observed that "if the spring bottling failed to make a brisk [sparkling] wine, they decant it into other bottles in the fall and it then makes the very best still wine." Jefferson went on to say that "they let it stand in the bottles, in this case forty eight hours, with only a napkin spread over their mouths, but no cork. The best sparkling wine decanted in this manner makes the best still wine." And it gets even better, he added, if it's allowed to age. "The brisk wines lose their briskness the older they are, but they gain in quality with age." They reach perfection between two and ten years of age, he said, with some maintaining their quality for fifteen.

Jefferson obviously consumed a goodly amount of champagne, for he could easily rate numerous vintages as to their quality. He must have been very pleased to find that one of the very best years was 1776, even though so much champagne had been lost in the tsunami of exploding bottles.

In this, as in all of his wine purchases, Jefferson revealed a refined and discerning palate. His favorite, Dorsay, was praised as one of the two best white wines in France, the other being a white Hermitage. Dorsay's quality was reflected in the cost, which was more per bottle than many of the great Bordeaux. (Today, the vineyards of Dorsay are the property of the Bollinger Champagne House and provide the grapes for its top cuvées.)

Jefferson emphasized that he preferred champagne made from Pinot Noir grapes to that from Chardonnay. The former provided structure and backbone and resulted in a "harder" champagne, he said. Chardonnay was softer and lacier, more delicate in terms of what connoisseurs call "mouth-feel."

One of the other things that impressed Jefferson was how selective the Champenois were in picking the grapes they used for their champagne. "They choose the bunches with as much care to make wine of the very first quality as if to eat," he said.

Jefferson had no patience for lesser-quality wines or producers who took shortcuts. On his trip to Champagne, while passing through the city of Nancy in the province of Lorraine, he remarked, "This is a place where bad wine is made."[5] By 1788 the still wines of Champagne had become so popular that some feared sparkling champagne might disappear altogether. As one historian at the time noted, "It is not more than a hundred years since the fashion for making the wine of Champagne sparkle began, and it has not been twenty since it stopped. All that remains are mentions in drinking songs in which foaming Champagne is celebrated. Only a few old Drinkers still remember the ecstasy of seeing a cork hitting the ceiling."[6]

The historian went on to say that it was "the still wine of Champagne that was generally favored in more genteel society." Or, to put it more succinctly, as Jefferson did in a letter to a Philadelphia merchant, "The Mousseux or Sparkling Champagne is *never* brought to a good table in France. The still, or non-mousseux is alone drunk by connoisseurs."[7]

This style was reinforced by changes at the top, that is, at the French royal court. Louis XVI, unlike his flamboyant predecessors, was a "quiet monarch," content with his clock-making and occasional hunts. He wanted his champagne "quiet" too, no bubbles. Only once is he known to have had the sparkling version—at his coronation in Reims on June 11, 1775.

The king was only nineteen years old when he succeeded his grandfather Louis XV to the throne. He could still be considered a "growing boy" because, on waking up one morning sometime later, he asked if he could have chicken and chops. "It's really not much when they bring me eggs with gravy and a bottle of champagne," he reportedly complained.

Louis XVI, however, must have loved his still champagne, because when he and his family were captured as they tried to flee the ravages of the Revolution in 1789, what they had with them to drink was six bottles of water and one bottle of still champagne.

After he and Queen Marie-Antoinette were guillotined, the champagne house of Gosset collected original manuscripts and prepared an inventory of the royal cellar. In it was red wine from the Champagne villages of Bouzy and Verzy and several bottles of still white champagne. There is no mention of any sparkling champagne.

But sparkling champagne had not disappeared. Far from it. Fizz, as the English called it, still continued to attract new followers, albeit slowly. As early as 1764, the house of Ruinart received a letter from one of its customers saying, "I have been so content with the first two baskets I have received from you that it is with great pleasure that I would like to order two more, but must ask most earnestly that they be as sparkling as possible. I am not unaware, messieurs, that fine gourmets prefer the non-sparkling, but as there are very few of them you must surely content the multitude who prefer the sparkling."

Sparkling champagne also had at least one champion in the American diplomatic community: Benjamin Franklin, who was in Paris garnering support and funds for the new Republic. Franklin had settled into a comfortable life on a large estate overlooking the Seine River in the suburb of Passy, today part of Paris's sixteenth arrondissement. Between diplomatic meetings and other adventures, he found time to build up a wine cellar of more than one thousand bottles. In addition to Bordeaux and Burgundies, there were Sherries *and* a quantity of sparkling champagne.[8]

Franklin, who served as ambassador from 1778 to 1785, was a frequent and generous host. His dinners, which took place nearly every night, attracted most of the American community in Paris, including Jefferson and another future president, John Adams, along with his wife, Abigail.

Adams was in France to help negotiate an alliance with the country. He was also "an enthusiastic wine-drinker" and, like Franklin, collected an impressive number of French wines which he would take with him to England as America's first minister to that country and then, later, to America.

Unfortunately, he soon tired of the dinners and complained that Franklin was not doing his job as ambassador. In his diary, Adams wrote: "These incessant dinners and dissipations were not the objects of my missions to France." Adams, however, failed to grasp the purpose of these parties, that French society combined politics with pleasure in a way that he was not accustomed to.

Franklin, by contrast, mingled effortlessly in the atmosphere of high society, telling jokes and flirting with women. He later admitted that it sometimes got out of hand, confessing that "the hard-to-be-governed passion of my youth had hurried me frequently into intrigues with low women that fell my way."

Nevertheless, it did help him generate much support for America and substantial sums of money from the French. Generous servings of his sparkling champagne probably helped, too.

||||||||

As important as wine was to Champagne, it was not the driving force during this time. Rather, it was wool. Textiles had dominated the economy of the region since the Middle Ages, and it was still that way at the end of the eighteenth century.[9]

Wine, or champagne, however, was never far away. Many textile entrepreneurs also owned small vineyards. They had long ago learned that being able to offer a glass or two of wine to customers was always good for business.

They also discovered that it helped to speak a foreign language, something they were reluctant to do. That reluctance sprang from a multitude of factors, one being pure chauvinism. French was considered the language of diplomacy; it was precise, refined, cultured. As one merchant noted, "The unhappy but nevertheless very real French unwillingness to study foreign languages [forced many to hire young Germans] to take care of foreign correspondence. Many of these young people soon found themselves initiated into the secrets of champagne-making and well knew, with an intelligence we are first to acknowledge, how to profit from the exceptional opportunities they were offered, and set up their own businesses."[10]

Their success, however, provoked a degree of jealousy among many French, one of whom said, "We cannot avoid expressing one regret: that of seeing an industry based on French soil, an industry which is so clearly of national interest, slip almost entirely from our hands through our own mistakes."

The names swiftly became legion: Heidsieck, Krug, Roederer, Mumm, Deutz, Bollinger . . .

Robert Tomes, an American consular official who was working in Champagne, observed, "There is, in fact, not a single wine establishment in all Champagne which is not under the control, more or less, of a native of Germany. If the nominal head should chance to be a Frenchman, he is sure to have a partner or a chief clerk of that country. There was, however, a champagne house which happened to be controlled exclusively by natives of France. It became bankrupt while I was at Rheims, and it was a common remark that it perished for want of a German."

Tomes went on to confirm the prevailing view. "When I asked how it had happened that, to conduct so national a trade as that of champagne wine, France had called Germany to its aid, I was told that it was owing to the fact that there were so few Frenchmen, and so many Germans, who had a knowledge of foreign languages."

But Tomes thought it was more than that. In his book *The Champagne Country*, which he wrote after he left France in 1866 and in which he dissected the French, he said:

> I fancy that the French have a natural inaptitude for commerce. With an unquestioned superiority of taste, a precise attention to details, much thriftiness, an easy compliance, and a polite address, they make good workmen and excellent small dealers. Napoléon called the English a nation of shopkeepers. The saying in its literal sense is more justly applicable to the French. They are emphatically the shopkeepers of the world. . . .

While he is the shopkeeper, the German, Englishman and the American are the merchants. The Frenchman contents himself for the most part with adjusting a color, devising a pattern, inventing a toy, or peddling small wares; while he leaves the management of the great financial, manufacturing and commercial establishments of its country to the adopted citizens from Germany.

One of those "citizens" was Florent-Louis Heidsieck, a Westphalian who arrived in Reims in 1777. He was the first of many German immigrants to find fame and fortune in Champagne. Others included such names as Krug, Roederer, Mumm, Deutz and Bollinger.

Heidsieck had been working for a textile firm in Berlin when he was sent to Reims to try to settle a legal dispute with a cloth-making firm there. He became friendly with a French wool merchant named Nicolas Perthois, who, like many of his colleagues, also owned vineyards and made small amounts of wine. Perthois also had a daughter, Agathe. She and Florent-Louis fell in love and were married in 1785, and Florent-Louis, following his father-in-law's example, promptly set up his own textile and wine firm in Reims.[11]

It didn't take long, however, for Heidsieck to realize that wine, not wool, was the future. Wool had been the defining mark of Champagne ever since the region had been a natural crossroads of Europe and where giant trade fairs attracted thousands of people. Although wine was there, it was usually just something offered by merchants as a courtesy to entice customers to buy their main products, like wool and other textiles.

By the end of the eighteenth century, however, all that had begun to change. Wine seemed primed to take center stage, and Heidsieck moved quickly to take advantage. Dropping wool from his business, he decided to concentrate exclusively on making champagne—not still champagne which so many like Jefferson still preferred, but *sparkling* champagne. It was a gamble. No more than ten other houses were doing that, Ruinart and Moët being two of them, but it was a gamble that paid off.

Heidsieck's new champagne house, the Maison Heidsieck, was so successful that he, a foreigner, was invited to accompany the aldermen of Reims to the royal court at Versailles where they presented samples of sparkling champagne to Queen Marie Antoinette. The queen was probably very happy to meet him because she was an Austrian by birth and pleased to be in the company of another German speaker.

Unlike her husband, the queen loved bubbles. Legend says she was so fond of sparkling champagne that she allowed the Royal Manufacture of Sèvres to use her left breast as mold for porcelain champagne coupes. In reality, the coupes, although definitely in the shape of a breast, were made for drinking something much different—milk—and were part of a large porcelain service that the "quiet" monarch, Louis XVI, had made for his wife to use at the Dairy. The Dairy, a gift from the king to the queen, was a kind of play farm located on the grounds of their summer residence at the Château de Rambouillet.

Because the gift was a surprise, it seems unlikely that Marie Antoinette was the model for the coupes, but she may very well have enjoyed the story.

As for Heidsieck, his champagne business had grown so rapidly that he realized he would need assistance managing it. His only child, a boy, had died very young, so he sent a call for help to his family in Germany. Three of his nephews responded: two brothers, Charles-Henri and Christian Heidsieck, and their cousin Guillaume Piper.

All three would eventually found champagne houses of their own, resulting in one of the great dynasties in Champagne.

But it would be another Heidsieck, one not yet on the scene, who would make an even greater mark on the world of champagne.

# 2

||||||||||

# Young Charles

Reims sat quietly on its hill above the marshes of the River Vesle in 1824, its glory days as the "royal city" of France nearly forgotten. The ancient ramparts enfolding the city were crumbling, and its massive Gothic cathedral was bleak, nearly blending into the prison that leaned against it. Mass sung in the church often was drowned out by the cries and moans of the prisoners.

Beggars roamed the streets; buildings once housing busy convents and other religious institutions had been turned into warehouses and factories. They sat drab and colorless.

Only the clicking and clacking of shuttles and the looms pouring out yards of woolen goods for markets throughout Europe reminded the city that it was still a major commercial center, one of the textile capitals of the world. Spindles there filled with a thread so fine that Casanova took time away from other pursuits to note in his memoirs that he only ordered shirts made from "cambric woven from thread from Reims, the finest there is."

But the city was run down, its population about one-quarter of what it once had been, and its position as a leader in the textile world was a fragile one. Most of the thread spun and woven in the Champagne town was now imported from other parts of France or from Belgium and other countries. The large flocks of sheep that had once covered the nearby slopes had all but disappeared when fertilizer became widely available and began being used to enrich the thin and chalky soil. Although farming of crops had taken over and more vines had been planted, most of the land remained in the hands of families in the textile business who saw their farms and vineyards as mere adjuncts to their main enterprises.

The textiles of Reims had been famous as early as the Middle Ages, when their outstanding quality drew crowds from all over Europe and Asia to the annual fairs of Champagne. Savvy merchants also had copious amounts of wine on hand for prospective buyers to taste, wine aimed at enhancing negotiations and enticing customers to spend their money. In hopes of turning big spenders into loyal customers, there might even be a barrel or more added to the wool order.

Reims was by then already an ancient city. It traced its roots back at least to Roman times; some even claimed it had been founded by Remus, the twin brother of the founder of Rome, Romulus. Less fanciful residents said the city's name came from the ancient tribe of Remi who made their capital there. Under Roman rule, Reims was a provincial capital and the second-largest city of the empire, right behind Rome itself. Its population grew to as many as fifty thousand people, possibly even a hundred thousand.

With the decline of the Roman Empire, Reims declined, too. The Romans, however, had left behind two things that would prove invaluable for the city's future: vines and a vast set of interconnecting underground tunnels and caverns called *crayères*. The Romans had mined them for chalk and building materials in the third century.

No one, however, was thinking about those in the fall of 1824 when exciting news shook up the city. For the first time in more than two generations, Reims would have a coronation. The new king, Charles X, announced he would do as his predecessors had done and come to the city to be anointed as the ruler of France.

It was stunning news, thrilling news, and it swept through the city. It meant hundreds of officials, dignitaries, and nobles would follow, all of them bringing money to spend in the once-again "royal city" of Champagne.

All of Reims rejoiced—the wealthy merchants and landowners who lived in luxurious mansions in the center of the city, and the

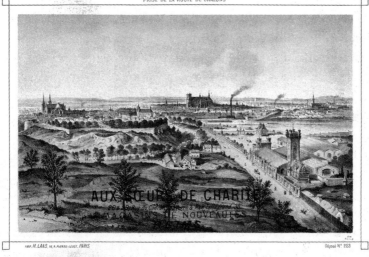

VUE PANORAMIQUE DE REIMS

PRISE DE LA ROUTE DE CHALONS

**3.** City of Reims, 1850s. Courtesy of Bibliothèque Carnegie de Reims.

poor and struggling workers who crowded into the suburbs on the city's edge. Everyone could see a way to profit from the coronation.

Reims had been campaigning for this event for more than a decade, from the moment when King Louis XVIII, Charles's brother, returned from his twenty-three-year exile after the defeat of Napoléon I.

King Louis had barely set foot on French soil when a delegation of notables from the city arrived at the Tuileries Palace in Paris to entreat him to plan a coronation in the traditional glittering style. From earliest times, they reminded him, French kings had knelt in Reims's Cathedral of Notre Dame to be anointed with the sacred oil said to have been brought from heaven by the Holy Spirit.

They also pointed out that Napoléon—the "Corsican upstart"—had eschewed Reims and crowned himself emperor in Paris.

You can't let that happen again, the leaders of Reims pleaded with the new king; this is your opportunity to outdo Napoléon and uphold tradition and validate your position. They unrolled plans for decoration of their cathedral and city along with samples of the fabric they could produce to make ceremonial robes for royalty, nobility, and ecclesiastics. They also reminded the king they could provide copious amounts of the wine of Champagne for the celebrations.

Louis said yes . . . well, maybe . . . let's wait and see. First, he needed to solidify his hold on the throne by establishing himself as a monarch ruling according to the new *charte,* or constitution. Plus, after years of financial difficulties in exile, he was a penny pincher; all the robes and decoration would cost the depleted French treasury money. In addition, the Congress of Vienna was about to begin, and resources and people would have to be directed there to make sure France did not suffer unduly in the peace treaty being negotiated after Napoléon's fall.

There was one other important reason Louis sent the representatives of Reims away without a definite commitment to a coronation: he was ill, obese, and already an invalid after a severe attack of gout which would soon lead to gangrene. He could only get around comfortably in a specially built large, mahogany wheelchair. There was no way he could manage climbing steps and kneeling in a long and elaborate ceremony.

When it became clear Louis would never agree to a coronation, the disappointed Rèmois rolled up their drawings and fabric samples and packed everything away. This king would not live forever, they reminded each other as they headed home. They would be ready when a new one came to the throne.

Now, more than a decade later after Louis's death in 1824, the time had come.

Charles X was a very different man from his brother Louis XVIII. He had grandiose ideas; he might not be able to say he ruled by divine right as his ancestors had done, but he could re-create the elaborate protocol and luster of the *ancien régime.* The Revolution and its guillotine had done away with the titles, regalia, and ceremony, but he was going to bring them back.

For the people and city of Reims, those words were more than welcome, especially so because Charles X also declared he wanted only French-made products used for the event. Manna from heaven, thought the people of the city's large textile industry. The vineyards and farms they owned would profit, too.

Nonetheless, city fathers must have been daunted by the amount of work and money required to bring the dilapidated city up to royal standards. They would also be responsible for providing the royal banquet following the coronation which would cost them even more money. The king was determined to get the spectacle he wanted, so he announced he would contribute sixty thousand francs, about a half million dollars in today's money, to refurbishing the city to make it an acceptable stage for a coronation. He also would commission a new mass by Luigi Cherubini and an opera by Gioachino Rossini, *Le voyage à Reims*, for the event.

Added to the royal shopping list was a gold coach that would have made even the Sun King, Louis XIV, blink. It was designed by the architect Charles Percier, who was the artistic force behind the Arc de Triomphe du Carrousel. The carriage was ornamented with sculpted figures and paintings by the leading artists of the day. Eight matched horses would pull its royal passenger through the newly resurfaced streets of Reims.

With the Rémois feeling the pressure of a deadline, work on the coronation began almost before the old king could be buried. Wagons loaded with lumber and other building material clogged the streets; the pounding and hammering, the rattling of harnesses and yelling of drivers nearly drowned out the great bells of the cathedral. Even the shouting and cursing from prisoners housed next to the church was muffled by the constant noise.

Roads quickly became mud and ruts; supplies piled up in every available space. Buildings and trees were ripped out to carve a new street from the Place Royale to the city hall. The city hall, or Hôtel de Ville, was itself was being rebuilt to be impressive enough to welcome the king. The Palais de Tau, where the king would stay during the festivities, was remodeled and its banqueting room redecorated. Along the streets six triumphal arches went up, as well as a huge marquee at the entrance of the cathedral. Finally, as the date neared, sand was hauled in and the roads were repaired.

|||||||||

Just steps away from the cathedral, the site of the greatest activity, a toddler named Charles-Camille Heidsieck was watching from the windows in his home on the rue d'Anjou. All the construction and all the sounds would have been a source of never-ending wonder and curiosity; he could hardly absorb it all. Every day something new was happening; every day more people filed into the city—carpenters, masons, artists, musicians, actors, priests, monks—also more beggars, prostitutes, and thieves. And more police and military to deal with concerns about crime and, more importantly, labor unrest, fears of which were haunting manufacturers as they rushed to prepare their products.

None of that concerned young Charles-Camille. The sounds and sights of history were unrolling before him, and he could feel the excitement building right in his own family.

His father, Charles-Henri, actually knew the king, so the Heidsiecks felt a personal connection to what was going on. Charles-Henri had been decorated by Charles X for his role in preventing Russian troops from destroying Reims when they moved in to occupy Champagne after Napoléon's fall. He had been able to sway the Russian commanders by calling on connections he had made a few years earlier in Moscow.

Now the city he helped protect was being renovated and transformed to evoke "medieval pageantry and nineteenth-century luxury," as the official historian of the coronation wrote. It would do everything possible to replicate coronations of earlier French monarchs, including the most famous one in 1429 when Joan of Arc personally escorted Charles VII to Reims to be crowned. But the city would add even more dazzling effects this time, elaborate decorations people began calling "troubadour style."

Banners went up, buntings were hung from every window railing, and garlands were draped along the streets. Little Charles-Camille Heidsieck easily could have imagined he was back in days of knights in armor.[1]

For his mother, however, all the joy and excitement were suddenly extinguished. Just as the coronation work began, Charles-Henri died unexpectedly, and then, only a few weeks later, her youngest child, a mere baby, also passed away. At twenty-six, Emilie Henriot Heidsieck found herself a widow with three young children.

At the same time, she was weighted down with responsibilities in the family's businesses that her husband had been running. These included a successful wool-trading company built up by her father as well as vineyards outside the city. Although her mother had stepped in to take over, she, too, was a widow and had five children, some still very young. Emilie was the oldest. Emilie was later to tell her son that she took over responsibility for the accounts and "yet had to be a comfort to *Maman*. The work was non-stop."

On top of that, she was teaching herself German, something she had vowed to do when she married. Family was of paramount importance to her, and now, more than ever, she was determined to remain in close contact with Charles-Henri's prominent and deeply religious German family. She had also promised her husband she would remain on good terms with local Heidsiecks, his cousins in the champagne business, so Charles-Camille someday would have an opportunity to pursue that should he wish.

Champagne had been her husband's first love; it was what had brought him to France from Germany when he was just a teenager. His uncle, the pioneer champagne maker Florent-Louis Heidsieck, was childless and needed help in his growing business. He promptly contacted his nephews in Germany, promising them a share in the concern if they did well. Three responded; Charles-Henri was one of them.

It quickly became clear that Charles-Henri had a flair for the business and a love for it. Being in the vineyards and familiarizing himself with the rhythms of life there as grapes ripened, or didn't, depending on the weather, constituted much of his day. Since the family's holdings were relatively small, he also bought grapes from other vineyards for making sparkling champagne. Mastering yeasts and fermentation was still a work in progress, and workers were still getting injured when bottles exploded, so Charles-Henri had to learn about that, too.

Gradually, his uncle Florent conferred more responsibility on him. In 1811 he was handed a major assignment: develop the market in Russia for Heidsieck Champagne. The country had proved to have an insatiable thirst for the sparkling wine, but Heidsieck had yet to grab a significant share of the sales.

The Russian market, until then, had been the almost-private preserve of Veuve Clicquot Champagne, whose agent, Louis Bohne, had built up such strong personal relationships at the court of Tsar Alexander I that they kept other champagne makers at bay.

Plus, there was a war going on: Napoléon was at the height of his power and ambition, successfully fighting his way across Europe to bring one area after another into his empire. Now he had his sights set on Russia.

Under those conditions, it would take something extraordinary to cut into Russian sales, but twenty-one-year-old Charles-Henri was unfazed. He had an idea that he was convinced would do the trick.

In 1811 he purchased an enormous white stallion, loaded it and a packhorse with *paniers*, or baskets of bottles of champagne, and then, with a servant carrying even more champagne, set off for the Russian city, nearly two thousand miles away. His goal was to plot a route away from the battle zones and beat Napoléon to Moscow. He would then be in position to sell champagne for the victory celebration, no matter who the victor was.

Charles-Henri's entry into the city on his white charger caused a sensation, just as he'd hoped. Within no time he had sold all his champagne and filled his saddlebags with orders for more.[2]

Veuve Clicquot's agent was furious and embarrassed. Writing to the widow Clicquot, Bohne detailed Heidsieck's "charge" into the city and complained bitterly about his success.

Once more back in Reims, Charles-Henri garnered almost as much attention there as he had in Moscow. At six-foot-four, he towered over most of the locals; he was a wavy-haired blonde with bright blue eyes, and he probably swaggered a bit after his successful Russian adventure. That's when he caught the eye of the beautiful Emilie Henriot and she caught his, as well. But there was a problem: he was Protestant and German; she, Catholic and French, this at a time when Protestantism, previously persecuted in France, had only recently been legalized and the only recognized Protestant place of worship was the chapel in the Swedish Embassy in Paris.

Nonetheless, both families agreed to the marriage on the condition Charles-Henri agree to allow any children to be raised as

Young Charles

Catholics. Each of the newlyweds would bring a dowry of twenty-five thousand francs to the marriage, and Florent-Louis Heidsieck, Charles-Henri's boss and uncle, would add an additional twenty-five thousand. They would be able to live comfortably—but only if they could get the required official permission to marry. Months went by, and they waited, growing ever more frustrated and impatient. Nothing was forthcoming. Finally, after two long years, Charles-Henri succeeded in becoming a French citizen and permission arrived. In 1818 he and Emilie were married.

Emilie's mother, already widowed, had been nearly as impatient as her daughter for the wedding. She needed help with the family businesses, and in Charles-Henri she saw the man she wanted to take over. Leave your uncle, she pleaded, and you can run Henriot Frères et Soeurs et Cie.

It was a tremendous opportunity for an ambitious and creative young man, to be head of a business rather than wait to inherit a share of one. Granted, the primary business was wool, but there were those vineyards, too; he might be able to do something with them. He agreed, but only with the understanding that Florent-Louis would honor his commitment of a twenty-five-thousand-franc dowry for the young couple.

The dowry, however, never arrived. There were repeated entreaties from the family, polite requests, then stronger ones. More than six years went by.

In November of 1824, as work on the coronation was beginning, Charles-Henri decided to make one more appeal for the dowry. He went to see his uncle, but a "particularly livid" argument ensued, according to one family member. In the aftermath of the confrontation, Charles-Henri suffered a stroke, a *congestion cérébrale*, and died. He was thirty-four years old.

⁕

As the coronation of Charles X approached in May of 1825, nearly all twenty-five-thousand residents of Reims were thinking about wool and worrying whether they could produce enough of it for the event.

Textiles still remained the city's leading industry and its main source of income, but the merchants had long ago proved themselves sensitive to trends and changes in fashion, both in wool and wine. They moved from offering heavy cloth to ever more elegant merinos. When their pallid red wine was eclipsed by that produced in Burgundy, they concentrated on their light white still wine. There was a problem, though. When temperatures warmed up in spring, the wine began to "work," or effervesce. With the trade fairs in Champagne beginning at Easter, merchants fretted that their clientele would be turned off. They needn't have worried. Customers said they liked bubbles and sparkle; it was different and, well, fun. When coronations came along like the one in 1429 when Joan of Arc brought Charles VII to Reims to be crowned, there were numerous banquets and the wine of Champagne was poured liberally. Bubbles indeed made it special, attendees said; worthy of a royal event. So began a perfect and long-lasting marriage: celebration and champagne.

This coronation would be no different: celebration with the wine of Champagne. There were already plenty of bottles sitting below the city in the cool climes of the *crayères*; they had no worries there. The problem was not that.

The real problem was making sure they had enough cloth to meet the needs of the celebration. Textile manufacturers called up every available hand and set the spinners to work. Shuttles flew around the clock as the looms rolled out bolt after bolt of fabric nonstop. Undoubtedly many of those bolts came from the very factories Heidsieck had been in charge of at Henriot Frères et Soeurs.

Spring arrived, and the six-hundred-year-old Gothic cathedral became the focal point. It had been built with an extra long nave for the express purpose of hosting coronations—also to make its nave longer than the one going up in Paris. Even in cathedral building there was rivalry.

Through the years, however, there was damage from weather and neglect; the labyrinth had been lost and works of art had deteriorated. The French Revolution left its mark, destroying some of the statues and, more importantly, breaking the Holy Ampulla, which contained the God-given oil for anointing kings. But some drops reportedly had been scraped off the ground and saved by a priest and a pious parishioner. Or perhaps most of the oil had secretly been emptied the day before, leaving only a small amount for the revolutionaries. Whatever had happened, the drops that had been "recovered" were decanted into a new ampulla ready to be opened to anoint Charles X.

In the meantime, Reims artisans retrieved plans and designs they originally made for Louis XVIII's coronation and set about transforming the cathedral into a magnificent stage set. Sumptuous, fringed red draperies, most woven within sight of the building, were hung to embellish the ancient structure.

Galleries were built to accommodate the thousands of spectators, and stairs were added; hundreds of chairs and benches were lugged in.

The church was so disguised for the May 29, 1825, ceremony that the Reims correspondent for the newspaper *Le Constitutionnel* wrote, "No real vestige of the Reims Cathedral can any longer be found; it has completely disappeared underneath the ornaments."

Victor Hugo, one of the invited guests, said, "For the coronation of a king of France, a theatre had been constructed inside the church, and it has since been said, with perfect accuracy, that on arriving at the entrance I asked of the guard on duty, 'where is my box?'"

The banquet after the ceremony, for which the city of Reims had to pay, followed the strict etiquette of the *ancien régime* with the king served first and nobles and others seated by rank. The feast was sumptuous, according to the official historian, but he was not concerned with the menu, noting only that the food had been tasted before being given to the ruler. The *grand échanson*, the royal cupbearer, also tasted the king's wine before it was served. It was undoubtedly champagne—or the wine of Champagne, as it was then known—but the historian failed to mention that. He did say the king's meal took a half hour. Then everyone else was permitted to eat.

The royal stay in Reims included stops at several wool manufacturers, and it was recorded that some of the princesses were impressed and purchased "merinos." There is no record of anyone, royal or otherwise, visiting the champagne houses.

4. Coronation of Charles X in Reims, May 29, 1825. Anonymous lithograph.
Courtesy of Bibliothèque Carnegie de Reims.

Although all went off without a hitch—even the weather cooperated with warm sunshine—the coronation and the pomp surrounding it were viewed skeptically. The city was jammed, but crowds were not as big as hoped. Transportation was difficult, and householders had no hesitation about setting exorbitant fees for rooms.

Another writer present, François-René de Chateaubriand, looked back on the event and wrote, "It was the performance of a coronation rather than a coronation." He said he actually preferred the stage version of a coronation he had seen in an opera in Berlin.

Dozens of engravings were made for a book about the event. It was never published.

It would, in fact, be the final coronation of a French king. Charles X lasted less than six years on the throne, his conservative policies pushing the country once again to the brink of revolution. He abdicated in 1830 and was succeeded by the elected King Louis Philippe, who had no coronation.

It would also represent the apogee of the Reims textile industry. The wine, which had been almost an afterthought for vineyard-owning wool merchants through the centuries and which was barely noticed at the coronation, was about to explode into prominence and turn the city's once famous wool industry into little more than a footnote.

Champagne, the wine of celebration, the wine of romance, would become the city's and the region's major industry, its *raison d'être*, and it would "rule" long after the kings and queens of France and their beautiful woven robes had slipped into obsolescence.

Young Charles-Camille Heidsieck who had watched with wonder would arrive on the scene just in time, and it would be he who would take the exciting drink to even greater heights and carry it to places it had never been.

||||||||

Even with all the demands placed on her in business and at home, Charles-Camille's mother remained a woman firmly in charge of her own life. She was also strikingly beautiful, adept at business and extremely religious.

Working with the archbishop of Reims, Emilie established the Dames de l'Oeuvre de la Miséricorde, Ladies for the Work of Mercy, an association designed to coordinate aid for the city's charities. It was a major undertaking. Reims was considered one of the two most charitable cities in France and, as such, a magnet for beggars and people who were struggling to make ends meet.

At the same time, Reims was also becoming more divided as the textile industry, struggling to survive, turned to mechanization, increasing wealth for the owners but costing the jobs of many workers. The latter were forced to crowd into tenement-like lodgings on the edge of the city where they had little access to hygiene and few means to feed their families. Emilie and her organization labored to improve the conditions.

Her work, not to mention her beauty, soon caught the eye of the widowed mayor of Reims, who had recently been ennobled as the Vicomte de Brimont and was head of Ruinart Champagne. He came calling and asked Emilie to marry him. She said, "No, but thank you for asking." Her life, she explained, was already full with work for her church and especially her family.

Her thoughts particularly centered on Charles. His school did not include the kind of religious education she wanted for him, so at age ten he was sent to Paris to the Collège de Vaugirard, a boarding school run by priests.

It was a difficult decision. She missed him terribly and her letters to him reflected it, saying how eager she was for vacations when he would return home and she would have her family together again.

In 1836, however, she would send sad news: the death of his older sister, Apolline. "What a sacrifice to no longer have the sweetness she brought to our family," she wrote. Charles and his sister Clementine were now her only remaining children, and she watched over both with an eye to their futures. Clementine, she told Charles, was very popular and had been invited to dances at homes of the most prominent people in Reims. Nearly all were champagne makers.

Emilie also had people she wanted Charles to meet: "Monsieur Franz Abelé de Muller of that esteemed champagne house was here last night and asked for news of you. Your cousin Henri Piper has also inquired and thinks that when you finish schooling in Paris you should study in Germany." It was Emilie's way of prodding Charles toward a career in the champagne business, something she dearly wanted since she knew it would have pleased her late husband.

But Charles had other plans. After obtaining his *baccalauréat*, or high school degree, he was determined to stay in France and study law. Leaving the country and going to Germany was out of the question as far as he was concerned. He didn't explain but the reason was clear to everyone: he was smitten, head over heels in love.

The object of his adoration was a young cousin. Like his mother, she was named Emilie. She was seventeen years old.

The family, however, was alarmed, since the Catholic Church forbade marriage between first cousins. They urged Charles to reconsider his decision about Germany. "You can continue your education there and live with your Protestant uncles and their families," his mother said.

In January of 1844, Charles finally consented. He was twenty-two when he left and immediately plunged himself into perfecting his German and pursuing an advanced degree in business at the University of Lübeck—all the while nursing his hopes and dreams of

Emilie. Perhaps, he thought, a dispensation from the archbishop would allow the marriage. After all, his mother was very devout and worked tirelessly for the parish.

Meanwhile, Charles's uncles, including some who were ministers in the Lutheran Church, were filling him with stories about the father he barely knew and the perilous journey he made to Moscow to sell champagne to the Russians. "You had a father you can be proud of," said one, "and if you can emulate him in his way of thinking and doing things, then surely you will secure your own way."

But in 1845, Charles received a carefully worded letter from his mother: his sweetheart Emilie had become engaged to someone else. It was to another cousin, Georges Delius, whose father earlier had left the champagne business created by Charles's great-uncle, Florent-Louis Heidsieck, to become a banker. It's unclear how Charles dealt with his heartbreak, but the news must have been shattering. He would remain in Germany for another year before returning to Reims. By then, his thoughts were focused on a job awaiting him.

During his absence, his mother had worked out a deal for him to go to work at Piper-Heidsieck, the champagne house headed by his cousin Henri Piper. He'd begin at twelve hundred francs a year, which was a substantial entry-level salary. After a year he would qualify for additional benefits.

Precisely what his duties were is unclear. What is certain is that two things soured him about working there. One was personal; the other was professional.[3]

Georges Delius, the cousin who had married Charles's sweetheart, joined the firm instead of following his father into banking. Suddenly, Piper-Heidsieck began to feel very cramped to a young man who was the loser in a romantic contest.

Then there was Jacques Kunkelman—no family relation—who had gone to the United States as an agent and salesman for Piper-Heidsieck. When he came home, Henri Piper decided to make him an associate in the company.

Charles was furious. First Delius, the man who had stolen his sweetheart, was given a major position in the company, and now

Kunkelman. What was left for him? What about his opportunities for advancement or a share in the operation? Hadn't he been promised those? What's more, he was part of the family and Kunkelman was not. There was a nasty row and Charles stormed out.

His mother must have been devastated and probably very angry. She undoubtedly felt twice betrayed by that branch of the family. Once, when Florent-Louis refused to pay the promised dowry and the ensuing battle about it had precipitated her husband's stroke. Nonetheless, she had persisted and faithfully honored her commitment to her husband by cultivating the relationship with Henri Piper and the family firm he was running. Piper, in turn, had let her know he was following Charles's education and promised her there would be a place for him at Piper-Heidsieck. Instead he had brought Kunkelman into what was a family business at the expense of her son. It was a second betrayal, a slap in the face, and she viewed it as an affront to the memory of her husband, who had done so much for the family firm. It opened a deep wound that would fester between the two branches for the family for years.

As for Charles, his future was now uncertain. At age twenty-eight he was unemployed and still unmarried, but his mother had an idea. Rather, she had a young, unmarried niece, Amélie Henriot.

Amélie had been largely ignored by Reims society because of her grandmother's "tarnished reputation." That reputation actually should have been attached to her grandfather, who was known to have "a roving eye," but blame, as was so often the case, fell instead on his wife, Amélie's grandmother. At the "advanced" age of forty-five, she apparently had had an affair with a much younger man, a very handsome one who was known as *le lion de la jeunesse rémoise*, the idol of all the young people in Reims. Some said the affair was revenge or payback for the serially unfaithful grandfather, but that did not protect Amélie's grandmother from scorn. Gossips castigated her, metaphorically all but branding her with a scarlet letter "A" as an adulterer. Plus, she was considered a "cradle-robber" for taking a younger man as her lover. The resulting talk and finger-pointing upset her youngest son to such a degree that he left home and became a monk.

The lingering whiff of scandal and the fact that she was not a beauty may have been the reasons Amélie was still available at age twenty-two, a relatively advanced age for a woman to be unmarried at the time.

Emilie looked at it practically. She knew Amélie was sensible and extremely intelligent and, if not precisely attractive, she was "well-made." A marriage to her would extend the family even further and make Charles cousin to nearly all the major champagne makers of the day—the Delamottes, the Ponsardins, the Clicquots, the Roederers, the Delbecks, and others. There was also plenty of money in that branch of the Henriot family as well as a brother who was eager to try something new.

Was there any affection involved in this union? Was it a love match? Or was it merely a good business arrangement? Whatever it was at the beginning, it would become a marriage of truly deep and long-lasting love. It was also one that would prove very satisfying in the bedroom, as their letters to each other would later reveal.

Fittingly, Amélie and Charles were married in the cathedral he had seen decorated and "disguised" for the coronation of Charles X. The archbishop of Reims himself performed the ceremony, reflecting the deep devotion of Emilie Heidsieck and her family. With so many large and interrelated families, the church must have been nearly as full for the wedding as it was for the coronation, while the banquet afterward surely included some outstanding champagne, probably better than the king had been served. The young couple moved into a *hôtel particulier*, a large, private townhouse, next to the city hall.

Soon after, Charles and his new brother-in-law Ernest set up business together and named their fledgling company Charles Heidsieck & Cie. They were financed by family funds. Charles's mother had inherited money when *her* mother died, and she put some of that into the business; the Henriots also provided capital. It was hardly a surprise when the brothers-in-law announced they were going to make champagne. Apparently neither of them had any thoughts of going into the family textile trade. They also took over another champagne house, Champagne Auger Godinot & Cie, which had come into Amélie's family from the infamous grandmother, who had been born a Godinot. They said they would keep it as a separate marque, or brand, apart from Charles Heidsieck Champagne.

Charles and Ernest outlined a careful division in their duties, one that had become traditional in champagne making and in winemaking families in general. It was a bit like the Gothic cathedral that dominated their hometown: one partner would provide the handsome facade and the basic structure—Charles, in this case—and the other would handle administration, finances, and sales. Ernest, in other words, would be the flying buttresses of the operation taking care of purchasing, the cellars and all the technical aspects of champagne making. Each partner agreed he would keep the other "scrupulously informed" of what he was doing.

Charles seems to have been very pleased with what his life had become, for almost immediately he decided to take his new wife to Germany and introduce her to his uncles and other family members there. Although it was a sort of honeymoon, it was also about business, for Charles spent part of his time making contacts for his new company and employing agents.

It was the first of several trips he made in 1851 visiting Belgium, the Netherlands and Great Britain. At the end of his travels he came back to Reims with a conviction and a vision: Europe was nearly saturated with champagne. If a young man wanted to build a profitable business, it wouldn't be here. It had to be somewhere else.

Images of his father on a white horse "conquering" Russia flooded his imagination. He would have to do something as spectacular as his father had done, yet something radically different. That was the only way to achieve what he wanted: a tremendously successful champagne house of his own.

*America*, he thought excitedly, *the New World*. That was where he would go. That was the answer, the great untapped continent across the water where champagne was almost unknown. That's where he could lead the charge.

And make a name for himself.

# 3

||||||||||

## Discovery of the New World

Travel was in his DNA. From the earliest age, Charles-Camille Heidsieck had been on the move. To his grandparents' place in the country every summer, to boarding school in Paris when he was ten, to Germany for university, to nearly every country in Europe as he set up his champagne house.

But this was different. As he stood on the docks in Liverpool, England, that day in 1852, he knew this trip was the most important he had ever attempted. It was a matter of life and death, life *or* death for his new business.

He knew, as well, that other champagne producers had tried to gain a foothold in the American market and had failed. Still others had dismissed the country as barely civilized and full of "wild Indians."

Charles knew the arguments by heart, but the things they warned him about were the very things that excited him and convinced him America was the place to make a name for himself and his champagne. In his gut, he knew he could make it work.

Liverpool at the time Heidsieck arrived was the king of the maritime world. New docks were going up to accommodate the port's ever increasing traffic of larger ships sailing in from all over the world. Shipbuilders worked on the Mersey River alongside the docks, turning out iron ships to replace the wooden ones they had crafted for centuries.[1]

All around Heidsieck was motion and commotion. The port was a forest of masts as ships sat nearly on top of each other. Smoke blew across the waterfront from the smokestacks of steamers jockeying for position in the harbor. Stevedores loaded ships and unloaded exotic goods from Asia, Africa, and the Americas; passengers pushed their way aboard, sailors scoured decks and repaired the bulkheads, workers hauled timber and supplies of every sort from wagons clogged on the roads.

Everyone and everything seemed to be moving, and the noise was overwhelming. Sights and sounds mingled and blurred as Heidsieck tried to find his way through the crowds.

But if he had strolled down the streets by the harbor, Charles would have seen remnants of another and very different aspect of Liverpool's shipbuilding supremacy: the slave trade. Only forty-five years earlier Liverpool had been the capital of the British slave trade and the place where nearly all the slave ships had been built. Trade in human beings was the backbone of the city's economy and the source of the wealth of many of Liverpool's leading citizens. Several streets in the city even carried the names of slave traders like James Penny, whose name found its way to a certain Penny Lane.

Until Great Britain outlawed the transatlantic slave trade in 1807 (the United States did the same in 1808), as many as one-fifth of all slaves shipped to North America had been transported on ships built especially for that purpose in Liverpool. They had been loaded with trade goods in the Merseyside city before heading to West Africa, where the cargo was exchanged for slaves who were jammed into ships with almost no ventilation, water, or light. Frequently ships designed to hold four hundred slaves crammed in shoulder-to-shoulder were loaded with as many as seven hundred, making the six-to-eight-week voyage across the Atlantic a veritable hell.

There are few firsthand written accounts of what conditions were like on slave ships, but one of them comes from an Irish clergyman, Reverend Robert Walsh, who was with a British patrol boat that intercepted a slave ship in 1829. His report practically defies imagination.

The slave ship had been at sea nearly three weeks and was crammed with five hundred slaves. They'd been stuffed below the main deck, each deck being only three feet, three inches high. They were packed so tightly that they sat between each other's legs; everyone was nude. According to Walsh, "there was no possibility of their lying down or at all changing their position by night or day." Each had been branded, "burnt with the red hot iron"; many were children, little girls and little boys. "The heat of these horrid places was so great and the odor so offensive that it was impossible to enter them even if there had been room." They sat in their own feces, urine, vomit and that of others. If another person sat between your legs, their bowels emptied out on you. Many became sick or went mad, and were thrown overboard. Others simply jumped. "There was so much human flesh that went over the side of those ships that sharks learned to trail them."

Those who survived the torturous journey were sold into lifelong servitude, and the profits they generated bought goods like cotton, tobacco, and rum for the British market. Then the circle of trade, rather the triangular trade, would begin again in Liverpool.

|||||||||

At the time Heidsieck passed through, the transatlantic slave trade had been outlawed. Now, the Liverpool docks were touting their fame as the place where Jenny Lind, the "Swedish Nightingale," had set sail for America at the behest of P. T. Barnum. Liverpool was also known as the launching point for thousands of emigrants who crowded onto ships and as the departure stage for explorers of long ago who had set out for new lands and adventures.

Heidsieck could identify with them—all of them, like him, bound for something new, something exciting, something risky.

As he gazed out from the docks, the Atlantic Ocean lay in front of him, an unending vista of nothing but blue. Beyond the water and the horizon, however, the New World—America—waited. He was going to see everything he could of that country and then plant the flag of his company there and make sure Americans discovered the pleasures of champagne. *His* champagne, of course.

Yet, Charles would have admitted to himself that he was apprehensive, maybe nervous and a little scared. He was risking every-

5. Charles-Camille Heidsieck, 1852. Courtesy of Champagne Charles Heidsieck.

thing on this trip: his new business, his reputation, his family's love, even his own life. Don't do this, friends had warned. It's too dangerous. You'll regret it, you could lose all you've worked for, they said. The ship could hit an iceberg or capsize in a storm.

Charles knew they were right, but he had inherited not only his father's height, which was six-foot-four, but also his panache, fearlessness, and flair for business. If his father could ride a white stallion through the midst of a war to sell his champagne, certainly he could survive an ocean trip and manage to cope with a few new, unusual, and maybe even difficult situations.

Still, he wasn't naive; quite the contrary. Charles knew the risks; he was aware of the problems other champagne houses had faced in the United States, but he was going to make this trip anyway, and he'd do so in person rather than rely on the word of someone else. He would see for himself what America was all about and find out what was needed to make his business succeed there.

In March of 1852, full of dreams and plans, and armed with a bit of English, he kissed Amélie good-bye and set off from Reims, first across *la Manche*, the English Channel, and then to Liverpool and its massive international port to catch a steamer bound for America.

|||||||||

Twenty years had passed since someone from a champagne house had been in America. That someone was Edmond Ruinart, who had been head of Ruinart Champagne for five years. "My business with the United States having expanded well for several years, I contemplated this journey overseas," he wrote in his journal. "All the more since it became crucial to establish our commercial relations on solid bases and stop relying on vague information."[2]

Ruinart had had several people advising him about what he labeled "the particulars of the American market," but they sent conflicting and sometimes discouraging reports.

One of his contacts was Louis Mark, an American consul in Germany. Mark was not pleased with the champagnes Ruinart had been sending him. The reason is unclear. The champagnes may have been "off," that is, spoiled, or perhaps they were too sweet. Whatever the problem was, Ruinart was determined to fix it and change Mark's opinion. "We have noticed that you are not finding the wines we sent to you appropriate for America," Ruinart wrote to him in 1829. "According to your request, we are sending an assortment of our sparkling wines like those we usually ship to the United States of America. We are persuaded, Sir, that the choice we have made of these wines, which are of a distinguished quality, will give you satisfaction." Consul Mark must have indeed been satisfied, because there were no further complaints from him in the Ruinart files.

||||||||

Ruinart was exhausted when he arrived in New York. It was June 24, 1831, and the city was hot and busy. He had weathered thirty-eight miserable days onboard the *Henri IV*, a three-masted sailing ship overloaded with poor immigrants hoping for better lives in America. The ship had spent days dodging icebergs and fighting storms, making the long trip a frightening one as well. New York came as a relief, and it was, Ruinart conceded, "a very lively city. Everyone is a merchant."

Although Ruinart wrote almost nothing about his business in America, he proved to be an observant tourist. The steamboats that traveled on the country's waterways, he noticed, were much different from those in Europe. They were wider and could carry six to eight hundred people.

The big difference, however, was in the way of life. "In my hotel they wake everyone at 7 a.m. by beating on an Indian tambourine in copper making a penetrating sound. It calls a second time at 8 a.m. sharp for breakfast, at 3 p.m. for the hotel dinner table attended by ladies. Dinner is well served. One always finds on the table brandy, then maize or Turkish corn which is the usual food of people. Fruits are not abundant apart from peaches and apples. One takes tea at 7 p.m., and has supper at 9 p.m.," he wrote. "I always avoided this last meal that I found unnecessary."

It was the drinking habits he was most interested in, and he noted that Americans were downing plenty of spirits. "Common people were so stupefied with alcohol at a point that they thought it necessary to solve the problem." Ruinart did not elaborate.

But he noted that even though Madeira "is preferred, our French wines are consumed more frequently . . . and consumption can only grow."

Ruinart traveled from New York City to Philadelphia, where he toured a museum. "There is a strange collection of Indian objects taken from the tribal chiefs during the wars," he wrote. He also visited what is now Independence Hall where the Liberty Bell hung. Then it was on to Baltimore, where he wrote about the luxuries of his hotel, and finally to Washington, where he briefly met President Andrew Jackson. If they shared a glass of his champagne, Ruinart does not mention it.

By then the champagne maker was eager to leave in order to be home in time for the harvest. He scribbled down his lasting impression of the United States: "I dare say that Americans are extremely enterprising, they fear nothing. They even look for difficulties to overcome. The national motto is 'We must get along.'"

It is unclear whether Ruinart was able to set up the "solid bases" he wanted in America, or whether his business picked up there as a result of his trip. If so, it didn't have a lasting effect because by the end of the century sales of Ruinart champagne in the United States were on the decline.

||||||||

At the time of Ruinart's trip, America looked like a giant box of candy to champagne makers, and every one of them wanted a piece. But no one was quite sure how to get it.

Small amounts of champagne had been making their way to America since 1750, when the enterprising Jean-Rémy Moët of what is now Moët & Chandon sent some bottles to the French islands in the Caribbean, but the United States got only a trickle. Some diplomats like Thomas Jefferson made a point of seeking out champagne and other wines, making contact with producers and sending home baskets filled with bottles.

Although the Champenois were experienced exporters—they had been peddling their wine throughout Europe ever since Louis XV gave permission for them to ship champagne in bottles in 1735—no real market had yet been established in the new republic. They were shipping only small amounts, and those on a haphazard basis.

Several obstacles stood in their way of selling to America. Most important was the weather, something they hadn't had to worry about when the market was confined to Europe. Now, with a possible market across an ocean, weather became a preoccupation. A transatlantic crossing by sailing ship of the kind on which Ruinart traveled took more than a month; hence every departure had to be carefully calculated to avoid seasonal problems. It was too cold to ship in the winter and risk the wine's freezing, and summer with its murderous heat was out of the question because bottles would explode. That left a couple of months in the spring and fall—if the ship was not lost at sea to a storm or a chunk of iceberg. How could they hope to develop a market that left customers uncertain of supply and high and—literally—dry for months on end?

Ruinart's concerns about the weather were shared by Thomas Jefferson when he was placing orders for President Washington. "I am anxious this wine should not move from Champagne til the heats are over, and that it should arrive in Philadelphia before the heat comes on," Jefferson wrote.

In addition to worrying about weather and shipping problems, champagne makers were also bedeviled by American preferences in taste. Jefferson bemoaned the fact that America's taste had been "corrupted" when it was still a colony by England's commercial interest in brandy and fortified wines like Port and Madeira, drinks high in alcohol which he said were forced down the throats of Americans. Every country was different, however. Russia craved champagne that was sickly sweet and so thick that you could splatter it against the wall and it would almost stick. By contrast, England's preference in "fizz," as they called it, leaned toward bone dry and was crafted for connoisseurs. "In Germany," said one critic, "they like their champagne to be very sparkling and are less mindful of quality."[3]

America was somewhere in the middle. Some liked it lacey and light, while others insisted on something heavier and "full-bodied." Still others liked it with a bit of sugar or syrup added to round out the flavors and tone down the acidity. It was all very confusing for champagne producers. The United States was a young country, an "infant" compared to other countries, and considered culturally unrefined. At the end of the day it was hard to picture a cowboy just off the trail with mud and straw clinging to his boots, bellying up to the bar and saying, "A glass of champagne, please."

To better understand what America was all about and how to penetrate the market, the champagne house of Perrier-Jouët hired a group of historians to study the country. One of the first things they became aware of was that meals were eaten much more quickly:

There is no question of spending time around the table, even at a restaurant. For these meals, the usual drink is black coffee or coffee sweetened with cream. In the countryside, one drinks water but in the cities there is a fear of cholera so that prohibits that beverage of water. However, that also serves as very useful excuse for adding cognac or rum to the water under the pretense that the water isn't safe to drink. Another solution adopted by the middle class to avoid drinking water is to consume root beer. Outside the upper classes, wine is practically unknown.

It was said at the time that "perfect ladies" didn't drink but instead would wet their lips from a glass of sherry. Gentlemen found refuge in their clubs or bars, such as the Metropolitan Hotel in New York or the famous Gem Saloon on Broadway. There they drank gin slings, mint julips, sangarees, sherry cobblers, timber doodles, hot-buttered rum, blue blazers . . . and champagne.

Which raised another question: what color should it be? There seemed to be a distinct preference for white champagne over pink, though this was probably because, as one champagne maker noted, rosé, or pink bubbly, was considered the champagne of prostitutes. In 1828 another producer told its representative in America, "We thought best not to send any pink, but all white, there being so little demand for the pink champagne." But the representative responded, "The only complaint, if any, is if it is of a brownish color." Apparently moral considerations didn't enter into it.

One thing everyone seemed agreed on was that Americans were extremely conscious of appearance. Champagne should be "straw colored, quite pale." Bottles had to look good, too, preferably with gold labels or labels with gold print. Customers also wanted the name of the importer on the bottle, someone in America, not just a producer in far-off France. If there could be special decoration, say, like an American flag on the neck label, so much the better.

Even the baskets champagne was shipped in had to be attractive. This was something the widow Clicquot was especially sensitive to. "I took particular care over the packaging to please the eye and the taste at the same time. The baskets are decorated with a colored wicker trim while the bottles have elegant labels," she wrote in 1831 when she filled an order from John Mel, who was hoping to become Clicquot's agent in America. In response, Mel requested that he be sent "wines always with abundant mousse, limpid, as light colored as possible and packed in pretty baskets, because appearance is very important in these regions."

Madame Clicquot could not have agreed more, saying she was "eager to provide you with every means to please your buyers, as much with the real quality of the wine as with the external adornments to which it seems importance is attached." She went a step further and ordered "elegant labels made to be placed on the bottle."

These labeled bottles destined for the United States were the first ever to use the name Veuve Clicquot.

Clicquot had been exporting champagne to the United States since 1782, when the founder of the company, Philippe Clicquot, sent one hundred bottles with a shipment of wool from what was then his family's main business. It went well, and by 1797 he was dealing with an agent in Paris who had business with the United States. Clicquot wrote him, "I engage you to transmit a few cases to your house in Philadelphia where this liquor is much sought-after."

Monsieur Clicquot had another idea as well for launching a market in the New World: a charm offensive on the American community in France. He was rightly convinced once they tasted his champagne, they would take their love of it home with them and ask for more. He was echoing Jean-Rémy Moët who had allowed invading Russian soldiers to plunder his cellars after the Napoleonic wars. "All those soldiers who are ruining me today will make my fortune tomorrow," he said. "I'm letting them drink all they want. They will be hooked for life and become my best salesmen when they go back to their own country."

When Clicquot died, his ideas were carried forward by his widow, the legendary Barbe-Nicole. In 1804 she sent wine to the "Naval Ministry in the United States" and received word that it was "most satisfactory." Over the next two decades, however, she faced a bumpy ride. She had to deal with extensive fraud, had to change agents several times and reorganize her American distribution system. When California became the thirty-first state, one merchant suggested she send champagne there, as it "will become the world's premier market." She demurred, saying she would wait for more information.

Two years later, as Charles Heidsieck was getting ready to leave for America, the widow told a San Francisco merchant she was still "waiting for more favorable circumstances." It was a position she would stick to until 1858, when she finally agreed to send champagne to "San Francisco of California."

Maison Joseph Krug made a stab at the United States as well and, like other champagne houses, was told "the wine has to be crystal clear, dry with a fine effervescence, and contained in nice bottles and with beautiful labels."

Another correspondent added, "The packing must be very careful. One cares much for the label to be with gold and silver. Same for the corks that have to be of good quality and covered with a silver foil. The only suitable packing is in white baskets as flat as possible and comprising never more than twelve bottles or twenty-four halves."

Americans, it was clear, were not hesitant about making their preferences known. On March 15, 1846, Krug got a rebuke from the firm Loison & Sylvestre in New Orleans, a firm it had been dealing with for two years: "The ship docked today. But the wines arrive[d] too late. We had previously informed you of the best times to receive some champagne. And we remember [sic] you of those favorable periods and the causes that command them in order to help you understand the importance of complying with these requests. Business here starts on October 15 when foreigners come for the winter. The city is deserted in summer that is to say from July to October because of the extreme heat."

Loison & Sylvestre went on to list "favorable periods," which included Christmas and early January. "By March and the beginning of hot season previous deliveries of champagne can be disposed of . . . much activity happening at that time [i.e., Mardi Gras]. But it is also the moment when the place is well crowded and receiving wines is not safe anymore."

Perrier-Jouët likewise was hankering after a piece of the American market, so when it received a letter from New Yorker John A. F. Rachau in 1836 offering to serve as an agent for its champagne, the firm jumped at the chance. It was, as company historians later said, "an improvised arrangement."

The American market, however, was not a stable place to be in the first part of the nineteenth century. Growth was unsteady and irregular, and financial crises always seemed to be around the corner. One hit the very next year, in 1837, but Rachau managed to weather it. Yet, it became clear that Rachau's financial footing was not solid, and debts accumulated. At the same time, he and Perrier-Jouët faced the same problems other champagne houses had: identifying *le goût américain* (American taste), working out transport schedules, and designing labels that would appeal to the American market. Like Veuve Clicquot, Perrier-Jouët found that too often their American agents were, at best, unreliable and at worst, outright crooks. Trying to manage sales from a distance was a recipe for disaster.

By 1842 losses had soared and the company concluded that, while America might become an "essential market," it wasn't worth the trouble. It was difficult to understand, they said, and even harder to master.

Perrier-Jouët sold off its remaining American stock at a loss and called it quits. It would concentrate on Britain.[4]

At the time, America was little more than fifty years old and still trying to define itself. Perhaps it was too soon for the citizens of such a young country to be interested in something from the old continent, a part of the world that so many of them had recently and gladly left.

|||||||

Charles Heidsieck could hardly wait to get there. Steamships had taken over transatlantic crossings by then, and he made the trip from Liverpool via Halifax, Nova Scotia, in only ten days. It was a bright, spring day when he bounded off the ship in Boston.

His enthusiasm practically leapt off the pages of the letters he

6. Haymarket Square, Boston, 1852. Boston Public Library.

wrote home to Amélie. "This is one of the most beautiful cities I've ever seen, and the people are so full of energy!" Charles was surprised by the number of different churches there were in Boston, how many Protestant denominations compared to the limited Protestant presence in France. "The people here are also great churchgoers, but very puritanical. Rules of conduct are severe," he went on, "and smoking and spitting in the streets are prohibited."

He told Amélie he wanted to see everything, and quickly set about doing so. He crossed Massachusetts to get to Albany, the capital of New York State, but his goal was Buffalo. He wanted to see the port that was the gateway to the "Wild West," the staging point for everyone heading for the wilderness. It was, however, nearly three hundred miles away. Over land it would be at least a three-day, four-night trip, changing trains and stage lines numerous times. That was the route express messengers followed with their suitcases and strongboxes of documents, letters, securities, and packages for those who found the postal service too slow and too risky.

Although it was faster, it was far less comfortable than the ten-day trip on the Erie Canal. The canal, which had been open for more than twenty-five years, was still the pride of America. It connected the commercial and industrial centers of the East Coast to the American West. Everything—merchandise and people—moved on this man-made waterway. Its barges were considered masterpieces of design.[5]

"The boat was long and narrow, with a row of windows on each side. There were Venetian blinds, painted red, before these windows, and the boat itself was painted white. This gave it a very gay appearance," observed one traveler in the same year Heidsieck arrived. "The top of the boat, which formed a sort of deck, was nearly flat, being only curved a little from the center toward each side, so that the rain might run off. . . . The deck was four or five feet above the water. At the bow, and also at the stern of the boat, there was a lower deck, with steps to go down to it; and from the lower deck in the stern, there were other steps leading into the cabin.

"The cabin was a long and narrow room, which occupied almost the whole of the interior of the boat. It looked like a pleasant little parlor. . . . There were seats on the sides, under the windows, covered with red cushions. . . . There were one or two tables in the middle, with some books and maps upon them."

In the evening a change came over the cabin when a red curtain dropped down to separate the women's sleeping quarters from the men's. The "Ladies' Saloon" had a table with a bouquet of flowers and more books, the traveler observed.

When Charles arrived, there was one book everyone was talking about: *Uncle Tom's Cabin; Or, Life among the Lowly*, by Harriet Beecher Stowe. It had been published just at the time Heidsieck was stepping off his steamer onto American soil, and it became almost instantly "the most popular novel of the day."

The book had first appeared in serial form in the abolitionist paper *National Era*. Its popularity there was so astounding that Mrs. Stowe had to write additional episodes.

The book itself caused an even greater sensation, becoming immediately a best-seller of never-before-seen proportions. Three hundred thousand copies were sold in the first year alone, this in a country of about twenty-three million people, at least one-fifth of whom were totally illiterate and others, such as immigrants, who had only

# UNCLE TOM'S CABIN;

OR,

# LIFE AMONG THE LOWLY.

BY

HARRIET BEECHER STOWE.

## VOL. I.

ONE HUNDRED AND FIFTH THOUSAND.

BOSTON:
JOHN P. JEWETT & COMPANY
CLEVELAND, OHIO:
JEWETT, PROCTOR & WORTHINGTON.
1852.

7. Title page of first edition of *Uncle Tom's Cabin*. Missouri University Archives.

a minimal grasp of English. Eight presses ran nonstop to keep up with the demand, although publishers reported that nearly all sales of the book were in the northern states. It would go on to sell three million copies in the United States within the next year and another three and a half million around the world.

*Uncle Tom's Cabin* also stirred the waters of the slavery question which were thought to have been calmed two years earlier by what was labeled the "final settlement," or the Compromise of 1850. The compromise admitted California to the Union as a free state, and allowed territories recently gained in the war with Mexico to determine their own status as either free states or slave.

Written in straightforward prose free of the usual railings and ravings by abolitionists, Mrs. Stowe's book touched a nerve. As one historian was to write, "the northern attitude toward slavery was never quite the same after *Uncle Tom's Cabin.*"

For the first time, hearing about the book and the fraught discussions that went with it, Charles would be exposed to the contentious issue that would upend his life.

But slavery was not the only issue keeping Americans up late at night talking and arguing. As they sat in their comfortable seats on barges gliding along the Erie Canal, they were also spouting phrases like "Manifest Destiny" and "the '49ers." "Manifest Destiny" claimed that it was America's God-given right to extend from coast to coast, and now, thanks to the recent war with Mexico and a little horse trading with Great Britain, it finally did, they would have explained to the visitor. The slogan probably sounded pretentious to a foreigner like Heidsieck, but hearing of "the '49ers" would have thrilled him, for it carried the same sound of romance and adventure that inspired him to set off for America.

ııııııı

Discovery of gold at Sutter's Mill in California four years before Heidsieck arrived in the United States had inspired people in the thousands to decamp and try their luck mining.

There was a French connection, too. In Paris it gave the government an idea: this was a perfect way to get rid of the country's "undesirables." We can ship all of them—the unemployed roaming the streets, the criminals, the renegades, the drunkards—off to the goldfields. Plus, Emperor Napoléon III calculated, it was a clever way to get a toehold in the New World so he could begin rebuilding the French Empire. There was, however, one stumbling block—money. Getting from Paris to the famed goldfields cost more than a thousand francs per person, or nearly four thousand dollars in today's terms. The voyage itself would take at least half a year.

How to pay for it, how to put the idea into practice was unclear. The answer came in the form of a semi-private lottery sanctioned by the government, *la loterie des ingots d'or*, the gold ingots lottery. A gold ingot then worth four hundred thousand francs was announced as the first prize, along with some other substantial prizes. Chances were sold for one franc, then the average daily salary of a worker. "Four hundred thousand francs for one franc" was the slogan. Money raised by the lottery ticket sales would be used to send five thousand Frenchmen to the goldfields, the publicity said. The ingot itself went on display in the window of a bank on the Boulevard de Montmartre.[6]

Ticket sales were slow at first, and there were charges of the government misappropriating the money for its own use. These combined to push the company running the lottery to seek a way to add legitimacy and, at the same time, promote the scheme. A celebrity, that's what we need, they decided. Someone famous and respected to endorse the scheme. They chose Alexandre Dumas *fils*, author of the popular *La Dame aux Camélias*, and son of the writer of *The Three Musketeers*. He promptly produced a pamphlet on the supposed history of lotteries, pointing out that all of life, including love, is a lottery. He suggested a lottery ticket would be the perfect gift for a woman, because "women are so fond of gambling and the unforeseen!" If she won something, he went on to say, "she will be eternally grateful to you, and who knows what might come from the eternal gratitude of a woman?"

Apparently Frenchmen had no trouble imagining what that might be, for Dumas and his pamphlet did the trick: seven million tickets were quickly sold. By this time, everyone in France seemed to have "gold fever." "It was California at the top, California at the bottom,

California everywhere and all the time," one writer noted about the newspapers of the day. Even fashion retailers joined in; it was France, after all. They announced collections of clothes "perfect for California." If, however, you did not plan to go prospecting yourself, you could, for twelve francs, purchase *un chapeau californien*, a Californian hat, made by a well-known designer, and be part of the excitement that way.

In Paris, six thousand people crowded the Théâtre de la Cirque des Champs-Elysées to witness the drawing for the lottery. And the winner? Someone Charles Heidsieck must have known: Louis-Médard Yvonnet, a fellow champagne maker. The news was all over Champagne, and so too was Yvonnet's decision about what to do with the windfall. He gave much of it to help build a new, larger church of Saint Basle in his hometown of Bouzy, a village renowned for the quality of its grapes. He was, perhaps, too generous, because he died in poverty not long afterward.

Some of the five thousand men sent to California in the government's program to rid itself of its "deplorables" did not fare much better. One group mutinied along the way and were thrown off the ship in Brazil; others continued their drunken ways in the Golden State, but many settled down and succeeded, nearly all in professions unrelated to gold prospecting. They became solid citizens of their new country, and many of their descendants still reside in California. Almost none of those shipped off by the lottery ever returned to France.

Many of those wayward Frenchmen chosen by the government were en route at the time Charles arrived in America, so the idea of "the '49ers" remained vivid and the dream of finding a fortune in a stream still exuded its magic for Frenchmen and others.

So, what we need now in America, fellow travelers would have told Charles as he traveled across New York, is a transcontinental railroad, one to connect the east coast to the west. They might have argued about whether the train line should take a northern route or a southern one, but whichever one, it would be the ultimate realization of Manifest Destiny, they said. It would bring not only the goldfields but also the huge swaths of empty land into the reach of all Americans, especially those newly arrived immigrants longing for homes. People could settle there and create farms and ranches. Oh yes, they confirmed to Heidsieck, who was steeped in tales of savages and danger, there were "real live wild Indians" out there on part of the land, but they could be "removed."

ıllıllı

Charles's French accent, which fell so prettily on American ears, his earnest but halting English, his curiosity, as well as his elegance and sophistication would have made him a sought-after companion on the slow, monotonous trips. He, in turn, was absorbing all the other travelers had to tell him. His interest in everything around him fired up not only his newfound friends who were eager to share their knowledge but also his own eagerness and determination to learn even more about the country.

Now, hearing of the idea for a railroad stretching thousands of miles from one side of the country to the other, both the businessman and the adventurer in Charles were intrigued. He had seen what the enlarged railroad system was doing for France, especially for its champagne industry, so he could well imagine what it would mean for America.

Nonetheless, it would not have been a train that caught Charles's eye and imagination when he arrived in Buffalo, but a stagecoach—a stagecoach totally different from those he knew in Europe. This one was high and wide and its body curved to provide extra stability and a bit more elbow room for passengers. Most surprisingly, there were no steel springs. Instead there were thick strips of bull hide to stabilize and cushion the ride which, as Mark Twain was later to say, could make you feel as though you were in "an imposing cradle on wheels."[7]

It was called the Concord Coach, named for its "birthplace" in Concord, New Hampshire. Under the driver's seat was a green box made of Ponderosa pine, oak, and iron. Inside might be gold bullion, coins, checks, or securities of another type, but whatever it was, it was sure to be valuable and sure to be conscientiously guarded by the man sitting next to the driver and holding a sawed-off shotgun, "riding shotgun."

Throughout his time in America, Heidsieck sought out every means of transport available, and his eagerness to experience everything he could would have undoubtedly made him a passenger in one of the new vehicles.

Heidsieck's cross-country travels, his varied experiences, including his look at the "shattering waters" of Niagara Falls—nothing could do more to prove to him that what Ralph Waldo Emerson had written was true: "America is the country of the future. It is a country of beginnings, of projects, of vast designs and expectations." That was exactly what Heidsieck himself had felt: America was the country for *his* "vast designs," for *his* future. Now it was time for the plunge.

Thanks to the Erie Canal and Hudson River connecting it directly to the "West," New York City already had become both the commercial heart of the country and its major port, so it was the perfect location for a sales agent for Champagne Charles Heidsieck in America. Fully aware of the problems other champagne houses had faced in the New World, Charles was, nonetheless, confident he could find someone there who would understand and appreciate his vision and be able to carry it out.

Other houses had merely tested the waters, he thought as he headed for New York City; he was going to dive straight in. Not just a few hundred bottles of Charles Heidsieck Champagne for America each year. No, Heidsieck had his sights set on a few *hundred thousand* bottles annually. He was determined his champagne would become a fixture of American life and taste buds.

At a time when so little champagne was being sent to America, it was an almost preposterous idea—but just the sort of thing that appealed to a pair of young brothers, Thomas and Theodore Bayaud.

Their father, Jean, had left France for New York in the early 1800s and opened a business importing a variety of items from his native country, including spirits. His sons, who were about the same age as Charles, joined their father in the company and set about buying up warehouses and making contacts all along the eastern seaboard.

The two Bayauds, like their father, were open to new ventures and eager to expand. Plus, as Charles was to discover, the older one, Thomas, shared his fascination with stories of the California Gold

Rush and the American West and hinted about his own hopes to go there someday, perhaps to "start a new life."

It was an idea that resonated with Charles, for here he was, doing much the same thing. He'd started a new business and was pursuing it in a country everyone had warned him against. Charles encouraged Thomas to take a chance and follow his dreams.

It appealed to Charles that the Bayauds spoke French and that, like the Heidsiecks, they were a family business. It seemed like a perfect match. He hired them to represent and sell his champagne.

In a letter to Amélie, he wrote: "They're honest and one of the best. We're in good hands."

# 4

||||||||||||

# Reading the Stars

If Charles-Camille Heidsieck had glanced up at the stars that autumn of 1852, he would not have been surprised to see they were perfectly aligned and shining more brightly than ever. Everything—technology, finance, transportation, even Mother Nature—had fallen into place to turn his daring bet on a starting a new champagne business into a winning one.

Good fortune, in fact, seemed to be everywhere. The whole of France was smiling. In less than two years, with a classic Gallic shrug, the country had managed to shuck off a revolution that toppled its bourgeois King Louis Philippe I and install a republic presided over by a man with a heroic name: Louis-Napoléon Bonaparte. He was the nephew of the first Napoléon, who had raised France to new levels of glory before his crashing defeat at Waterloo. Even though he died in exile, his aura and successes still enchanted his countrymen. Perhaps, they thought, some of his magic ran in the veins of this new Napoléon. Victor Hugo's newspaper, *L'Événement*, certainly thought so. "We have confidence in him; he carries a great name," it editorialized. Most of the country agreed with the paper. In 1848, by an overwhelming majority, Louis-Napoléon was elected president of France. That title was not quite grand enough, however. He proclaimed he would now be known as the prince-president. No one was going to be allowed to ignore or forget his imperial connection.

The prince-president also announced he would honor the new constitution drawn up by a commission that included Alexis de Toqueville, the diplomat and historian who had chronicled the state of America and its democracy seventeen years earlier.

Toqueville's views were set down in *Democracy in America*, a two-volume set written when westward expansion and Jacksonian democracy were transforming the American way of life. His goal was to help his country better understand its position between a fading aristocratic order and the emerging democratic one. Despite the Revolution of 1789, most French still relied on a central authority: the center of political gravity, Toqueville said, resided in a chaotic bureaucracy answerable only to the monarchy form. In the United States it was just the opposite; there private individuals formed the basis of economic and political life. In his writing, Toqueville emphasized that democracy was a balance between liberty and equality and respect for the individual. The United States, he said, was a society in which people looked out for themselves rather than to the state for their needs, and where working hard and making money constituted "the dominant ethic," values that set it apart from France and other European countries.

These were ideals that Toqueville tried to incorporate into the new French constitution, and which Louis-Napoléon swore to uphold. Louis said he supported "religion, family, property, the eternal basis of all social order," and intended "to give work to those unoccupied; to look out for the old age of the workers; to introduce in industrial laws those improvements which don't ruin the rich, but which bring about the well-being of each and the prosperity of all."

To meet those ambitious goals, Louis-Napoléon immediately set about modernizing France, which was lagging well behind Great Britain and other industrialized countries. One of his first moves was eliminating tariffs, thereby opening France to products from all over the world. Suddenly faced with an onslaught of imported goods, French companies had no choice but to update and reorganize to stay alive and compete. To assist them, the new government jumped in with improved banking practices and credit programs.

In addition, the press was given greater freedom, and educational opportunities began to be expanded.

Expanding, too, was the railway system, making it easier and faster for people to get around and for producers and manufacturers to get their products to market.

The prince-president took great satisfaction in his role, and especially in the powers that went with it. So it came as no surprise that with his term coming to an end, he indicated he was not ready to leave office. The constitution of the Second Republic, however, the one written by Toqueville's committee and the one Louis-Napoléon had sworn four years earlier to uphold, said otherwise. It did not permit a second term for the nation's president, no matter what he called himself.

As a result, in December of 1851 the prince-president staged a bloodless *coup d'état* to continue as president. A year later he completed his takeover of the French government by naming himself Emperor Napoléon III. The empire was back.

There would be no big coronation in Reims as there had been for Charles X, but champagne makers did not let the event go unnoticed. They produced special labels for their bottles showing the new emperor galloping at the head of his troops.

Louis-Napoléon must have been thrilled with that image. As he said in a speech in Marseille soon after establishing the Second Empire:

> Some people say the Empire is war. I say the Empire is peace. Like the Emperor [Napoléon Bonaparte I], I have many conquests to make. . . . Like him I wish . . . to draw into the stream of the great popular river those hostile side-currents which lose themselves without profit to anyone. We have immense unploughed territories to cultivate; roads to open; ports to dig; rivers to be made navigable; canals to finish, a railway network to complete. We have, in front of Marseille, a vast kingdom to assimilate into France. We have all the great ports of the west to connect with the American continent by modern communications, which we still lack.

Those words would have made champagne makers, who were always eager to expand their markets, their own empires, committed Bonapartists—at least for the moment. Any doubts about that were washed away when the archbishop of Reims announced he would celebrate a Te Deum mass on January 1, 1852, in the city's cathedral to celebrate Louis-Napoléon's *coup d'etat*. Reporters were to note, however, that support for the new emperor was less than overwhelming. The cathedral was only half full.

But no empire can be complete without an heir, the emperor knew, so he began a search for a wife who could add prestige, as well as an heir, to the Bonaparte regime. The choice he made was a Spanish noblewoman named Eugénie de Montijo. The new empress had a family background that encompassed half of Europe and more. Although her father was a Spanish grandee, her mother was one-half Scot, one-quarter Belgian, and one-quarter Spanish. Her Scottish grandfather was the United States consul in Málaga, but as far as champagne producers and others in the wine trade were concerned, his most important role was that of a wholesale wine merchant, a very successful one. Wine producers were hopeful they would now have a sympathetic ear at the Tuileries Palace, someone who understood and supported the needs of their business. The new empress, they said, could remind the emperor of how much his uncle had done to promote their sparkling wine.

Reminding was hardly necessary. Napoléon III readily grasped champagne's power to win friends and influence people and had already been wooing the army with bubbly. Hoping to become as popular with the troops as his uncle had been, he regularly staged military parades at an army base outside Versailles. Before each ceremony, he distributed champagne to all the soldiers. If nothing else, one historian pointed out, "It got champagne into the news." And also into the popular satirical press, which proclaimed, "The wine of Champagne is now intoxicating soldiers with politics. Government is to be found at the bottom of a bottle; we will soon have a Champagne Caesar." Another edition of the same paper featured a cartoon of the newly appointed military governor of Algeria arriving at his post with crates of champagne, saying he was now equipped to have military parades just like the emperor's.[1]

Even before he declared himself emperor, Louis-Napoléon was, in the historian's words, "an excellent propagandist for champagne." At parties at the Elysées Palace, the presidential residence, he had champagne laid out in rows of two hundred bottles.

Once the empress arrived on the scene and they had moved to the Tuileries Palace, the entertaining became even more spectacular. They organized balls, welcome parties for ambassadors, charity soirées, gala events—one after another. No dinner could be given without a parade of toasts made with the frothing wine in crystal flutes.

Although the champagne coupe, the glass said to be molded on the breast of Marie-Antoinette, continued to be popular, connoisseurs denigrated it, preferring the slim and elegant glass being used at the Tuileries. One went so far as to defend it by claiming the glass had been named a flute because of "the heavenly melodies it pours into our hearts."

No matter what glass was used, it was clear champagne had become *de rigeur* in the Second Empire.

||||||||

In Champagne itself, changes that previously had inched forward were now moving at a many-miles-per-hour pace.

Until the middle of the nineteenth century, still wine—in other words, wine with no bubbles and pale red in color—dominated the area. Only a small percentage of the total production, about two-sevenths, was turned into sparkling wine.

Vines grew in a manner known as *en foule*, with branches from one vine pushed into the ground and covered with earth and manure to create another vine capable of producing grapes within two years. The young branches circled the "mother" vine like dancers around a maypole, making care of the vineyards a time-consuming, labor-intensive, and, as a result, expensive operation as workers had to carefully maneuver around the baby vines. Neither machines nor horses could work in such a hodgepodge. Everything—pruning, fertilizing, harvesting, even hauling soil that had washed down the slopes back up to the vines—had to be done by hand. It was backbreaking work that endured from one New Year's Day to the next, eight and a half to twelve hours a day every day. No one in a wine producer's family was exempt from the labor. Engravings from the mid-nineteenth century show women bent nearly double with *hottes*, or baskets, on their backs loaded with manure to be shoveled around the vines. Children, too, were pressed into helping.

But with Paris and its thousands of consumers only one hundred kilometers down the road, Champagne's red *vin ordinaire*, or everyday wine, was easily and quickly sold, and so the unending work continued.

That is, until the railroad came to town. Suddenly the City of Light was awash with cheaper red wine hauled in from the southern part of France, the Midi and Languedoc. The vignerons of Champagne, with their mercurial climate and higher costs, could not keep up, let alone compete, with their cousins from the sunny south. Many simply gave up. Reports from Champagne sent to the emperor's ministers said, "Each day the sons of vignerons are abandoning this difficult work."

Another report in 1858, from the Champagne village of Sainte-Ménéhould, where Dom Pérignon had been born, said only twenty-two hectares of vines remained. "Vines disappear day by day because they produce only losses and the finished product has no commercial value."[2]

The good monk would have been appalled. Two hundred years earlier Dom Pérignon had identified and laid down the rules for making quality wine: prune vines aggressively so fewer but better grapes are produced, pick in the early morning when it's cool, discard bad grapes, press quickly but gently. Those rules had been accepted and followed religiously by serious winemakers in the years that followed. But now, in his own hometown, his guidelines were not only ignored, they were tossed onto the trash heap.

Yet, elsewhere in Champagne, the positive signs, those aligned stars that Charles Heidsieck had bet his future on, were beginning to appear and multiply.

Chemical pesticides and fungicides came onto the market even as wine producers in Sainte-Ménéhould were abandoning their vines. Although chemical treatments were expensive and labor-intensive, they significantly reduced damage from pests and diseases and increased production of healthy, quality grapes. Wine producers quickly realized application of the new products was easier when vines were planted in rows rather than tangled *en foule*. Equipment and horses could move through vines planted that way, too.

Even more importantly, technical progress in champagne production itself had now begun to pay off.

Champagne's "big bang"—exploding bottles—had been all but eliminated with a better understanding of the relationship between sugar and wine. It was a pharmacist from the Champagne village of Châlons-sur-Marne (now Châlons-en-Champagne), Jean-Baptiste François, who discovered the "magic formula" for determining how much sugar could be added without causing bottles to explode. Up to then, champagne makers used extra sugar to preserve their product and create bubbles, but it was largely guess work—that is, until François created what he called a *gleucoenomètre*, or glucose meter, in 1835. Thanks to his invention, champagne makers now had a quick and accurate way of measuring how much sugar to use and ensuring that their wine and their workers were safe.

As Eugène Perrier of Perrier-Jouët said in 1868, "What his research has shown has saved the champagne industry millions." Producers no longer had to plan on a loss of 50 percent or more of their annual production; they could bottle, sell, and ship with newfound confidence. They could forget about the cheap red wine they'd been making and concentrate on the far more profitable sparkling wine.

The new railroads that now carried champagne to every corner of France were also accelerating and contributing to changes in the entire country's economic landscape. People had the means to leave the countryside and seek better-paid, less physically demanding employment in urban centers. As a result, a middle class was gradually developing, expanding the market for all products.

Champagne took advantage of the changes to use its new technology and means of transport to break out of the narrow world of nobility and aristocracy that had been its principle market. With articles and cartoons, newspapers popularized the beverage among the increasingly literate, middle-class population. So did the theater.

Serious playwrights included scenes with it to attract the highbrow audience, while those with more pedestrian tastes were drawn in by the songs music hall composers wrote about the wine with bubbles.

Sparkling champagne escaped into the streets as well. It was the favorite drink of *lorettes*, the prostitutes of Paris who got their name from the area around the church of Notre-Dame-de-Lorette, where many of them plied their trade. The *grisettes*, or working girls of Paris who labored daily in gray or *gris* dresses, loved it, too, and would order it whenever their after-hours flirtatious behavior caught the attention of a moneyed man. They called it "champ."[3]

No restaurant worth its menu would be caught without what was still called "the wine of Champagne" on its list. And in their *cabinets particuliers*, where men entertained and were entertained by their mistress of the moment, champagne automatically appeared before the doors were firmly closed for the evening.

In more public settings, corks were usually popped at dessert. "Like fireworks at the end of an evening," one writer said, but across the Channel the English had other ideas. They liked their sparkling wine at the start of the evening, something to tickle the taste buds and stimulate conversation. They also preferred their champagne very dry, not sweet. The classic French *apéritif* was being born to British parents.

Champagne was now being poured and drunk in every European country and attracting such a big following that the French began to complain there was no longer enough of it left at home for them to drink. The lyrics of one popular song lamented,

Sweet Aÿ, dear wine of our fathers,
We no longer know your taste;
It is only beyond our borders
That your splendour is justly honoured!

There was some justification for the complaint. In the ten years after 1850, champagne sales doubled, but three times as much was sent abroad as remained at home.

To make matters worse, it was the best champagne that was exported, leaving the French with only the lesser-quality wines. *Le*

*Vigneron Champenois*, the industry's newspaper, moaned that "the wine of choice is today a royal rarity here, like the black pearl or the 'white blackbird'; foreign countries pay for it and take it away; a person in a good position cannot even be sure of drinking one bottle a year."

Devoted connoisseurs in France, however, were not to be stymied. Some got around the problem simply by ordering their bubbly from foreign merchants.

|||||||||

In the spring of 1852, a jubilant Charles Heidsieck returned to Reims after making his first trip to America. He was thrilled with how it went and enthusiastic about everything he saw. With a sales agent now in place in New York to handle his business, he moved quickly to capitalize on everything that lay ahead. In a whirl of activity, he organized the packing of thousands of bottles of champagne into straw-filled baskets, which were then transported by rail or boat on the Vesle-Aisne canal and the Seine to the Atlantic, where they were loaded onto ships bound for the United States. Charles was confident that what he was sending off would be enthusiastically received.

Other champagne houses watched and drooled with envy. Three hundred thousand baskets a year, he said he'd sell! It was beyond imagining, all those thousands and thousands of new consumers in the American market. More than enough customers for everyone.

All they had to do was reach them. It was not an easy task, however. Fraud had reared its ugly head, complicating the already difficult conditions of transport and distance.

As early as 1844, in the *Pétition des Négociants en Vins de la Champagne*, producers complained to the government that, "not content to usurp the names of 'Champagne' and the famous towns of our department, in order to apply them to any liquid that has been made to sparkle, [fraudsters] now seize the names of the most well-known merchants, to sell wine abroad, using this honourable and respected passport, thereby prostituting the reputation of houses that until now have inspired complete and unquestionable trust."

Unfortunately, there was little the French government could do to change the situation. It was a battle that would continue to be fought into the twenty-first century.

Charles, at the same time, had a private battle to fight, and it touched him where it hurt most—within his family. No sooner had he opened his company than Piper-Heidsieck, the firm where he had begun his career and which he had left only months earlier, filed a lawsuit against him. Piper-Heidsieck argued that Charles should be barred from using the name "Heidsieck" for his business and asked the court to disallow its use.[4]

The suit opened old wounds that reached back through at least two generations of the extended family. Charles's uncle Christian Heidsieck ran the Heidsieck champagne business after the founder's death, but like Charles's father, Christian died at a young age. His widow married Henri Piper, who took over the firm's operations, renaming it Piper-Heidsieck. Charles had begun his career there but quit in anger when it became apparent that Henri Piper had plans for the future of the company that did not include Charles.

In creating his firm, Charles registered it in his own name, which, as he told the court, he had every right to use.

In 1853 the court handed down its decision: Charles did indeed have the right to use his own name. The company Champagne Charles Heidsieck would continue.

But so would the rift in the family. The scars left by the legal battle would not heal completely and would be reopened time and again down through the years.

||||||||

Other champagne houses were less concerned about what name Heidsieck had given his firm than they were about what he was accomplishing in America.

Soon after Charles returned to France in 1852, Ruinart, which had dabbled in the U.S. market by sending a few baskets from time to time, decided to take a chance. For the first time, it sent champagne to the West Coast, shipping twelve hundred bottles to San Francisco. More would follow.

At the same time, Veuve Clicquot opted for a trial run to New

Reading the Stars

Orleans. The company sent fifteen baskets of twelve bottles each to the Crescent City and then, pleased with the result, appointed an agent there to handle the southern states.

Chief among those feeling the magnetic pull from across the ocean was Perrier-Jouët, a champagne house that had blundered into the United States twenty years earlier only to withdraw not long after with its proverbial tail between its legs.

Now a new opportunity appeared when Edmund Poirier, a cousin of the owners by marriage, announced he was moving to New York and said he would be glad to represent the company. The Perrier brothers, who were running the firm, decided they were ready for another try at the market which their father years earlier viewed as "essential" but "impossible to master." Knowing Heidsieck had launched his champagne in the United States in person, the brothers believed having a family member overseeing operations could be the key to success this time around. They gave Poirier the go-ahead to set up shop and start trading. But with Heidsieck's recent success in mind, they also issued a note of caution: "We have perfectly understood what kind of individual buys champagne, that if the price is equal, [he] will choose the one that is best known."

It was a not-so-subtle reminder to Poirier of how well Heidsieck was doing, how hard *he* would to have to work, and how much publicity he would have to generate if he expected to compete.

Poirier, however, was not directly from the champagne business, even though his family in Paris had some dealings in wine, so the Perriers wanted to make sure he was prepared for what he would face.

Worries soon began creeping in. Within a few months, Charles Perrier was querying their new representative, "We know the Heidsieck champagne is there and has such a big reputation, but we don't understand why wines that are just as good [like ours] aren't being sold as well." But Perrier, at the same time, was also careful to sound an encouraging note for his younger cousin: "We have the goal of doing better than the marque Heidsieck and we believe with confidence that we can establish our business in New York."

Poirier's response was disappointing. Instead of going head-to-head with Heidsieck and being aggressive, Poirier asked for wines of "second quality" that he could sell for lower prices. The Perriers were appalled. "Let us be clear," they said. "We want to confirm to you our intention of selling *quality* champagnes. Those are the ones which will make our reputation. We'd rather reduce the amount we're sending than reduce the quality. We think wines of the best quality are the ones you should try to sell. That's what Heidsieck does and that's what we intend to do!"

But their frustrations with Poirier only grew deeper. His request for a delivery each month of one hundred baskets seemed risky and excessive to the Perriers. They explained why and gave him a short course on handling champagne. Don't build up a large stock, they admonished him. "Wines that sit too long in the warehouse always suffer. Here we take all precautions—double cardboard in the baskets, double paper around each bottle—all to preserve our wine. Your care [when it arrives] will do the rest."

"And don't forget," they added. "You should watch the unloading of champagne very carefully. Don't let it sit on the quay." The Perriers were concerned about temperature changes where intense heat could create extra pressure in the bottles and make them explode. They worried, too, about freezing cold in the winter months which could freeze the wine itself.

Their concerns about Poirier's suitability as the company's representative finally reached a tipping point when a sales agent from New York, armed with a glowing letter of recommendation, came to Épernay and convinced the brothers he would be a better representative. The Perrier brothers transferred their American representation to his agency.

They were undoubtedly frustrated, since this was the second time Perrier-Jouët had attempted to break into the U.S. market. The brothers knew that having a succession of agents made it harder to develop a loyal clientele. Exactly whom should clients deal with now? Was there still another new agent to contact? What was wrong with the old one?

The Perriers also felt more strongly than ever that Perrier-Jouët was "a name without a face." Unlike the Heidsieck marque, they had no one in America who could "incarnate" their house. A cousin by marriage like Poirier was clearly not enough. They saw that Heidsieck's active presence was responsible for the advantages his champagne house had.

Although the two brothers had talked about it, they realized they had not understood the importance of publicity in a country as vast as the United States. They could not rely on a "royal warrant" or the backing of a nobleman to promote their marque, as had been the case in Europe. They needed a way to get their name into newspapers and before the American public.

Heidsieck's foray in America, his time traveling with Americans and seeing the country, had shown him how important the press was there and how important publicity was in such a vast land. Already fluent in French and German, with a good knowledge of Russian, he went to work improving his English—American English, that is. He knew it would be the key to understanding the culture and establishing his business in the New World.

Perrier-Jouët would finally find its own way by perfecting *its* language skills, not in the United States but in the United Kingdom, where they had developed a thriving market. They also made sure their champagne was served at high-profile events to give them publicity and extra exposure to mass audiences. In the coming years, this would give them an opening into the United States.

|||||||||

Charles Heidsieck, meanwhile, had a new role, one he relished and would cherish his entire life. He had become a father; daughter Marie was born in 1853, and it was no surprise that she was his great delight. Her birth solidified the base and strength he found in his family. Although he was inspired and counseled by the men of the family, it was the women who were his most important advisers and provided unstinting support and comfort for him. Of his eight children, Marie would grow to be the one he was closest to.

His letters reveal the respect and love he felt for the women of his family as well as his enduring devotion to Amélie. As the years went on, he relied more and more on her judgment and business knowledge.

8. Amélie Heidsieck, ca. 1853. Courtesy of Champagne Charles Heidsieck.

For her part, Amélie brought her own commitment to family—and an even bigger and better-known family—to her marriage. Hers was a family peopled by men and women every bit as bold and driven as her husband and as his father, Charles-Henri Heidsieck, the man who had taken Moscow by storm on his white stallion during the Napoleonic Wars. There was, of course, Amélie's notorious grandmother Appoline, whose affair with a younger man left a "stain" on the family escutcheon.

However, her grandmother on her father's side, Marie Perrette Barrachin, was nearly as famous or, perhaps, infamous. She was a devout Catholic who, as a young woman during the French Revolution, refused to play the role of the goddess "Reason" in a tableau of "The Nation" being enacted in front of the altar of the cathedral in Reims. It may have been her youth and beauty that allowed her to escape the wrath of the revolutionaries. It was undoubtedly that which caught the eye of a Knight of the Order of Malta, Nicolas Louis

Reading the Stars

de la Motte. He, too, was devout and from a long line of deeply religious and celebrated nobles. But, there was no question in his mind when he met Perrette, as she was known, that she was the one for him. He immediately sought—and won—release from the vows of poverty, chastity, and obedience he had made as a Knight of Malta so he could marry the young and strong-willed woman.

She found a place for her faith in the watchwords of the republic, *liberté, égalité et fraternité,* and those words were to guide her to a crucial decision.

This was no time to flaunt connections to the discredited nobility, she announced, and argued that her husband should weld together the elements of his family name, wiping out any hints of elite status. He agreed. Henceforth, they were citizens Perrette and Nicolas Delamotte. They were, however, very wealthy citizens, with property, land, and vineyards throughout the Champagne region. Their holdings included a much-loved home in the village of Ludes where the entire family, now including Amélie, Charles, and their growing brood, would spend the summers.

For the Heidsiecks and Henriots, there was almost no line between family and business. While her brother Ernest managed the vineyards and oversaw the winemaking for Champagne Charles Heidsieck, Amélie's father, François Henriot, took over much of the financial management for the new company. He, like Ernest, he would have advised Charles to stay home, consolidate the business in France and Europe, and not become overextended in a faraway market. He knew from experience what he was talking about. He had mechanized and extended his wool business too much and too soon and gotten far ahead of the market. It led to financial disaster and forced him to sell the business.

Henriot's advice to Charles was not misguided. All aspects of French life were changing rapidly as a result of the grand plans coming from the Tuileries Palace—and not just from the emperor.

There was another voice on the scene as well. The empress herself was pushing new ideas. She was known for her passion for sports and for her rebellious streak. As a young girl, Eugénie tried to run away to India and got as far as a ship in the docks before being caught.

As empress she became involved in programs for the education of women, something that would have resonated with the women in Charles's family. She campaigned fiercely but unsuccessfully to have Aurore Dupin, a.k.a. George Sand, elected to the Académie Française, the French Academy, the respected body responsible for producing the official dictionary of the French language. Although it would take another century before a female was elected to the august assembly of *les immortels*—the immortals, as the forty members of the academy are called—the empress had made them squirm.

Undeterred by her failure, Eugénie, who herself had been educated in Paris and by a succession of famous intellectuals, managed to convince the Ministry of Education to award a woman, for the first time ever, a *baccalauréat* diploma. It was the equivalent of an advanced high school degree.

Eugénie's championing of new, modern ideas reflected the optimistic, forward-looking tenor of the times, and the emperor's goals as well. He had implemented a massive renovation of Paris under the direction of Baron Haussmann. There would be new, wide streets, "modern" buildings, and, among the urban-renewal projects, an aqueduct to bring fresh water to the city.

In Heidsieck's hometown of Reims, now only a short train ride away from the nation's capital, there was a growing awareness of the need to emulate what was happening there. In the years since the coronation of Charles X, when Heidsieck was a toddler, the city's population had nearly doubled. Any glamour Reims claimed as "the Royal City" was thoroughly tarnished. No one who saw champagne as an elegant, aristocratic drink would have believed this was its hometown.

The *faubourgs*, or suburbs, were overcrowded shanty towns where woolen workers struggled to make ends meet as increased mechanization cost more and more jobs in the mills. The water supply, which came from the River Vesle, was poisoned from centuries of washing sheepskins in it and then with chemicals used in the wool industry. The river had been used by residents as a sewer for so long that the land along it had absorbed its poisons. Even wells dug to provide fresh water produced only polluted water. Few streets were paved, and epidemics regularly ravaged the *faubourgs*.[5]

People like François Henriot were campaigning to "save" the city. He immersed himself in the archaeology of his hometown and was one of the founders of Ami de Vieux Reims, an organization dedicated to preserving the patrimony of Reims. The election of 1852 then brought in a new mayor, Edouard Werlé, the director of the champagne house of Veuve Clicquot and a friend of both the Heidsiecks and the Henriots. Werlé dusted off an old plan for modernization of Reims, added some ideas of his own, and went to work.

Much like the emperor would do in Paris, he brought in a city planner or architect to oversee the work. Down came the old ramparts, up went new buildings, and in came new cobbled streets, as well as an aqueduct for fresh water. Using land confiscated from religious institutions during the Revolution, the Vesle-Aisne canal was extended, making shipping to ocean ports easier.

At the same time, as the champagne industry was taking off, the wool industry, as Henriot had discovered, was feeling the pressure from other areas, particularly eastern France and Belgium. Jobs were leaving, wages were dropping, but rents were not. Reims's new mayor thought about grouping each industry in one section of town to make the city more efficient and also clean up the *faubourgs*—but then the money ran out.

The *faubourgs*? Well, they would have to wait for another plan, another round of urban renewal.

More important was *centre ville*, the center of the city, which presented a sharp contrast to the filth and squalor of the suburbs. With its imposing private homes, impressive limestone offices, and modern services, along with paved streets capable of supporting heavy wagons loaded with thousands of bottles of champagne, the heart of Reims was the ideal base for international business.

And Charles Heidsieck, with his company now solidly established, was ready to become its most visible and notable representative.

# 5

||||||||||||

# The Panic

Five years after his first trip to America, Charles Heidsieck had reason to celebrate. He had reached his goal; he was selling three hundred thousand bottles of champagne a year to the United States, a figure nearly equal to the amount exported by all other champagne firms put together.

But Heidsieck could not relax. There were some problems, and they concerned Bayaud & Berard, the agency he had hired to represent his champagne house. Although they had done a good job of selling his champagne, he sometimes found them difficult to deal with. They often seemed distracted and reticent about providing information. When it came to payments, they frequently temporized. *Sorry to be a little late*, they'd say. *We'll get to it. We were a little busy last week.* Heidsieck realized it would be best if he went to New York and sorted it out face-to-face. Nonetheless, he still believed America was the land of opportunity and that now was the time to take advantage of it.

Bursting with optimism, Heidsieck boarded a steamer on October 3, 1857, and set off for New York again. Onboard with him were twenty thousand *paniers* of champagne, each containing fifteen bottles, enough to double his sales. He did the figures in his head; he would make a killing.

Heidsieck arrived in New York City twelve days later, but the moment he stepped off the ship he was hit with the worst news imaginable. Stunned, on October 19 he dashed off a letter to his wife: "Four days ago, all the banks closed and suspended their payments. People who were millionaires twenty times over have gone bankrupt. Someone who would have spent a hundred dollars yesterday without giving it a thought now hesitates to buy even a sandwich or glass of beer. At this moment, ships in the harbor are being loaded with merchandise to be returned to Europe because it no longer has the slightest value. It's a disaster!"

It was called the Panic of 1857, a sudden meltdown of the American economy that saw banks fail and thousands of companies go out of business.[1] So swift and steep was the downturn that ripples were felt worldwide. In France, champagne houses, including Heidsieck's, were forced to suspend or sharply curtail operations. Not long afterward, a letter from Amélie arrived. "October 27—My dear Charles, the crisis seems to becoming more and more severe and we are feeling the repercussions. Other champagne houses such as Piper and Roederer have had to let their workers go. It's terrible for everyone. The children and I are doing the best we can but it's not easy. It's now harvest time, and because of that we went to early mass at five o'clock in the morning. As for you, my darling, please try to remain calm and not get agitated, for that won't change anything."

But Heidsieck was in deep depression. He fretted about everything, including the weather. Rain seemed to fall continuously. "Heaven is in tune with earthly things," he moaned. He also complained about his sales agent, who was "sick" and "making it impossible for [him] to get things done." Among his concerns were ninety thousand bottles of champagne that had been shipped to New York after his first trip but which his agent hadn't paid him for: "November 3—My dearest Amélie, our business keeps me awake at night with worries. I lie on the sofa but sleep never comes. I try to read but it doesn't help. I'm trying to keep my pain locked in a tiny corner of myself, hoping it will not escape and invade everything I am trying to accomplish. If it would save us, I'd willingly cut off my arm. Really. To save us financially I would do it. I wouldn't hesitate."

What made the Panic so painful is that it felt like it came from nowhere. The period leading up to it had been one of prosperity. Gold had been discovered in California in the late 1840s, and railroads were stretching tracks across the nation. America was on a roll. Literally. Or so it seemed.

But on August 24, 1857, the New York City branch of the Ohio Life Insurance and Trust Company—a major financial force—had suddenly collapsed following widespread embezzlement. Its failure, said one scholar, "struck the public mind like a cannon shot." There was a run on banks as people, fearing financial ruin, sought to withdraw their money. Unemployment soared. Those who had invested in the stock market lost heavily. Five thousand businesses failed within a year.

This was not the first financial crisis in American history—there were two other "Panics," one in 1837 and another in 1819—but the Panic of 1857 was the first to spread rapidly across the entire country, thanks to the telegraph. When Samuel Morse invented it in 1844, he said, "I trust that one of its effects will be to bind man to his fellow man." Fifty thousand miles of wire, fourteen hundred stations, and ten thousand operators now indeed tied America together. Few were more excited than Gordon Bennett, editor of the *New York Herald*. The telegraph, he said, made it possible for "the whole nation" to have "the same idea at the same time." Or, in this case, the same reaction.

Unfortunately, in 1857 the reaction was disastrous. Panic spread; the run on banks continued without letup. "It was like a contagious virus that could not be stopped," said the *New York Times*, resulting in a crisis of confidence that engulfed the country. But public confidence was about to sink even deeper.

On September 3, a little over two weeks before Heidsieck arrived in the United States, a side-wheel steamer named the SS *Central America* set off from Panama for New York. People called it the "Gold Ship" because of the cargo it was carrying: thirty thousand pounds of gold consisting of coins, ingots, gold dust, and bullion from the California Gold Rush. It had been stored at the San Francisco Mint until it could be shipped to the East. Also on the ship were 425 passengers.

A week into its voyage, the vessel was struck by a raging hurricane. Sails were shredded by 105-mile-an-hour winds and the vessel began taking on water, pitching so violently that the crew could no longer feed coal into the boiler to keep it on course.

By the evening of September 12, with the crew working frantically to bail out water, the ship had made it to waters off the coast of South Carolina. That's when the 280-foot-long steamer was struck by a giant wave. Timbers splintered and the vessel shuddered, then suddenly slipped beneath the waves at a sharp angle. Distress signals went unanswered. All aboard, passengers and crew alike, were lost. Lost, too was the cargo of gold worth two million dollars, the equivalent of three hundred million today. It was the worst economic catastrophe in U.S. maritime history.

Without the gold, banks had no way to back up their paper currency and were forced to close. Investors and speculators went broke. Nearly every segment of society was affected.

It fell particularly hard on the Black community because of a decision by the U.S. Supreme Court earlier that year. In *Dred Scott v. Sandford,* the court ruled that under the Constitution, people of African descent could not become American citizens. This applied to free Blacks as well as those enslaved. They were shackled for life to owners now feeling the effects of the financial crisis. Many slaveholders found themselves hard-pressed to afford the care and feeding of their workers, and put them on rations. The *Dred Scott* decision added significantly to the uncertainty then prevailing. It would not be overturned until the Fourteenth Amendment was adopted in 1868.

Meanwhile, New York City, where Heidsieck had landed in mid-October, was in turmoil. It was the country's major port, and immigrants were flooding in from Europe, primarily from Ireland, which was still facing the effects of its potato famine. But increased numbers were also coming from Germany and eastern Europe. The city's population of a half million people in 1850 had nearly doubled in the intervening seven years, putting pressure on housing, employment, and every aspect of daily life in the city.

Nevertheless, most immigrants were thrilled with their new country, praising it as having "advantages which are not to be found in Europe nor in any other quarter of the globe." Writing home, one new arrival said, "Tell Miriam there is no sending children to bed without supper, or husbands to work without dinner in their bags." Another observed that there was no military conscription, no overbearing aristocracy, and that a workman "did not have to call his employer 'master.'" He wrote how relieved he was of "the absence of overbearing soldiers, haughty clergymen, and inquisitive tax collectors."

Like Heidsieck, most had been drawn to America by romantic and attractive stories. They'd heard "tall tales of miles of virgin trees and acres of fertile soil." The Panic of 1857 served as a sudden reality check and put the brakes on what had been a tidal wave of immigrants into the country.

Making things worse, two rival police forces in New York City were locked in a battle for supremacy. Riots had broken out between them in July. The new Republican Party, composed mainly of native-born men, had gained power in the state legislature and promptly abolished the New York City Municipal Police Department. It wanted to curtail the power of Mayor Fernando Wood, a Democrat, who was backed by the large Irish community. The legislature replaced the Municipal Police with the Metropolitan Police, but the Municipal Police had no intention of going quietly. Internecine wrangling between the two forces continued until the state militia was brought in and Mayor Wood yielded.

So absorbed were the two police forces in battling each other that the New York City underworld had virtually a free pass. A crime spree erupted that finally led to another riot, dubbed the Dead Rabbits Riot. The catalyst for it was Independence Day, a day that the state legislature ruled should be honored by closing all saloons and bars. Irish immigrants in the Five Points area had other ideas about how to celebrate the Fourth of July and flocked to the saloons of the neighborhood, which flagrantly remained open in violation of the order.

It was the provocation rival New York gangs needed in their battle for turf. The Bowery Boys, who supported the new Metropolitan Police, faced off against the so-called Dead Rabbits or Roach Guards, the Irish gangs of Five Points who backed the ousted Municipal Police. The riots turned deadly and were only put down by the arrival of the state militia which had just forced the city's mayor to yield.

The city's upheaval, however, *did* produce some good news. With the fast-growing population, officials knew they had to do something to improve the quality of life. They decided on the creation of a park. In a competition organized to choose a design, two landscape architects, Frederick Law Olmsted and Calvert Vaux, submitted a "Greensward Plan" that won. In 1857, shortly before Heidsieck arrived, the first shovel was turned on what would become America's first great urban green space. It was called Central Park . . . and it became the anchor of a citywide program to establish parks in every borough.

|||||||||

Meanwhile, the financial crisis rolled on, relentlessly and with no end in sight. Heidsieck, like the city itself, wavered between hope and despair. He did whatever he could think of to kill time and take his mind off the crisis, at the same time praying it would soon be over so he could finish his business.

At the rooming house where he was staying, he played endless games of whist during the evenings with other guests. He also managed to put on some extra pounds as he made a surprising discovery: "The cuisine is good here," he wrote home in another letter. He felt sure the Panic couldn't last forever and asked Amélie to send some champagne he could use as samples for potential customers along with her tasting notes on recent vintages. "And also my good eaux [eau de vie] and my Northern Pines Syrup." Was he trying to fend off a cold, or seeking something stronger than champagne to fend off his worries?

Adding to his stress was his awareness that he had to present a relaxed, happy face to the world in order to sell his champagne. His jovial facade worked, and it wasn't before long that Americans began calling him "Charlie."

What also helped him relax was a change of pace which arrived when a friend invited him for a weekend trip outside the city to go hunting. "Given the possibility of having to stay here longer than I expected, I'm glad to have a little distraction."

One concern kept gnawing at him, however, and it involved his sales agent. Heidsieck's business was now being handled primarily by Theodore Bayaud, the younger of the two brothers, but for some

9. Heidsieck's hunting rifle. Courtesy of Champagne Charles Heidsieck.

time payments for champagne shipped to New York had been irregular and were frequently less than the amount due. Amélie, who dealt with the finances, was especially worried. She was convinced they were being shortchanged.

Charles was not so sure. On a visit to the agent's office, he received the warmest welcome possible. He was treated not just as a client, he told Amélie, "but as a real friend." Everyone there, he said, was enthusiastic and expressed their pleasure about being associated with Charles Heidsieck Champagne. He reminded Amélie that they had been doing business with Bayaud for five years and that sales were increasing. "Even if we're not getting everything we should, I'm still convinced Bayaud is an honest man," he wrote on November 20. "He's been open and straight with me, so I still have confidence in him."

Right then, however, Heidsieck knew his most urgent challenge was surviving the financial crisis that was gripping the country. He was somewhat encouraged. "Curiously," he noted in another letter, "the importers of liquids such as our agent are those who are suffering the least."

By December, as the holidays approached, sales of champagne had picked up. It would take several months before they reached previous levels, but Heidsieck was feeling more and more optimistic and began making plans to return home. "Our business is waking up!" he told Amélie happily.

Unfortunately, it was waking up to a problem that left producers, including Heidsieck, gnashing their teeth.

The Panic

The problem was phony champagne, bubbly that was bubbling with ingredients that had nothing to do with grapes. Fraudsters, keen on cashing in on champagne's popularity, were using apples, pears, and a variety of other foreign substances to make their bubbly.[2]

That fake champagne was pouring into America was obvious to anyone who glanced at the figures. In 1860 France exported just over two and a half million bottles of champagne to the United States ... but Americans *consumed* twelve million. How could that be? Where did those extra bottles come from, and what did it all mean? The answer was all too clear—nearly four out of every five bottles sold as champagne were fake. America wasn't just being inundated with fake fizz; it was drowning in it.

"Most of the champagne drunk in America comes from suspicious quarters," one critic said. "We may be very thankful when we get the fruit of the grape for, except in rare cases, we are sure to be deceived. Like Jeremiah's figs, the good are very good, the bad *too* bad to give to pigs."

Another critic noted: "We drink more champagne in America than all the rest of the world put together. Every quality of it is sent here, and most are without labels. That permits dealers to put on any label they wish to best suit his customers, varying the price as he can make for it, for it is absolutely within our knowledge that we have drank champagne of all prices and all brands, at the same table, when there was *but one quality of champagne under all the brands*, and that of the most infamous description." But it wasn't only champagne; it involved every wine on the market.

The capital of corruption was Sète, a French seaport on the Mediterranean which, at the time, was second only in importance to Marseilles. "You name it, we make it" could have been the city's official slogan. Given its location, wines from Spain, Portugal, Italy, and many other places were regularly shipped there. "From these wines," wrote James Gabler, who chronicled Thomas Jefferson's travels through the wine regions of France, "Sète wine chemists were able to manufacture in their laboratories any type, kind, or style of wine. Sète gained the reputation of being able to concoct any of the world's wines, from Falernian of ancient Rome to new claret or old Burgundy."

Such was not lost on Agoston Haraszthy, a pioneer California winemaker, who visited Sète in 1861, nearly a century after Jefferson. If anything, the counterfeiters had only become more skilled in what they were doing. The city, Haraszthy wrote, "is the great manufacturing place for spurious wines. Millions of gallons of imitations being here made, of every brand in existence, and sold to all parts of the world, a few drops of the genuine being used to give the taste of the different qualities. So perfect are some of these imitations, that it is with difficulty you can distinguish the spurious wines from the genuine. The manufacturers buy up cheap wines," he wrote, "and by their chemical preparations, fix them up, and sell them, mostly to the American market, for good prices."

Champagne was at the top of the list. So skilled were these con artists that no one except experts could be sure if the champagne they were drinking was the real thing. "The only security for the consumer who desires to purchase a genuine brand, is to buy of the authorized agent or of him whose integrity is undoubted," one expert said.

That might help, but it was still no guarantee. As one French historian pointed out, "The name of one of the great houses was not enough in itself to prove the authenticity of a product because [unscrupulous makers] of sparkling wines took over the names of the most fashionable brands."

One of the names "borrowed" was Champagne Charles Heidsieck.

In a letter addressed to the American public and published in the *New York Times*, Heidsieck expressed his frustration. He railed against "dishonest adulterators and worthless traffickers. Among the brands that have suffered more than any other by this means, the one bearing my own name, of Charles Heidsieck, may be mentioned. Wines have sprung up as plentiful as mushrooms, and possessing about the same amount of purity as that well-known fungus."

Heidsieck reminded readers that more of his champagne had been introduced into the American market "than all other brands combined" and that buyers should beware of "gross imitations and forgeries of labels." He said he "deeply regretted" having to write such a letter "but the gross impositions which your country suffers under having champagnes imposed upon them with all kinds of figurative names, with ornamental labels, various colored sealing-wax on the corks, and which pretend to represent superior brands of wines, when in fact they are only strengthened with brandy and colored by artificial means—these facts compel me, in justification of my family reputation, to write this letter to the American public."

The problem had been festering for years. As early as 1844, producers had been clamoring for authorities to do something about the situation. In one petition, they complained: "Not content to usurp the names of 'Champagne' and the famous towns of our department, in order to apply them to any liquid that has been made to sparkle, [fraudsters] now seize the names of the most well-known merchants, to sell wine abroad, using this honourable and respected passport, thereby prostituting the reputation of houses that until now have inspired complete and unquestionable trust."

Normally, making champagne is at least a two- or three-year process. In the heart of Paris, however, large quantities of *sham*-pagne were being turned out in twenty-four hours. Fraudsters used minor white wines from Bordeaux, added sugar, then employed a machine normally used for making carbonated water to inject carbon dioxide into each bottle before corking. Afterward, they slapped on phony labels to lure the unwary customer with fantastic names like Ai Mousseux du Schah de Perse (The Shah of Persia's sparkling wine) or Sillery du Grand Turc (Sillery of the Sultan of Turkey).

But it was about to become more outrageous. By the end of the nineteenth century more than four thousand different brands of champagne would be registered, each one seemingly more fantastical than the rest. When learning Esperanto was popular, there was Esperanto champagne, and when electricity made its debut there was Electricity champagne. Other labels commemorated cyclists (Champagne de la Pédale), showing a champion crossing the finish line. Great horses also got their own champagne, such as the famous

10. Heidsieck champagne label, 1850s. Courtesy of Champagne Charles Heidsieck.

Gladiateur. There was also Champagne du Vatican, Champagne for Freemasons, and Nuptial champagne.

And there were no restrictions, not even for those of dubious taste such as Plus je te bois, plus je t'aime (The more I drink you, the more I love you) and Champagne de la Jarretière (Champagne of the garter), the label of which did little to evoke finesse. During the Dreyfus affair there was even a label for Champagne anti-juifs (Anti-Jewish champagne).

As for the quality of the champagne, it was often dreadful. Lovers of champagne could even make their own, they were told. In *Le trésor de l'amateur de bon vin* (The wine lover's treasury) there was this recipe: "Take sixteen bottles of white wine, three pounds of loaf sugar, a demi-gros of vanilla extract (about two grams), two ounces of bicarbonate of soda, two ounces of tartaric acid: when everything is well dissolved, add sixteen ounces of spirits of wine, filter and bottle."

Or, if you were British, you might add gooseberries or a pinch of rhubarb. Everyone, it seemed, was getting in on the "act." Corruption had become so endemic that one American champagne expert asserted that he didn't believe "there is a single bottle of genuine wine that ever reaches our shores." The British, who had been producing sparkling cider for years, now applied themselves to imitating champagne by using gooseberries. "They are the greatest rogues in Christendom," complained one champagne maker. Gooseberries, the Brits claimed, if picked green, resulted in a sparkling wine with a real kick. Rhubarb could also be used but resulted in something less pleasant. An illustrated English weekly in 1853 published a humorous complaint about *champagne à la rhubarb* made in England which ended, "I conclude, Monsieur, not wishing to associate myself any longer with a vegetable whose specialty is to give one colic. Please accept my most vigorous spurts of foam!" A graphic cartoon accompanied the complaint.

If there was a chief culprit when it came to making counterfeit champagne, it was Germany. They are clearly the "front runners," claimed one French journal, especially when it comes to labeling. Bottles were decorated with labels in French invoking charming villages and famous figures in the history of wine. Counterfeiting in Germany reached such levels that prospective purchasers would be asked which brand they desired and then given a label and cork virtually identical to those of the real champagne house.

The United States also had its share of con artists, including one who produced large quantities of a champagne labeled Moët and Montebello. "Unbelievable," said one Frenchman who saw it. "Who would ever believe that champagne with such a name could possibly come from America? What's worse, it is made entirely from the meager, acidic juice of the rhubarb plant!"

Legitimate producers gnashed their teeth and lost money. Veuve Clicquot was particularly hard hit and stopped doing business in California and other parts of the country. Another champagne house pulled out of the United States altogether.

As in France, there was little American authorities could do or were inclined to do, which left it up to local officials to resolve. In 1854 the details of counterfeiting were revealed by the *Washington Star* in an article headlined "Machinery of Fraud Exposed." A champagne dealer on Wall Street had been tried and convicted of selling fake fizz. Most of it, the paper said, had been made with cider from New Jersey along with "other liquors more hurtful" to provide effervescence. Prosecutors showed how the culprit used lithographic stones to make phony labels and stamp corks. They described how he and other fraudsters collected empty champagne bottles from hotels, filled them with their own concoction, and then resold them.

The defendant was sentenced to several weeks in prison. According to an editorial in the *Star*, a more appropriate punishment for someone "making French champagne out of Jersey cider" would have been to compel him to drink a case of his own concoction in the course of a week. "That would have been a severe punishment, perhaps a fatal one. It would have extended the Eastern custom of suiting the penalty to the crime—just as, in Constantinople, when a baker is detected using light weights, he is put into his own oven with the next batch; and when the loaves are drawn, a baked baker is drawn out also."

‖‖‖‖‖

In a way, champagne's soaring popularity had become a double-edged sword. It was, perhaps, only natural that artists and con artists alike would leap to take advantage. Protection for consumers and producers was practically nonexistent. Rules and regulations to keep what was now a big business in check had not kept pace with the demand.

To protect himself from fraud and assure customers his champagne was "the genuine article," Charles Heidsieck, working with his sales representatives, flooded newspapers from New York to New Orleans with ads. In New York, buyers were alerted that "this celebrated wine has attained a reputation solely from the fact that energetic measures have been taken to make it worthy of the name it bears. The varieties of brands of champagne tend greatly, no doubt, to confuse the purchaser; but lovers of good and genuine wine must look for 'Charles Heidsieck' in full on the lable [*sic*], as well as on the corks and capsules."

Another ad, this one in the *New York Daily Times*, ballyhooed the "superior qualities" of Heidsieck's champagne before adding:

P.S.—IMPORTANT: Connoisseurs of Champagne Wine are respectfully notified that the genuine wines from the above house are branded "Charles Heidsieck" in full, on the label, and that all other wines assuming the same name are not genuine. The baskets of our Charles Heidsieck have also a distinct mark, as follows, "Chs. H," with four red stripes of willow on the cover. This change from "C.H." to "Chs. H" ought to be especially observed, in consequence of the appearance of baskets in the American market bearing [solely] initials. A careful observance of these marks will prevent all mistakes.

In the South, readers of the *New Orleans Daily Crescent* were assured that "Charles Heidsieck has given his whole mind to the perfection of his wine, and to making it worthy of the name. His visits to the United States have enabled him more fully to understand and appreciate the tastes and wishes of consumers."

While the ads were no cure-all, Heidsieck hoped they would help insulate him from fraudsters who were damaging the industry and give consumers confidence that when they pulled the cork on a bottle of his champagne, they were getting the real thing.

# 6

||||||||||

## The Lion of New York

"Where's Charlie?" they asked in bars. "Where's Charlie?" customers queried agents. It was Charles Heidsieck they were looking for. America was on a first-name basis with him. In restaurants almost nobody ordered "a bottle of champagne." Now it was simply "a bottle of Charles."

In Reims, Heidsieck heard the call.

It was 1859, two years since his last visit to America, and the plea for "Charlie" was growing louder than ever. In that time the United States had become the world's biggest market for champagne. Of the eight and a half million bottles exported, nearly half were bought up by thirsty Americans. Russia was second, followed by several European countries and Great Britain.

"It's always on our dinner tables," rhapsodized one American enthusiast. In the March 1859 edition of *Southern Planter*, the anonymous writer said: "We call for it from the frescoed ceiling of our New York hotel dining rooms, till we reach the outskirts of our Western wildernesses. We call for it in the cabin of the steamship, no matter on what ocean she is floating—we drink it at the head-waters of the Missouri, at the cataracts of the Nile, at the sources of the Amazon, on the vales of the La Plata, and at the falls of the Ganges. If there be a good genius in wine (and a thousand inspired odes to Bacchus have said there was), that good genius lurks under the champagne cork."

That "genius," he might have added, was none other than Charles Heidsieck, whose champagne, he said, was "the most popular and most reliable." No wonder Heidsieck believed that America was the place to be. If what poet Walt Whitman said was true, that America was "essentially the greatest poem," it was poetry Heidsieck could embrace because it encapsulated precisely what he believed in: progress.

"No word in the English language," one writer observed, "is used so much as the disyllable 'progress.' In America we use it so much that we have made a verb out of it."

It was time to push ahead, to make more progress, Heidsieck realized, time to write another stanza for "the greatest poem." Time to go back to America. His only regret was saying good-bye to the family, especially now, because Amélie was expecting another child. It would be their fifth.

On December 13, 1859, Heidsieck mounted a horse and made his way "very quietly" out of Reims, riding across northern France to the port of Le Havre. He'd stolen a march on other champagne producers and knew how envious they were of his success. They watched his every move, and he was determined to stay ahead in the game.

The trip to New York was miserable. It took thirteen days, much longer than his two earlier trips. Winter storms lashed his ship, the *Arago*, causing it to collide with numerous ice floes.

Heidsieck arrived just in time to celebrate Christmas mass. And then it was on to parties and receptions for New Year's, where he was welcomed like a returning hero. "Our Charlie is back again!" screamed one newspaper headline. Another paper noted: "His visit is chiefly a pleasure tour, to do some hunting and shooting in our vast preserves and to see how our ladies compare with those of La Belle France. Mr. Heidsieck will meet a cordial and friendly welcome not only where his name is known, but wherever courteous manners and refined gentlemanly bearing are appreciated."[1]

Receptions were held in his honor, and his picture was carried in newspapers throughout the Northeast. In his fashionable French clothes as he strode from one party to the next, Heidsieck was hard to miss. He stood six-foot-four, sported a goatee and mustache, and had large, deep eyes that seemed to smile.

Before long, everyone was referring to him as "Champagne Charlie," a nickname that would soon inspire a music hall performance.

The nickname seemed meant for him, even though it was not original. It had first been given to Charles Townshend, chancellor of the exchequer in Britain in the eighteenth century. It was Townshend, some Americans may have remembered from their history books, who imposed the infamous tea tax on the American colonies, the tax that led to the Boston Tea Party and American Revolution. Townshend earned his nickname after giving what became known as "the champagne speech" in Parliament. The speech was supposed to be about the East India Company, but Townshend, a bon vivant, was drunk on champagne, so when he stepped to the podium he rambled on to other topics and spliced in a few off-colored jokes along the way.

Afterward, everyone was asking, "Did you hear Townshend's champagne speech?" From that day on, Townshend, who was noted for his wit and charm but not political aptitude, was known as "Champagne Charley," spelled with an "ey" instead of the "ie" Americans used.[2]

Had Heidsieck known he was playing second fiddle to a long-ago British parliamentarian, he probably would have laughed it off or turned it into one of the stories he told so well at the long list of parties and receptions he attended.

In a letter to Amélie, he boasted, "I must tell you that for the moment I am the most important person in New York. I can't make a move without journalists on my heels. It's sometimes a nuisance but the more noise made about me, the easier it will be to sell my champagne."

More than any other champagne salesman of his time, Heidsieck grasped the value of publicity. Newspapers were unanimous in their praise.

*Public Ledger*, Philadelphia: "This is the purest article of champagne on the market and it's called Charles Heidsieck."

*New Orleans Daily Crescent*: "This celebrated wine is a line unsurpassed for its rich bouquet and general excellence."

11. Cover of "Champagne Charlie" sheet music. Authors' collection.

*Baltimore Sun*: "This is now the most important wine imported, and consumers of Heidsieck hereafter will be careful that 'Charles Heidsieck' is on the label."

*Public Ledger*, Memphis: "Heidsieck is the oldest winegrower in France and his champagne is immensely popular in America. If you purchase his champagne, you will have the best in the market."

Such reviews surely delighted Heidsieck, but it was one in the foreign press that may have made the biggest impression for it confirmed that his name had become synonymous with champagne— not only in America but around the world.

It was not really a review as such but an article describing a visit to London by Prince Kung, brother of China's emperor. Published by a cheeky London tabloid called *The Press*, the story coincided with the signing of a peace treaty ending the Second Opium War (1856–60).

That war, like the first, had seen countries like Great Britain, eager to expand commerce, force Imperial China to open itself to the West. A major thorn, however, involved opium, which merchants with the British East India Company sold to private traders who then smuggled it into China. In the beginning, opium was first seen as a kind of medicine but when people began smoking it and millions became addicted, the emperor banned it, a move that set off two bitter and costly wars.

Judging from the tone of *The Press*'s article, hard feelings still existed when Prince Kung arrived in London:

There is a certain sublimity in the superlative of ignorance. Prince Kung, next brother to his Celestial Majesty the Emperor of China— traditional Brother to the Sun and Moon, and first cousin to the Stars—must be a sublime creation for he is excessively ill-informed. After he recently signed the Treaty with Great Britain, his Imperial Highness paid a friendly visit to Lord Elgin, and was attired, we are told, in a puce-colored satin robe with the Imperial dragon embroidered in gold on the skirt, and smaller animals of the same alarming class creeping up over his breast, shoulders and back. He remained to lunch, and became chatty and confidential after he had imbibed

## CHARLES HEIDSIECK.

### THE HEIDSIECK FAMILY.

It would seem, for the continued accession of European sportsmen to this country, that the forests of Great Britain and France presented too narrow a field for the adventurous sportsmen there. Snipe, plover, quail, woodcock and hare shooting, in particular deer-stalking, seem to have lost their charm. There are many reasons why it should be so, most of the game in Europe being kept in preserves; it is true these are of immense extent, and crowded with the finest species of the smaller game, yet the habit of feeding them by the keepers tends to tame them, and when their lordly owners are prepared to destroy them it is simply a general slaughter, unattended with that glorious excitement of surprises and dangers which accompany the pursuit of game in this country. Then another objection in Europe is the severe game laws, which prevent any but the privileged from enjoying the sport. We can imagine with what interest the true sportsmen across the water must peruse the romantic accounts of our backwoodsmen—the long marches through the deep forests—the encampments at night far away from civilization, when they form a circle around the blazing fire and recount the ventures of early life—the wondrous combats with bears and buffalo and sometimes with the red men. Then, when the sun has hardly risen and the dew still bathes the leaves and grass, the recital of morning tramps in search of the elk, the deer, the

CHARLES HEIDSIECK, ESQ.,
ONLY DESCENDANT OF THE GREAT CHAMPAGNE FAMILY.

buffalo, the bear and other game of equal size. The varied scenery through heretofore untrod paths—the voyaging in canoes on rivers —the ascent of mountains, from whose peaks new worlds of beauty open to the view. All these things told by the returning traveller, and highly colored in numerous volumes, have awoke a feeling of interest in American sport.

Sir George Gore first visited us. His retinue was lordly. Horses and dogs to the number of a hundred accompanied him. He had twenty wagons and forty men, and guns, rifles and ammunition enough to destroy tons of game. His adventurous spirit led him onward as far as the Rocky Mountains, and for three years he continued the excitement of the chase. Then we had Lords Grosvenor and Conyngham, besides Mr. Grantley Berkeley; the latter made himself unpopular and ridiculous by his Cockney assumption.

Now we have a sportsman from France, the first of note from that country. It is no less a person that the celebrated Charles Heidsieck, from Rheims, the representative and successor of the great Heidsieck family, whose wines have become the most popular of any introduced into this country.

Charles Heidsieck is known in Rheims as one of the finest shots in France. His love of sport is almost a mania; all the time which he can spare during the dull season of the wine trade he devotes to sport. The French papers state that for days he would ramble off from his estates, and venture into the swamps, morasses and woods for hundreds of miles, in the hope of discovering new species of birds or animals to bring home as trophies. But the sport has become too tame for this adventurous spirit, and he has determined to venture into regions where the excitement is spiced with a little danger. We have had the pleasure of examining some of the weapons which he has brought with him. More perfect specimens of the firearm we have never seen; they are marvels of beauty, strength, and, withal, so light, that the sportsman can never tire of their weight.

We believe Mr. Charles Heidsieck purposes taking an extended tour through the Southern States, Cuba, Florida, Texas, &c., when he will visit Minnesota, and afterwards ascend the Missouri river. Mr. Charles Heidsieck is young and agile, and we do not doubt will bear the fatigue as well as the backwoodsmen and trappers who will accompany him. In this connection, and considering the celebrity of the family which he represents, we have taken the pains to collect a few facts connected by their history, which may not be uninteresting to our readers.

The great establishment of Heidsieck & Co. was founded and received its world-wide celebrity through the continued and energetic exertions of his father, Mr. Charles Heidsieck, his uncle, Mr. Christian Heidsieck, and Mr. Walbaum. During the existence of that firm, they not only brought the cultivation of the grape to the highest state of perfection, but, by repeated experiment, they were enabled to improve the quality of champagne to an extraordinary degree. The fame of Heidsieck soon spread all over Europe. It became the popular wine at Court, and so great eventually became the demand, that though new vineyards were purchased, though the vines bore more each successive year, yet it was impossible to supply the orders.

Thus did this firm continue to gain in wealth and popularity until 1834, when the male representatives of the Heidsieck family who were engaged in the business died. The laws of France requiring that any firm bearing its name must have a representative of that name in the firm, and there being none, with the exception of the present Charles Heidsieck, the son of one of the founders of the firm, who was under age, it followed, as a necessity, that from 1836 to 1845 there existed nowhere in the champagne trade a single person of the name of Heidsieck.

In 1846, a gentleman by the name of Piper invited Mr. Charles Heidsieck to join him in business, probably for the sake of continuing the name of Heidsieck, promising him a good position. The contract with Mr. Piper ceased in 1850, when Mr. Charles Heidsieck immediately continued the manufacture of wine, which his family had been engaged in for a generation.

There can be no doubt that Mr. Charles Heidsieck is now the only representative of the famous Heidsieck family—with the exception of a young man, who, until 1845, was engaged in a business entirely foreign to the wine trade. His estate is a perfect model, the vines are trimmed and tended with all the care of delicate exotics. It matters not what new wines may be introduced to the market, the world-wide fame of the Charles Heidsieck brand will maintain its position, even as the diamond does among precious stones.

### A LETTER FROM VINE LAND.

*Champagne—Good Champagne—Champagne as a royal wine—Charles Heidsieck Champagne—Raising Champagne grapes—The Champagne vintages—A little more Champagne!*

There are ladies *and* ladies, there is luck *and* luck, there is champagne *and* champagne; and as there can never be too much of a really good thing, I have deemed it not *malapropos*, after giving you the account of one champagnery, to say something about another. A great moralist and lexicographer—*c'est la même chose*—once declared that he never had at one time as much fruit as he could eat. In like manner I boldly declare that I never got enough of cham-

RACKING CHAMPAGNE—CHARLES HEIDSIECK INSPECTING THE WINE.

PACKING CHAMPAGNE IN PRESENCE OF CHARLES HEIDSIECK.

**12.** Article about the Heidsieck family, *Frank Leslie's Illustrated Newspaper*, January 28, 1860. Courtesy of Champagne Charles Heidsieck.

some Heidsieck. In this free and easy conversation, he confessed that the Chinese did not know that India was merely a province of the British Empire and that he, with the rest of his nation, had formerly believed Great Britain to be a very small island, the population of which was so large that more than half were compelled to live in ships.

Most telling in the article were two words: "some Heidsieck." The writer might easily have said "some champagne," but instead he wrote "Heidsieck," a clear sign that the brand had become synonymous with champagne.

||||||||

Of all the newspapers that covered Charles Heidsieck, none was more enthusiastic than *Frank Leslie's Illustrated Newspaper* of New York. Leslie's real name was Henry Carter. He was an English-born American engraver and illustrator who arrived in America in 1848. Upon landing in New York, he adopted the pen name Frank Leslie.

His newspaper, founded in 1855, was the first successful pictorial paper in the United States. One of his first clients was the promoter P. T. Barnum, who commissioned him to produce a posh illustrated concert program for Jenny Lind, the opera singer known as the "Swedish Nightingale," who sailed from the same Liverpool docks Heidsieck left from.

Leslie was one of the few writers to actually travel to France and visit Heidsieck's champagne house. He toured the cellars, strolled through the vineyards, and came away almost starry-eyed. "I wish to impress firmly on the minds of my readers that in my travels in Champagne-land, among the simple-hearted Champenois, I have as yet seen no estate in which such extraordinary pains are taken to procure a pure wine as in those of Charles Heidsieck."

Leslie chronicled the Frenchman's every move almost from the day he first set foot in the country. His reviews, often accompanied by full-page pictures of Heidsieck, were unfailingly supportive. "It matters not what new wines may be introduced to the market," he

13. First ball of the season in New York, which Heidsieck attended, January 1860. Courtesy of Champagne Charles Heidsieck.

said. "The worldwide fame of the Charles Heidsieck brand will maintain its position, even as the diamond does among precious stones."

And it happened almost overnight. In just eight years, from the day he set off for America, Heidsieck had become something of an institution, something much more than a champagne salesman. To most newspapers, he was news of the day. Tucked between two articles—one about a Frenchman banished by Napoléon III for writing things that were "a little anti-Napoléonic," the other concerning a fellow who was killed after being kicked by a horse—the *Daily Exchange* of Baltimore revealed how avidly Americans were following Heidsieck's every move. "Mr. Charles Heidsieck, the famous wine merchant from France, is now in this city. He is traveling through this country on business, but intends to learn something of 'Wild Western sports' before he leaves us."

To that effect, Heidsieck asked Amélie to send him his pistols and hunting rifles and to "put them on the first ship possible." He knew full well that the spectacle of a pistol-packing champagne magnate would surely tickle the fancy of Americans, and he was right. The weapons, wrought by the finest gunsmith in Paris, drew almost as many rave notices as his champagne did when they arrived. "More perfect specimens of the firearm we have never seen," said one newspaper. "They are marvels of beauty and strength." The paper went on to say that Heidsieck knew as much about guns as he did about champagne and was one of the best shots in France. *Harper's Weekly* followed by informing its readers that "Monsieur Heidsieck will soon be heading west to hunt buffalo." Included in the report was a large picture of the dapper Heidsieck holding a rifle.

"I have invitations from people in high society nearly every day," he told Amélie. "It never stops." He did not try to conceal his exhilaration as he described how, on January 14, he was among the invited guests to attend the first ball of the season at New York's Metropolitan Hotel.

Heidsieck's agenda reads as though it was ripped from a novel of the Gilded Age. As one writer said:

Champagne salesmen are just as much at home dancing the night away or entertaining customers in the finest restaurants. They dine in the best places and have a horror of intemperance. They find it quite ordinary to be in the great literary salons, along the famous promenades, in the foyer of the Opera, and after a conversation there with you they very delicately mention the virtues of sparkling champagne. They always end those conversations with an air that is almost innocent. "Oh," they quickly add, "I will send you a case, no strings attached," and as they say it they pull on their white gloves and button them, then begin talking about race horses or taking the waters at the spa.

That was Heidsieck to a T. He nurtured this image as he and a business associate boarded a luxury steamship in New York bound for Boston. In a letter to Amélie, he wrote:

These ships are magnificently fitted up, differently from the Atlantic steamers, and are equipped for six to seven hundred passengers. The cabins are luxurious but the captain installed us in the honeymoon staterooms which are the largest and finest. Both of us had a colored man to wait on us, and supper was magnificent with fish, game, meat and vegetables of all sorts. And then we had another brilliant supper at half past ten in the evening. I remained on deck as long as it remained light, first of all because the landscape along the North River is extremely picturesque and later because a few miles out of New York, the river, which is three times as wide as the Seine, is obstructed by rocks making passage very dangerous.

At half past three in the morning, Heidsieck's ship reached Fall River, Massachusetts, where he and his friend climbed aboard a train for Boston. Eight years had passed since Heidsieck was last there, and the city had changed. It's still puritanical, he noted, "with very strict morality where smoking on the streets is still forbidden but it's now the center of the abolitionist movement, and foremost on everyone's mind is slavery." "It dominates everything and a certain prudence is necessary," Heidsieck said in another letter, "for it threatens to make trouble for the North and the South. It's already led to considerable financial unrest with numerous bankruptcies in just the past month."

Although business on other fronts was hurting, champagne sales in Boston were hardly affected. Heidsieck was able to brush off any financial worries but could not help noticing that Moët and Mumm had made significant progress in penetrating the market. "But we are still outselling them," he said. His name seemed to be as popular as ever. The *Boston Post* alerted readers, "Charles Heidsieck is with his friends at the Revere House in this city." But with the city in feverish turmoil over abolition and slavery, Heidsieck decided to cut short his visit and head to Philadelphia, Baltimore, and Washington.

American trains, he discovered, were much more sophisticated than those in France. Seats and benches were covered in velvet, while the ceiling of each car was decorated with fresco-like designs. What impressed him most, he told Amélie, was that each car was heated by a stove:

The cold in this country is not the same as it is in France. I'm now in a hotel in Philadelphia but I'm not suffering and only have a fire lit in my bedroom when I plan to write there. I go about town wearing a thin stock and low collar without feeling the chill. Up to now, I haven't had the slightest trace of a sore throat, although I am obliged, despite myself, to take a drink ten times a day just to keep warm . . . sherry, madeira, eaux-de-vie and a thousand other beverages each stronger than the other, and impossible to refuse.

In mid-February, Heidsieck was in Baltimore, where he was invited to sit in on a meeting of senators and congressmen: "In a few days, I am to return here for a reception where I shall meet some of the most remarkable men of the entire United States. I have also been invited to a private reception by Senator Stephen Douglas, one of the candidates running for President against Abraham Lincoln. In my opinion, I think Douglas has the best chance of winning."

Heidsieck spent an extra day in Baltimore, where his charm worked its usual magic. He told his wife their champagne was outselling all others. "There are two hundred thousand people in this city and I have been well-received. I've made many friends, all of whom are now our customers."

Next stop was Washington, which did not impress him. "It is a city of monuments of no character," he said, adding that they could not begin to compare to the grandeur of the cathedral or antiquity of the Porte de Mars in his hometown of Reims. What did impress him, however, was the welcome he received from government representatives. As one newspaper reported on February 25, "An elegant reception was given at the National Hotel in honor of Monsieur Charles Heidsieck." Senators from both sides of the aisle were present as lavish amounts of his champagne were enjoyed by one and all. "Monsieur Heidsieck has truly produced a miracle," the paper said, "for he has united opponents of both political parties!"

The highlight came when he was introduced to President James Buchanan at another exclusive function. That was something he was sure Amélie would be pleased about. And she was—but her pleasure didn't last long.

Her attention was caught by another story, this one appearing on March 10 in the *New York Times*, saying her husband was seeing another woman. Under the heading "Shall We Have Another Diamond Wedding?" the newspaper reported: "It is rumored that the celebrated dealer in Champagnes, who came to this country a few weeks ago ostensibly to hunt on the Western prairies, was himself wounded before he crossed the ocean, and that his trip hither was to claim the hand of a fair one whose heart he had gained while she was residing with her father, near Paris. The nuptials, it is said, will soon be celebrated, and Fifth and Madison avenues are in a whirl of excitement over the coming event of the season."

Other newspapers around the country quickly picked up the story. On March 15 the *Milwaukee Daily Sentinel* described how "the famous champagne salesman who came here a few weeks ago, supposedly to hunt buffalo, had in fact marked his game before he crossed the ocean." The object of his trip, the paper said, was to "win the affection of a fair lady whom he met in Paris. The New York upper ten are said to be in a flutter of excitement over what is expected to be the event of the season."

Even newspapers that dismissed the story as untrue could not refrain from writing about it. That included *Frank Leslie's Illustrated Newspaper* which published a lengthy account on March 17. Although Leslie was one of Heidsieck's biggest fans, he knew a good story when he saw one and that sensationalism and tell-alls were what sold. The story originally appeared in the *Home Journal*, a New York weekly, a few days before the *Times* reported it. "We are indebted to the Journal for the following delicious bit of romance, which we need hardly say is a work of pure fiction," Leslie said. "The hero, Mr. Charles Heidsieck, is in short a very happy husband and the father of several endearing little responsibilities. The romance, however, is too good to be lost." Leslie then proceeded to print the *Journal's* article with all the titillating details in its entirety:

The sportsman and his dear were seen rambling through the grove plucking buds and flowers, sailing on the silvery lake, and doing various tender and touching little acts common only to lovers who sigh and sing all the day long, and dream of paradise at night.... The rest of the story is made up of all those touching little incidents without which a love narrative would not be worth the telling. Charles won the heart of this peerless beauty, to bear her off in triumph, as the richest of trophies. We envy this young sportsman his good fortune, sincerely wishing it had been our own. . . . It is said the wedding is to be a grand affair and that a great fluttering has already commenced in Fifth Avenue society . . . but we have but one request, and we do it in the name of humanity, of charity, of peace, religion, good order—all that is merciful, and common decency, to say nothing of common sense and refined taste; spare us from another diamond wedding! We have no objection to a champagne wedding, only let care be taken not to invite our aldermen and county judges.

Even if it was all a complete fabrication, it was too much for Amélie. Every letter she'd received from Charles lately seemed to be about what a great time he was having while she was pregnant, struggling to help manage their business and take care of their four children. Jealous of the attention being showered on him, especially by "all the beautiful women at those evening *soirées*," Amélie had already warned Charles "not to get carried away" by all the wonderful things being said about him: "Put aside all the noise being made about you. If you were here, you wouldn't see things in such rose-colored glasses. Our agent Monsieur Bayaud has still not paid us for champagne that was shipped a year ago. He says nice things in the newspapers about our champagne and sends us a list of where it's being sold, but money? Nothing. Don't trust him. Stop having blind confidence. And quit paying attention to all the hoop-la around you!"

Heidsieck was stunned when he read Amélie's letter. Then he became angry. *How dare she doubt my loyalty or think I'm out carousing and just having a good time*, he thought. He wrote a hasty reply on February 17:

Every day, I'm running around some huge city, seeing people over and over again, submitting to unending presentations, being careful not to offend anybody, returning to my hotel exhausted, changing my clothes hurriedly, then having to go to dinner even though the food is atrocious, and drinking even if I'm not thirsty, for I can't refuse anything. I'm bored to death, and yet I always have to keep a happy face, a pleasant expression, all the while being eaten alive

14. Sign announcing a sale of slaves. Courtesy of the Historic New Orleans Collection.

by worries and problems and being far from those I love. If that's the existence that you are envying from Reims and you think it's so great, hurry up and change places with me. All of this is as bitter as the bread I have to eat here, or perhaps I should say there isn't any good bread here.

Though he was still upset, Charles ended his letter with a conciliatory tone: "When I got your letter, I wanted to throw it in the fire but I think I'll keep it instead. In spite of everything, please know that I love you, I embrace you and will always be faithful to you."

A contrite Amélie replied on March 9: "My Dear Charles, your letter that came this morning brought me to tears. I don't know why I wrote what I did. Please forgive me. I guess I'm sharing some of the bad moments you are experiencing. I only hope that we can put an end to our problems and that with your intelligence and determination those problems will soon be nothing more than a bad dream."

Heidsieck was eager to put all that behind and set off on the next part of his journey, his visit to the South. Before that, mindful of Amélie's worries, he went to see their agent, Theodore Bayaud. Charles laid out Amélie's concerns and asked why they weren't getting paid for their champagne. He told Bayaud that if they were to continue working together, he had to begin paying immediately. Bayaud agreed and promised to start sending weekly payments to Reims at once.

Heidsieck relaxed and turned his thoughts to the South. He thought everything was now resolved.

He was wrong.

# 7

||||||||||||

## Southern Comfort

Heidsieck could hardly bear to look out the window. He was on a train, and the car he was riding in was hanging over a cliff. He'd left New York for New Orleans a day earlier, but now he wondered if he would ever get there.

Gone were the luxurious trains he'd ridden in the North and raved about. This one was a lumbering beast belching fire and smoke and running on tracks that had been laid precariously close to the precipice to save money, or so Heidsieck had been told. That was terrifying enough. but because the train's wheels were set a foot and a half inward, most of the train, like Heidsieck's car, hovered directly over the gorge. Beneath was a drop of hundreds of feet. As the train chugged forward, it rocked back and forth. Heidsieck peered into the abyss before sharply turning away. "I prayed," he wrote Amélie. "I cast my eyes upward and prayed."

It was an unnerving start to what he considered the most important part of his American odyssey—an exploration of the Deep South. He'd already "conquered the North," as he put it, but had never visited the southern part of the country. Heidsieck considered the South the most lucrative area for his business. His "flying visit," as the *Times-Picayune* newspaper of New Orleans reported, was highly anticipated, "Those of you who have had the pleasure of a glass of Heidsieck will probably find him at the Saint Charles," the paper said, referring to the city's most luxurious hotel. "Mr. Heidsieck intends visiting all the leading cities of the South but he will hardly be able to find a place where his wine has not gone before him. Pass the Heidsieck!"

His goal, then, in the spring of 1860, was to see as much of the South as possible and get a feel for it. Over the next six months, he would travel everywhere and by every means possible: by stagecoach across Texas and Missouri; by paddle wheeler down the Mississippi; by horse and *iron* horse through Tennessee, South Carolina, Louisiana and Alabama.

"Frankly, a journey on a train going full tilt through mountains and gorges with their rivers, torrents and wooden bridges leaves you delighted to arrive safe and sound," Heidsieck observed. "However, it must be said that everything is so beautiful, the nature so varied, so smiling yet so wild, so sweet yet so daunting, that you can hardly think of anything else."

There were ancient forests that seemed as though they dated from the dawn of time, he wrote. Also alligators sunning themselves on the banks of rivers, blue herons and wild turkeys in flight, and magnolias as big as the largest oaks in France. Further on, he saw new settlements being carved out of the wilderness. Churches were the first things to be built, he noticed, and settlers slept on the ground, next to trees they had felled, until the church was finished. Only then would homes be erected.

"One tries one's best to see everything that flies past the windows," he wrote, "but the isolation in which I found myself caused a wave of utter loneliness to come over me."

Although his journey had barely begun, Heidsieck was already homesick. But he was also enthralled and recorded everything that happened for his family and friends. "My train has come to a stop outside Lynchburg, Virginia. There are people everywhere: a farmer smoking or chewing tobacco without twitching a muscle; strapping colored men loading and unloading luggage and merchandise; colored women offering oranges; piglets grunting and rolling under the train, and children, with or without clothes, whose laughter reveals two streaks of ivory."

Heidsieck had been traveling nonstop for a day and a half, but another two days and more than nine hundred miles lay ahead before he reached New Orleans.

With the terrain about to become more rugged, Heidsieck was forced to exchange his seat on the train for a spot on a *char-à-banc*, a huge wagon-like carriage with places for thirty passengers and drawn by three pairs of horses. It was a kind of forerunner of the bus with passengers sitting on benches. When it swerved one way, occupants slid in that direction and into each other as well. That happened all too frequently as far as Heidsieck was concerned. As the horses dashed forward "at full tilt over ghastly rocky roads no wider than the carriage itself," his heart was in his throat again. Once more, he found himself on a cliff, peering down into a deep gorge "to whose depths you were destined had some tiny stone upset the balance of our vehicle."

The harrowing ride ended without incident. Nonetheless, in Tennessee, Heidsieck was happy to switch back to a train for the rest of the journey. He also resumed writing, notes that were almost love letters to America:

> We are at ten leagues' distance from New Orleans. Here are flooded primeval forests; immense pines, their lowest branches one hundred feet above the ground; magnolias of a size that must be seen to be believed. Thousands of tree trunks float in the bayous, victims of age or the pioneer's axe. Spanish moss, hanging from every leaf and branch forming a graceful vault in which countless birds of many species live and sing day and night. Look downwards from these mighty trees to the inextricable thickets of bushes growing at their feet; count if you can these myriads of wild roses, these vigorously growing plants covered with brilliantly colored flowers, covered also with enormous butterflies.

The colors and sounds of nature were mesmerizing for Heidsieck, so different and dwarfing anything he had ever experienced in France.

> But having related the poetic thoughts inspired by flowers, butterflies and birds, let me briefly turn to a less pleasing aspect and, abandoning all that is great, tender and sweet, speak of creatures that are

merciless, hideous and treacherous. The tyrant is the alligator. They are the terror of the pigs, dogs, calves and all other animals that come to drink in their vicinity. I saw many of them from the platform of my train. The conductor, a Creole who spoke a French idiom with a remarkable soft accent, pointed everything out to me. I was truly wide-eyed before a Nature entirely new to me.

His eyes grew even wider when he finally reached New Orleans. "Never in my life have I seen so many beautiful women. Even the least among them have grace and charm, but without exception the most beautiful of all are the Quadroons." It was a letter that must have made the already wary Amélie squirm.

Heidsieck checked into the Hotel St. Charles, the best in the city and which he described as "a palace and a world in itself." American hotels, he said, "are unrivaled, particularly for comfort, and I should never finish if I were to give you every detail. For example, there are special entrances to the hotel for the two sexes, and separate bathrooms and sitting rooms."

After his grueling three-day journey from New York, Heidsieck was desperately looking forward to a bath—until he saw the tub: "The water was yellow. It came straight from the Mississippi, and it was used not only for bathing but also drinking. After my bath, I felt refreshed for a bit but I was dirtier than when I went in."

What Heidsieck could not stomach was the food. "Each day, four meals are served separately for gentlemen alone. Not only is it too much, it is ghastly. Why can't they make good bread here?" When he was introduced to turtle soup, he was even more disparaging. "You can throw that in the Mississippi!"

It was his first visit to the Crescent City, but Heidsieck felt right at home. Except for the bread and turtle soup, he adored the fancy restaurants, the French opera, and the city's buildings inspired by French and Spanish architects: "Everything is like Paris except that women's dresses are three times more luxurious and extravagant. Money is nothing here. It's earned with no effort and just as easily spent. As for the people, they are vivacious and hospitable, and they love to eat and drink! One is reminded from morning to night, by their behavior, that fifty years ago they were French. Even after all this time, they still retain their love of the 'old country' and most of them speak French."[1]

Heidsieck's English was practically nonexistent when he first arrived in the country in 1852, but it was now more than passable. Still, he was relieved to return to his native tongue for this part of the trip.

His arrival in New Orleans had been timed well. It was now April, nearly two months before the annual onslaught of yellow fever which sent residents fleeing from the city for the summer. His arrival also coincided with the unveiling of a statue of Henry Clay, the congressman from Kentucky who was hailed for putting together the Missouri Compromise of 1850. When the mayor learned Heidsieck was in town, he invited Charles to the ceremony. Charles wrote about it to Amélie: "The mayor offered me the occasion of seeing the town in full holiday dress, from the top to the bottom of the social ladder, by giving me a place in the grandstand as a guest of the town. It is here that I am beginning to become acquainted with Southern life."

Eager to learn more, Charles and his sales representative decided to rent horses to explore New Orleans. When they got to the livery stables, they were shocked to see a sign that slaves were about to be sold.

Inside were several dozen slaves, the men and women crammed into separate rooms.

A board listed their names, ages, skills, physical condition, temperament, and whether they were to be sold "with or without a guarantee." It also indicated whether they had attempted to escape from their former masters.

Although shaken, Charles stopped to read what was listed as "available for the day." He almost felt as though he was reading a menu. In a letter to Amélie, he recounted what took place:

A prospective buyer comes up. He wishes a plow-hand, an ironsmith, a farrier, a coachman, a valet, etc. Bob or Tom is called, the colored man rises, approaches his prospective master and tries to read his chances for the future in the features and manners of the latter. The buyer has him open his mouth, examines his teeth, feels his arms and legs, tries his arms and muscles, makes him walk and jump . . . all in silence, without a word being exchanged between him and the dealer. The colored man returns to his place. How much? $1,500. The buyer makes a face. No! He turns away and leaves, the deal has not come off.

In the neighboring room is the same number of colored women. The notice board lists their names, Elisa, Betty, Anna, etc. They are cooks, nursemaids and wet-nurses; they are sewing, singing and chattering. They are also well-dressed, some luxuriously, and many are attractive. Some are pregnant, others have a child nursing at their breast. A boy or girl squatting at the feet of his or her mother, looks at you with an astonished air, showing little white teeth and big wide-open eyes like enamel on jet. A buyer arrives and the scene is exactly as before except for minor details and the different skills demanded.[2]

Slavery was not unfamiliar to Heidsieck. He knew it existed in America, and he knew his own country's history. Under Louis XIII, France had legalized slavery in 1642, and it was further encouraged by his successor, Louis XIV. Throughout the eighteenth century and much of the nineteenth, France was one of the leading slave-trading nations of the world, capturing and selling nearly one and a half million people before abolishing it in 1848.

This, however, was the first time Charles had come face-to-face with it.

He tried to explain his feelings in a second letter to Amélie:

Ordinarily I would turn my eyes away from these awful places but today I was accompanied by a friend so I went in. I was curious. What can I tell you? I am now outraged, indignant and heartbroken. As the sale was going on, I couldn't keep quiet. I told my friend how wrong it was. When my friend tried to make excuses, I told him he should be ashamed of himself. He became angry. We continued to argue but it did no good. In truth, any discussion about slavery is futile. I lost my friend. I certainly didn't convert him, or anyone else for that matter. Their habits and interests have put a blindfold on the eyes of even the best of people. On the other hand, you know my ideas and beliefs, and they know my ideas and beliefs, and they now keep quiet in front of me. But I think that soon events will give a terrible lesson to them, inheritors of mistakes of another time.

Depressed, Charles returned to his hotel only to find its bar was closed. Instead, several long tables had been set up in the rotunda with a flight of steps behind each. Behind the steps was a circular bench. A member of the hotel staff told him that an auction was about to get under way—a slave auction.

Such events, if not regular, were enough to keep auctioneers busy and enabled the traders to conduct what one observer called "a brisk traffic in human flesh." Slave owners, however, were generally not eager to sell their workers for fear of looking like they were having financial problems. When sales did occur, they were often private transactions between neighbors. Local sales like the one Heidsieck saw were usually arranged through newspaper ads or through recourse to brokers or auctioneers. They took place for a variety of reasons. Sometimes owners had more slaves than they needed, or they had an estate that needed to be divided among heirs. However, when a slave owner found himself in trouble with creditors, an "execution sale" was seen as justified.

That was the case facing Pierce M. Butler, who owned hundreds of slaves on a rice and cotton plantation in Georgia. Butler had lost most of his money through gambling and risky investments during the Panic of 1857. To settle his debts, he held a two-day auction in March of 1859 at a racetrack near Savannah. Men, women, and children, 425 in all, were herded into a barn and confined to horse stalls for days as prospective buyers from around the country poked, prodded, and pinched to evaluate the worth of the "merchandise."[3]

The two-day sale netted $303,850, an astounding amount for the time. The highest price for one slave was $1,750. The lowest was $250. The amount collected was enough for their former owner to pay off his debts. When the last slave was sold, Butler broke out bottles of champagne and celebrated with buyers. It was the largest slave auction in U.S. history.

For the slaves, it meant facing a bleak and frightening future. Their

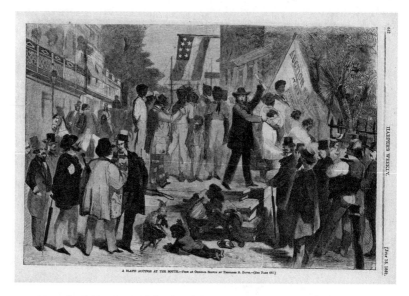

15. *Harper's Weekly* portrayed the almost festive atmosphere sometimes surrounding slave auctions on July 13, 1861. Courtesy of the Historic New Orleans Collection.

community had been ripped apart. Friends had been taken away, entire families separated. Although Butler had insisted families be sold together as a group, the slaves knew their new owners could do what they wanted with their "property," and they were proved to be right. As the auction wound down, sobs resonated across the race track. The spectacle became known as "the weeping time."

The auction that was about to take place at Heidsieck's hotel was much smaller and his first thought was to leave. He didn't feel he could face any more. The sale he had witnessed at the stables had filled him with revulsion. As he turned to go, however, the slaves were brought in. "The Negroes arrive," he wrote, and "some are from far away. I see a colored man, his wife and two children (a boy and girl) who have come from Key West, off the coast of Florida. There are many others, men, women, and children":

> The auction begins. One may read in French and English all the details about the slaves. One is a young Negro of about twenty-five years who is made to stand on a table. Before bidding begins, however, the auctioneer instructs him get down when a prospective

Southern Comfort

buyer announces that he wishes to examine the slave at close hand. The buyer looks him over carefully. When he is finished, the young Negro is told to step up on the table again. The auction resumes. Little by little, the bid reaches $150. "Going, going, gone!" The buyer has obtained a good coachman at a low price, but that's because he was warned ahead of time that the man drinks heavily whenever he can find any brandy or whiskey, hence the low price.

Next is a cook. She is sold for $1,000; a children's nurse sells for $750. The family from Key West costs $1,740 (the woman is a bit old); a fourteen-year-old boy goes for $1,250.

Heidsieck found the auction even more upsetting than the scene at the stables. He was almost speechless . . . and felt helpless: "As I watched the spectacle, I did not move a muscle of my face. I tried to remain calm, impassive and conceal my emotions while examining the buyers, dealers and the merchandise. I remained silent and said not a word, but how different was the language of my heart!"

Heidsieck would struggle with his emotions and reactions to slavery throughout the rest of his southern journey. In this he faced what one historian called "the perplexity and ambiguity" and "conflict of values" with which many Americans then approached the issue.

||||||||

In July, with the advent of yellow-fever season, Heidsieck, like many of the city's residents, fled New Orleans and headed inland. His destination was Louisiana's plantation country, where he planned to visit friends and relax. He was dazed by the sight that greeted him.

"The cotton fields of the great plantations are filled with Negroes of all ages and both sexes whose work ranges from plowing and sowing to pressing bales of cotton in hand-presses," he wrote. "They seem happy rather than otherwise, are easily moved to laughter and burst frequently into song. They lack for nothing and live more comfortably than a white farmer or laborer."

Charles began to question the stories of mistreatment: "In my opinion, they are whipped more frequently in novels than in real life, and their treatment is entirely humane. Each family has its house near that of the planter, as well as its kitchen garden, its poultry yard, and its fat pig living on the community. Each receives a weekly ration of corn, bacon, sugar and coffee. The children play up to the age of ten, after which they work at tasks suited to their strength. They are well taken care of when ill; they are faithful, devoted, active and intelligent stewards."

Heidsieck's words were startling, for they flew in the face of everything he said and felt after witnessing a slave auction in New Orleans. How could he have changed his mind—his heart—so quickly? One of his descendants theorized that he was "won over by the hospitality of the great planters and their well-ordered lives." A great-nephew opined that Charles constantly struggled to resolve a contradiction, to explain how he could be "pro-South but anti-slavery." There is no question that Southern culture, the elegance, even the language resonated with Charles. This was not the North with its factories, its noise, its filth, its nonstop rush to make money. Here, life moved with the seasons. Families—at least white ones—mattered, and so did friendships.

In letters home, Charles fairly gushed over the incredible hospitality that greeted him. People took him into their homes, made him feel part of their families. At times he seemed to be caught up in a fantasy world, especially when they included him on what he called "thrilling hunting expeditions." On one of them he sat near the marshy banks of the Mississippi and wrote about "the delicate egrets and rosy flamingoes which offered a scintillating target for the fervent hunter." On another outing he described his apprehension while moving through a forest: "Behind the screen of bushes lies unknown territory, the dusky haunts of the deer and black bear which first traced passages through it. The true American hunter silently follows these tracks. He makes little of the perils which surround him but is nevertheless not indifferent to them and occasionally, before thrusting his hand into a bush, he wonders if there might be a rattlesnake curled up with in."

Heidsieck learned the perils for himself when he went for a walk and stepped on what he thought was a tree trunk. It wasn't. "It was a huge snake I awakened from its nap!" Charles escaped, but he was quickly taught what to do if the worst did happen. "A snake bite is not always fatal but if one is attacked, there is a remedy. One must drink hard liquor or eau de vie until one is completely drunk. It's a sort of homeopathy but it works."

Heidsieck also wrote home about hunting alligators: "Alligator hunting is extremely easy, highly amusing and offers no great danger. Here they kill them by placing a bullet in an eye, in the forehead or in the underside of a front paw. They may be seen by the dozens, sleeping at the surface of the water like tree trunks abandoned to the current."[4]

It mattered little to Heidsieck what the prey was—alligators, bears, deer, giant squirrels, or "a curious animal called an opossum"— Charles relished every moment. And when the day's hunt ended, "the Negroes cut up the slain animals and roasted quarters of game over huge fires. Those were never-to-be-forgotten days of untrammeled liberty in the endless forest."

But if there was one day that was more memorable than any other, it was the day he took part in a cattle roundup, an experience totally alien to anything French and unlike anything he'd ever experienced. It was held on a plantation near Mobile, Alabama, owned by a Mr. Hall. Hall's plantation consisted not only of sprawling cotton fields but also of a vast forest in which hundreds of cattle roamed freely. Heidsieck must have seemed nervous, because Hall sought to reassure him. "Eli will look after you," he said. Eli, a mulatto, was an old hand and an expert with the lasso.

The roundup began, wrote Heidsieck, when

Negroes, mounted on enormous and very nimble mules, plunged into the trees to give chase, a whip and lasso hanging from their Mexican saddles. The cattle were in herds of twenty or thirty and immediately took off when they spotted us. No sight is so strange than to see these heavily-built beasts leaping over tree trunks, streams and ditches in an effort to escape. They are surrounded, however, and the Negroes, shouting and cracking their long whips, are now moving the animals into an enclosure. The most ferocious is Old Billy, a magnificent bull who escaped previous roundups but not this one.

Bellowing in deep low tones and foaming at the mouth, he knew why he was here. His eyes reflected, not terror, but a violent rage. I leaned over the fence at ten paces and stared at him, fascinated.

Branding was next, and Old Billy would be the first to feel the iron.[5] "This is where one risks one's death," Heidsieck noted. "Eli lassoes Billy's horns, then wraps the rope around a tree, drawing it gradually tighter until the bull's movement is restricted. He then slips a noose around the legs and brings the proud beast to the ground, incapable of movement. The burning iron is now applied . . . the hide sizzles . . . and the animal bellowed with pain and rage."

When it was over, Heidsieck, unlike Old Billy, was filled with contentment as he wrote,

> The day has been good. There are nearly five hundred horned beasts in the corral whose savage bellowing and furious hoof-beats constitute a diabolical concert. For dinner, we had a little ham fried for us in a pan and ate it with cornbread, washing it down with cold water. During that time, the Negroes unloaded the wagons and made our beds. Before long, rolled up in our covers, our feet toward the fire and our heads resting on Mexican saddles, we began drifting off to sleep, the monotonous bellowing of the beasts serving as a lullaby.
>
> As the sun set on a fiery horizon, we were bathed in an atmosphere of incredible purity. That night, with fireflies darting this way and that, not a breath of air stirred, the tall pines were completely still, the heavens were warm and clear, and there were millions of stars.

||||||||

Heidsieck didn't know it then, but these were the last moments of the idealized picture of life in the South. The days of ease and comfort on large plantations were nearing their end, and life was about to change for everyone.

Slavery was being eradicated in the Western world. Only in three places did it remain significant: Brazil, Cuba, and the American South. In the United States, abolitionists were on the march, and slavery had become a burning issue throughout the country. It crowded out all other questions, said one politician, "day after day, week after week. It meets you in every step you take, it threatens you in which-ever way you go."

Although Heidsieck's purpose for being in the South was commercial, slavery was a regular topic of conversation as he sipped mint juleps or some of his own champagne with friends on their veranda. There was no escaping it, for slavery dominated every discussion.

Senator Thomas Hart Benton of Missouri, two of whose nephews were to become army generals on opposite sides, one with the North and the other with the South, compared slavery and the debate it provoked to the plague of frogs in the Old Testament: "You could not look upon the table but there were frogs, you could not sit down at the banquet but there were frogs, you could not go to the bridal couch and lift the sheet but there were frogs. So, too was this black question, forever on the table, on the nuptial couch, everywhere."

It was even in music. A song called "Dixie" had just been written, and everyone was humming it. It had been composed as a "walk around," or a concluding number for minstrel shows, but it rapidly gained national popularity and would go on to become the unofficial national anthem of the Confederacy and entire South. Surprisingly, the song's name came from French. The "dix" in "Dixie" is French for "ten," and it's what was then printed on the ten-dollar notes issued by the City Bank of New Orleans to accommodate the French-speaking residents. Hence, the land of Dixies, or Dixie Land. More surprisingly, "Dixie" was written by a Northerner, a fellow from Ohio named Daniel Emmett. He wrote it for a touring minstrel company, and it was first performed in New York City in 1859.

As historians point out, visitors to the South usually came away with a narrow and distorted picture of what slavery and life was like on plantations. That included visitors like Heidsieck. Rarely did they venture into the fields where overseers often meted out cruel punishment to field hands who were forced to work long hours in the unrelenting heat and humidity. Seldom did they see the impoverished conditions in which slaves lived. What they saw was what owners wanted them to see: tree-lined alleyways leading up to white-columned mansions, massive oaks with Spanish moss hanging from their branches, verdant gardens gracing the property.

Visitors often registered surprise at the social intimacy that existed between masters and slaves in certain situations. Because domestics were frequently in the presence of the master and mistress as well as their guests, they were usually treated with great politeness and familiarity, more like pets than human beings.

That atmosphere was described by a Northerner who spent time on one plantation and explained how easy it was to be seduced by what was happening: "Every night the servant comes in and gets my boots and cleans them. Every morning, he comes in before I am up, brings me water to wash, brushes my clothes, and builds a fire when one is necessary. At night when I am down to prayers, the chambermaid comes in and turns down the bed clothes and puts things in order for me to go to bed. In fine, everything is done for me, I have nothing to do and I find it really convenient to be waited upon."

In his writings, Heidsieck continued to go back and forth, torn between what his conscience said and the pleasures he found in the daily life of Southerners.[6] In the journal Amélie had encouraged him to keep, he observed: "Life, though simple, was led on a vast scale in the huge properties of the rich planters who raised mostly cotton and sugar cane, and hospitality was generous. Family ties remained close in a typically French manner."

But then he wrote: "The heart of this otherwise so charming society has been nonetheless eaten away by the social evil of which I have already spoken: slavery."

And yet, in his next sentence, Charles writes: "It must be said, however, that the brutal planter of the melodramas is quite rare among the descendants of the compatriots of the Marquis de Bienville, the great eighteenth century colonizer of Louisiana."

Heidsieck was referring to the man sometimes called "the father of New Orleans." It was Bienville who, in 1717, discovered a crescent bend in the Mississippi River that appeared safe from high tides and hurricanes, a perfect place to build the capital of the new colony. He called it La Nouvelle Orléans in honor of Philippe II, Duke of Orléans, the regent of France during the reign of Louis XV.

Labor was scarce, however, and when French planters tried to enslave local Native Americans, they fought back. The planters then turned to Africa for workers, shipping in slaves from Guinea, the Gold Coast, Angola, and Senegal, as well as from islands in the Caribbean. By 1723 work on the new capital city was finished, and the benefits of slave labor had become clear. Although in 1712 there were only ten slaves in Louisiana, the numbers were growing. By 1795 there were nearly twenty thousand, a number that would soar to over three hundred thousand by the time Heidsieck arrived. The early French planters realized that to remain in control of this growing population they needed to do something. As a result, they moved to govern slavery with a series of restrictive laws known as Code Noir, the Black Code. It was only partially effective.

Although Heidsieck had described slaves as "faithful, devoted . . . stewards," day-to-day resistance was fairly common. They staged work slowdowns, feigned illness, sabotaged equipment, and committed acts of arson. They also, on occasion, plotted uprisings.

The largest occurred in 1811 on a plantation not far from where Heidsieck had once stayed.[7] The leader was Charles Deslondes, a slave who worked as a "driver," or overseer of slaves. On January 8, he and a dozen other slaves broke into the home of Manuel Andry, who owned a plantation on Louisiana's German Coast, an area on the eastern side of the Mississippi that had been settled by German immigrants in the 1720s. Andry was severely wounded when struck with an ax. His son was killed. Deslondes and the others then set off for New Orleans, about thirty miles away, torching crops, attacking plantations, and recruiting other slaves along the way. Deslondes, of Haitian descent, wanted to establish a Black state along the banks of the Mississippi. He'd been inspired by the Haitian Revolution, which had thrown off French colonial rule and abolished slavery on the island.

As the marchers neared New Orleans, their numbers had grown to several hundred. Many wielded cane knives, hoes, and clubs; others carried copies of the French Declaration of Rights of Man and chanted "freedom or death."

The revolt was brutally put down by the army and private militias organized by plantation owners. Dozens of slaves were killed before being decapitated. Their heads were then put on pikes over a stretch of sixty miles along the river as a warning to other slaves.

Deslondes was among the first to be captured after he fled into the swamps and was chased down by dogs. There was no trial, no interrogation. Instead, according to one witness, "Charles had his hands chopped off, then shot in one thigh and then the other, until they were both broken—then shot in the body and before he expired was put into a bundle of straw and roasted."

The uprising was over in three days. Only two whites had been killed. Official accounts at the time played down the revolt, saying it was merely a band of "brigands" out to pillage and plunder. In truth, it was a carefully organized rebellion that nearly destabilized the institution of slavery in Louisiana. It was the largest slave uprising in U.S. history and prompted the Louisiana legislature, along with those of several other slaveholding states, to pass new and tougher slave-control laws.

It's entirely possible, even likely, that Heidsieck was unaware of the uprising, since it took place before he was born. That may also have been true of Nat Turner's Rebellion, which happened on August 21, 1831, when Charles was only nine. But the fallout from both was long-lasting, especially from the latter, in which at least sixty-five people, most of them whites, were slaughtered. In retaliation and fearful of further uprisings, whites killed more than two hundred Blacks before authorities passed new slavery laws that were even more restrictive.

The Turner rebellion, however, was considered a major turning point in the history of American slavery, for it shattered previous points of view and opened the eyes of whites. "Turner's ordained mission," said one writer, "was to wake up the dead in the valley of the dry bones and awaken European Americans to their false image of the 'happy slave and benign master.'"

Heidsieck's wake-up call occurred on one of his hunting expeditions. He and several companions, loaded with camping equipment and supplies of champagne, were making their way through the woods when they happened upon a group of young men playing soldier. Not playing, really. They said they were part of a local militia training to protect their communities. Many such groups had sprung up in the South, especially in sparsely populated farming districts where it was often felt that extra protection was needed. There are robbers and thieves, one of the militiamen told Heidsieck, "but in an area like this there are lots of slaves and we have to be prepared in case of trouble." That surprised Charles, who, after spending time on friends' plantations, had assumed slaves were generally content and fond of their masters. The militiaman saw that Heidsieck was puzzled and explained that local people had to be on guard because uprisings were common. "Our group is made up of volunteers from New Orleans, Mobile and Baton Rouge," he said. "We train as often as we can."

Families and friends joined them for the evening meal, and Heidsieck found them to be delightful company. "I spent three days with them, during which time they consumed fourteen cases of my champagne!"

Groups like the one Heidsieck encountered reflected the growing concern about slavery and what the future might hold. Two years earlier, in the summer of 1858, the nation watched intently as Abraham Lincoln and Senator Stephen Douglas of Illinois squared off in a series of "Great Debates" about slavery. Douglas argued that citizens of new states should have the right to decide whether slavery is allowed; Lincoln was against it.

Tensions had already been sharpened the year before when the Supreme Court, in the *Dred Scott* case, ruled that Blacks were not citizens and could not sue for their freedom. It also declared the Missouri Compromise of 1820 unconstitutional, saying that Congress had no power to exclude or abolish slavery in territories west of Missouri or north of latitude 36°30' N.

The High Court's decision infuriated abolitionists such as John Brown, who, with his sons, went on a rampage in "Bleeding Kansas" in May of 1856 and butchered three members of a proslavery family with swords. Two people living nearby were also killed. Three years later, in October of 1859, Brown would carry his antislavery crusade to Harpers Ferry, Virginia (now West Virginia), and stage a raid on the U.S. Arsenal there—an act for which he was hanged.

All of this was dragging America closer to a terrible rupture.[8]

Despite the growing anxiety, Heidsieck remained captivated by the South. Even with talk of war, he was still fascinated by virtually everything around him . . . the friendships, the new adventures, everything.

Ahead now was an event that had Heidsieck, a confirmed and enthusiastic hunter, both puzzled and excited—a possum hunt. Opossums were ubiquitous in the South and in Southern culture, explained his host, Mr. Hall, proudly. In fact, he said, as "true Southerners themselves," the animals did not range any further north than the Mason-Dixon Line.

John James Audubon had even captured opossums in an illustration in 1851, Hall pointed out.

"Hunting the Opossum is a very favorite amusement among domestics and field laborers on our Southern plantations," Audubon wrote, but even "gentlemen" hunted possums on occasion. The best season for hunting, he said, was early fall:

> On a bright autumnal day, when the abundant rice crop has yielded to the sickle, and the maize has just been gathered in, when one or two slight white frosts have tinged the fields and woods with a yellowish hue, ripened the persimmon, and caused the acorns and chestnuts to rattle down from the trees and strewn them over the ground, we hear arrangements entered into for the hunt. The Opossums have been living on the delicacies of the season and are now in fine order, and some are found excessively fat; a double enjoyment is anticipated, the fun of catching and the pleasure of eating.

As for the "pleasure of eating," Audubon wrote, possum was "an excellent substitute for roast pig."[9]

An early Virginia colonist, William Strachey, had been introduced to it by Native Americans as early as 1612. He agreed with Audubon's assessment: "An opussum is a beast in bignes like a pig and in tast alike, of grey collour, yt hath a head like a swine; eares, feet, and tayle like a ratt; she carries her young ones under her belly in a piece of her owne skyn, like as in a bagg, which she can open and shut, to let

On Stone by W<sup>m</sup> E. Hitchcock

*Virginian Opossum.*

Drawn from Nature by J.J.Audubon, FRSFLS.

Lith. Printed & Col<sup>d</sup> by J.T. Bowen, Phil.

**16.** Opossum illustration by James Audubon, 1849. Courtesy of the Library of Congress, World War I Collection.

them out or take them in, as she pleaseth, and doth therein lodge, carry, and suckle her young, and eates in tast like a pig."

Now Heidsieck, more than two hundred years after Strachey first described the opossum, plunged into the woods with his host, two slaves, and three dogs to find out about the animal for himself. What happened next mirrored what an eighty-four-year-old former Alabama slave named Isaam Morgan recalled in a 1937 interview for the WPA Slave Narrative Project. "Some of de bes' food us ever ad was 'possum and 'taters. Us'd go out at night wid a big sack, an' a pack of houn's an' twarnt long befo' we done treed a 'possum. Atter we treed him, de dogs would stan' aroun' de tree an' bark. Iffen de tree was small, us could shake him out. Iffen it was a big, one of de n—— hadda climb up it an' git ole Mr. 'possum hisself."

Heidsieck recalled that the dogs Hall had brought on the hunt began barking as soon as they spotted a possum, sending it scurrying up the nearest tree. One of the slaves grabbed the trunk and shook it as hard as he could to make the possum drop to the ground.

That failed, and just as Morgan later recounted, the other slave began climbing. So did the possum, scrambling to the highest branch. But the slave was right behind, shaking branches as he went. Finally, the possum lost its grip and tumbled to the ground, unmoving.

Heidsieck thought the animal was dead and reached out to touch it before someone pulled his hand back. "One makes certain he is really dead before putting one's fingers within reach of his teeth, which are long and very sharp," he wrote in his journal. The possum was still alive, however, and Heidsieck said he was lucky he didn't lose a finger.

"Now you know what 'playing possum,' means," Hall told Heidsieck. The creature's body shuts down, almost like fainting, but the animal is very much alive.

As Heidsieck later recounted, "He gives a perfect imitation of death. Bitten by dogs or struck, he still makes not a move. Ours lay there, his mouth half-open, eyes closed and tongue hanging out. Someone put a bunch of dry grass between his paws and set fire to it. Still not a movement. I could hardly believe it."

Later, after the possum had been definitely killed, it was served for dinner. And an old religious melody filled the night, but the lyrics had been changed:

> De pos-sum meat am good to eat, Carve him to de heart;
> Yo'll al-ways find him good and sweet, Carve him to de heart;
> My dog did bark, and I went to see, Carve him to de heart;
> And dar was pos-sum up dat tree, Carve him to de heart.

> I reached up for to pull him in, Carve him to de heart;
> De pos-sum he began to grin, Carve him to de heart;
> I carried him home and dressed him off, Carve him to de heart;
> I hung him dat night in de frost, Carve him to de heart;

> De way to cook e pos-sum sound, Carve him to de heart;
> Fust par-bile him, den bake him brown, Carve him to de heart
> Lay sweet po-ta-toes in de pan, Carve him to de heart;
> De sweet-est eat-in in de lan', Carve him to de heart.

|||||||

Heidsieck was more than pleased with how his tour of the South had gone. He had amassed many new clients and developed a deep connection to that part of America. Now it was time to go home.

As he prepared to leave for New York to catch a ship for France, one of the slaves on Hall's plantation approached Charles. Her name was Dora, and she was a domestic worker. (Heidsieck recorded what happened in his journal, trying to capture the woman's speech.)[10]

"Master Charlie, can I talk to you about something important?"

"What is it, Dora?"

"They says you is leavin' soon for France, an' you is so good and kind I wants to go with you."

Before Charles could respond, she added, "I'll take care of your wife an' little children. I wants to so much! If you asks, the Master going to say yes and Dora will be so happy!"

Charles struggled to explain why that was impossible. He tried to make her understand that France was far away and that it would be wrong to take her away from her family. Dora did not understand, and she walked away in tears.

Heidsieck's nonstop journey from New York to New Orleans several months earlier had taken only three days. The return trip would be different, he decided. He would take his time and pass through parts of the country he hadn't seen yet.

In Texas he horse-backed across the eastern edge of the state where vistas seemed to go forever, "so different from anything in France." In the swamps of Louisiana he saw "enormous black vultures perched on different branches of a tree." Aboard a steamer named the *Duke*, he gazed in fascination at huge paddle wheelers churning their way up the Mississippi. "Why, they're just like water mills in France!" he exclaimed. Alabama, Georgia, and South Carolina were, he said, "the most beautiful part of America" he had seen thus far.

Never far from his mind, however, was business. From that standpoint, the time he spent in the South had been a huge success. He recorded that he'd secured orders for 3,000 cases of champagne in New Orleans, 2,000 cases in Mobile, 150 cases in Montgomery, 350 cases in Augusta, and 500 cases in Savannah. It helped that Charles was the only champagne producer actively traversing the region to promote and sell champagne.

In Charleston, South Carolina, however, he was greeted with what he called a "disagreeable surprise." Nothing was being marketed there—not a single bottle of Charles Heidsieck Champagne. His sales agent in New York had completely ignored what should be one of the primary markets for champagne. Clearly upset, Charles dashed off a letter to Amélie: "This market is dead! I've got to do something to wake it up!"

Amélie was not surprised. She had been warning Charles that Theodore Bayaud was not to be trusted, that payment for champagne shipped to the United States still had not been received or that the amounts were less than what was due. She had pleaded with him not to have "blind confidence" in Bayaud, but Charles had downplayed her warnings, believing he had worked everything out with Bayaud in New York. He had assured her the agent was "completely loyal." Now, he was no longer so sure.

Charles set off on a round of visits to restaurants and hotels in Charleston, explaining who he was and providing samples of bubbly for them to taste from the supply he had remaining. His instincts were right; this was an important market. He soon had orders for one thousand cases of champagne. "Now that I've thrown my net into the water, I've got to make sure that our agent pulls in everything that I've gathered," he told Amélie.

By September, Charles was back in New York. Despite growing misgivings about his sales agent, for some reason he did not try to see him again. Perhaps he was nervous about a meeting in which sparks were certain to fly. Or maybe he was still hopeful things would work out and that the money would come through. Then again, after six long months in the South, maybe Charles was simply homesick.

Whatever the reason, he wasted no time in booking himself on the first ship to France and headed home.

# 8

||||||||||||

## "It's War"

If Charles Heidsieck thought he would be coming home to a hero's welcome, he had miscalculated. What greeted him was a sea of red ink. His champagne house was drowning in it. All his hopes that Theodore Bayaud would settle his accounts were for naught. The agent was still holding out on them.

The situation was so dire that even though Charles had been home only two months, he immediately set plans in motion to return to the United States. It was a problem that would have to be dealt with quickly and in person. Letters demanding an explanation, even threats of legal action, had done no good.

But news from America was grim; the country seemed to be on the verge of civil war. Charles barely had had time to hold his new baby daughter or unpack his trunk than he was packing again.

On April 11, 1861, he received his passport to travel to the United States. It would be his fourth trip. He left France a week later, wracked with nerves and worries. Heavy winds on the English Channel only made matters worse. "I gave the fish plenty to eat and drink," he wrote Amélie as he made his way from the port of Calais to London.

Things did not get any better. He missed the first boat from Calais and had to spend two days in London waiting for another ship to New York. It was his first visit to London, so he went sightseeing in an attempt to distract himself. He went to the zoo, strolled the banks of the Thames, and walked in Hyde Park. He also toured the Tower of London, which, he told Amélie, "was more than enough."

But he still felt lost and out of sorts, adding: "I feel I'm living in another world. I hope the calm and solitude of the ship I take from Liverpool will bring me back to focus on my real goal. A thousand kisses my dear soul. I'll write more when I get to Liverpool."

Two days later, on April 20, he boarded a steamship, the *Arabia*, for the United States and wrote again: "I'm getting further away from you but I want to send you a few lines to tell you of my love for you. I received your letter of April 15 and it's giving me courage when I think of all the happiness you given me. It makes me want to throw myself into my work even harder."

Unlike his voyage the year before, when rough seas caused Charles's ship, to pitch so violently that a piano broke loose from its straps and nearly crushed him, this time seas were calm. The trip was uneventful—until the vessel reached Halifax, Nova Scotia. There the captain summoned all passengers to the deck. "It's war," he said. He did not need to explain. Everyone aboard knew immediately what he meant. For Charles the news that America was at war with itself was like a body blow: "Dearest Amélie, our captain has just informed us that war between the North and South has been declared. God only knows what will happen now. Although I am far away, I want you to know how much I love you. I will kiss the place where I sign my name and send this kiss to you from the bottom of my heart."

‖‖‖‖‖‖

President Abraham Lincoln's olive branch to the South had been brushed aside. In his inaugural address on March 4 he promised not to interfere with the institution of slavery in the states where it existed. "I believe I have no lawful right to do so, and I have no inclination to do so," he said.

His words inspired little confidence among Southerners. In the sixteen weeks between his election and inauguration, seven states seceded to form the Confederate States of America. Their exit prompted this from the president as he ended his speech: "In your hands, my dissatisfied fellow-countrymen, and not in mine, is the momentous issue of civil war. The Government will not assail you. You can have no conflict without being yourselves the aggressors. . . . I am loath to close. We are not enemies, but friends. We must not be enemies. Though passion may have strained, it must not break our bonds of affection."

But those bonds were broken early on the morning of April 12 when a South Carolina militiaman, Lieutenant Henry S. Farley, fired a single ten-inch mortar round at Fort Sumter. Another officer, a noted Virginia secessionist named Roger Pryor, had been "offered" the first shot but declined. "I cannot bring myself to fire the first shot of the war," he said.

What no one realized—certainly not Charles—was that that "first shot" was but a prelude to four savage years of conflict in which some 750,000 soldiers would be killed and another half million wounded.

|||||||||

Charles arrived in Boston on May 1. Nine years had passed since he first set foot in the city, and it had completely changed. Stars and Stripes were draped on every building. Union colors hung from every house, every store, and every monument. Small flags were even mounted on the harnesses of horses. In the streets, soldiers marched back and forth, drilling and filling the air with loud "hurrahs."[1]

Charles's bewilderment and fears came through as he tried to tell Amélie about the spectacle: "This country is in an indescribable state. Normal business has come to a stop. Stores are closed, Southern ports are blocked by Union warships, all young men, rich and poor, are under arms, and riots are breaking out everywhere. Blood is already being spilled in Baltimore and St. Louis and people have been killed. I fear what lies ahead."

The situation only intensified his concern about the meeting he was scheduled to have with his sales agent, Theodore Bayaud, for much depended on the outcome. Bayaud was several hundred thousand dollars in arrears for champagne he had already received. Unless this was settled quickly, Charles would be unable to pay his own bills. His whole future depended on Bayaud's payment.

It wasn't only about money, though. It was also about family, and Charles didn't want to let them down. They had been supportive even as others warned repeatedly that trying to do business in America was bound to fail.

Everything was weighing on him—time most of all. He'd get through this meeting with Bayaud, persuade him to pay, then head straight back to France. The last thing he wanted was to be trapped in a country wracked by civil war.

Charles arrived at Bayaud's office as a bitter argument was taking place. Theodore was arguing with his older brother, Thomas, who was in New York on a family visit. Heidsieck was surprised to see Thomas, whom he'd last seen when Thomas was planning to move west to hunt for gold. Charles, however, had no time for pleasantries and got right to the point with Theodore. He demanded an explanation and warned there would be no more champagne unless Bayaud paid up.

The agent was caught off guard by Charles's sudden appearance but denied any wrongdoing. "It's the war," he said, fabricating a story about an official "government moratorium" which he claimed allowed citizens to delay paying off any debts they owed.

Charles could barely control himself as his anger boiled over. "This has been going on long before any war started," he said. The exchange continued with Heidsieck becoming more and more agitated.[2]

HEIDSIECK: "You and I have been doing business for a long time but over the past couple of years, payments from you have gotten smaller and smaller and never correspond to what you have ordered. Amélie has written and so has Ernest, but you never reply."

BAYAUD: "There's a war going on . . ."

HEIDSIECK: "The war has nothing to do with it. I'm talking about last year and the year before that, *before* the war started. I'm talking about champagne you ordered then, which you never paid for."

BAYAUD: "Sales are off . . ."

HEIDSIECK: "What do you mean 'sales are off'? What have you been doing the past two years? I hired you to sell my champagne. You keep placing orders so it must be going somewhere."

BAYAUD: "A lot of it is in the South but payments from there have been slow."

HEIDSIECK: "So what! Look, this is not my problem, it's yours."

BAYAUD: "But what am I supposed to do? I can't just go down there and say 'pay up.'"

HEIDSIECK: "Why not? One thing's for sure, we can't keep shipping you champagne if you're not going to pay for what you ordered. So it's time to pay up!"

But nothing swayed Bayaud. Not Charles's appeal to the agent's sense of honor or hearing that Heidsieck faced possible bankruptcy. Threats of legal action were brushed aside, since most judicial processes had been suspended. Bayaud was at least three hundred thousand francs in arrears to Heidsieck, more than a million dollars in today's terms.

Angry and dejected, Charles made his way out of the office, only to be stopped by Theodore's older brother, Thomas, who said he was ashamed of what was happening. He promised that something would be done to help Charles, even if he had to do it himself. "I will not forget about this," Thomas said. "The damage my brother has done to you will be repaired."

With all that had just occurred, Charles was barely listening. All he could think about was that everything he had worked for was now in jeopardy. Bills were piling up, and angry creditors in France were demanding to be paid. Unless a solution were found soon, his entire business could collapse.

Charles felt he might collapse, too. He was exhausted, and the hot, humid weather of New York City only made things worse. In a letter to Amélie, he wrote: "We've been subjected to heat the like of which France has no *idea*. It lasts all day, all night. I sweat so much it's like being in an unending steam bath. I can't breathe and my nights go without sleep."

Extreme weather, in fact, was affecting much of the country—a reflection of the times, some said. On battlefields, morale fluctuated with the temperature. Torrential rains added to the misery, causing widespread flooding and making fighting sometimes impossible. Generals, it was said, "looked to the skies to decide when to launch their campaigns."[3]

People would later refer to it as "the little Ice Age," a lengthy period of bizarre, inexplicable weather conditions that affected everyone and everything. Summers sizzled and troops suffered from sunstroke. Winters were so cold that soldiers sometimes froze to death. And then there was rain, always the rain, constant and unrelenting and so intense at times that troops marching into battle often became lost. After one drenching downpour, the feet of Confederate soldiers got stuck in the mud as they attempted to cross a wheat field. It became known as the "field of lost shoes."

Charles was feeling lost as well.

"Everything has changed," he told Amélie. He described what happened in New York and his meeting with Bayaud. "I feel like I'm in the middle of the ocean without a life raft or glimmer of hope. Being away from you makes it worse. I'm missing you more than ever for it was exactly one month ago today, at this very hour, that I kissed you good-bye. I'm having a world of sad thoughts about our separation for I can't tell when it will end."

When he wrote those words, the war was barely a month old. He thought he would have been on his way home by then. Nearly everyone thought the war would be over soon, certainly by Christmas. Which is why, on July 21, a bright summer's day in Virginia, scores of high-spirited civilians and a few members of Congress carried picnic baskets and bottles of champagne to a bluff overlooking a field near Manassas Junction. Eager spectators armed themselves with opera glasses to get a bird's-eye view of what would be the first major land engagement of the war—the Battle of Bull Run.

They called it "the picnic war," but it was anything but a picnic for those fighting it. The battle was fierce. Union forces, composed of untested volunteers—"green as grass," as one officer described them—were routed and suffered nearly three thousand casualties. The Confederates lost two thousand. Stunned by what he thought would be an easy victory, President Lincoln signed a bill providing

17. President Lincoln with his commanders after the Battle of Bull Run.
Courtesy of the Library of Congress, Civil War Photographs Collection.

for the enlistment of another five hundred thousand men for up to three years of service.

No longer were there any illusions. The Civil War would not be settled by one grand battle. It would be long and bloody.

"The situation is getting worse," Charles wrote. "Bridges have been burned and neither side is willing to give quarter. Everything is going badly in this unhappy country and I fear torrents of blood will have to be spilled before the fury of the two sides is appeased."

Charles tried to think logically about what he could do. Much of the champagne he had shipped to Bayaud had been sent to the South. If there was any hope of getting his money, he realized he would have to go there and collect it himself. Over the years he had developed a vast network of clients in the South, many of whom were close friends. He'd been a guest in their homes and spent time on their plantations. Charles prayed that when they understood what he faced and how he'd been cheated, they would be willing to help.

He tried to sound upbeat when he explained his plans to Amélie: "I'm doing my best and believe that most of what is due us in the South will be paid. I'm sure that everyone wants to pay and will pay, but when and how I don't know. As for getting there, I'm not sure about that either. Roads have been cut and normal routes through Virginia, Maryland and Tennessee have been blocked by troops from both the North and South. I fear I will to have to travel hundreds of extra miles in order to reach my destination. I just hope my passport and French nationality will protect me."

In her reply, Amélie tried to be reassuring: "My dear sweet Charles, no matter what happens, trust in the future. Don't get down on yourself or let yourself be overwhelmed by those things you can't do anything about. We'll get through this. May God watch over you and give you courage when you need it."

Charles's destination was New Orleans, where hundreds of baskets of his bubbly had been sent. Normally, the trip from New York took three days. This time he expected it to take nearly three weeks. On a map, he sketched out the route, heading first through Albany, Syracuse, Rochester, and Buffalo. Once past Lake Erie, he would try to catch a train in Ohio which would take him to Cleveland, Columbus, and Cincinnati. From there it was into Kentucky, which was still debating whether to secede. After that he would make his way to Tennessee, Mississippi, and, finally, Louisiana which had already left the Union to join the Confederacy.

Transportation, however, was hit and miss. There was no regular schedule. Many trains were filled to capacity with private militias on their way to the front.

"Most are volunteers," Charles said in another letter. "They are badly clothed, badly nourished and badly armed. Only one out of a thousand has a gun but soon they will be slitting each other's throats with knives or killing each other with a revolver. The hate that animates them is unbelievable. . . . It would be ridiculous to say I'm not in danger."

The danger, however, was greater than Charles imagined, for coinciding with the larger conflict was another kind of warfare that had suddenly emerged, one fought from the shadows, in forests behind trees, on unguarded roads and trails, and often in the dead of night—guerrilla warfare.[4]

Like most people, Charles saw the Civil War as a struggle between two great armies. Those conducting it had been educated at the nation's military academies, such as West Point, and had "learned to think of war in terms of grand, climactic, Napoléonic-style battles." As historian Daniel Sutherland said, "They associated guerrilla combat not as did the public, with knights of the American Revolution, but with untutored, even uncivilized peoples. Their experiences fighting Indians and Mexicans in the decades before the Civil War confirmed this prejudice."

Often it involved ordinary folks hesitant to join the army and leave families and property unprotected. Instead of enlisting, they formed companies of "rangers" and "guards" for local defense, arming themselves with whatever they could lay their hands on—clubs, knives, even squirrel guns—in order to protect their neighborhoods.

But as hard-liners took over and outlaws, deserters, and misfits joined the ranks, exploiting the chaos of war for personal gain, violence soon escalated. Names like "Bloody Bill" Anderson and Quantrill's Raiders became famous. There were murders and massacres as Confederate guerrillas did everything possible to destroy Union morale. Some lay in wait to bushwhack Union soldiers. "I shall hunt the Yankees as I would wild beasts," one said. Guerrilla fighters also cut telegraph wires, blew up bridges and derailed trains carrying Union troops to the front. Those who were caught were often executed. "Boys are resolved to take no more prisoners but shoot every man they see in the woods," one said.

Union troops were often at a loss as to how to retaliate. As one frustrated soldier said, "They cannot catch guerrillas in these mountains any more than a cow can catch flies. We might just as well quit, throw down our arms and make friends with the South."

There were atrocities on both sides, and it was often difficult to tell who was who. Some claimed to be loyal Confederates while others said they were Unionists, "but most had no allegiance to anyone but themselves." "It is an old saying," observed one Southerner, "that the Devil is fond of fishing in muddy waters, and as soon as war has stirred up the mud of confusion you see Devils turn out in droves like avenging wolves. I predict that if the war lasts 12 months longer, the country will be completely overrun with vagabonds and [they] will have to be killed in some way."

For Charles, that meant his journey south was suddenly fraught with even more uncertainty and anxiety. Plain robbery and other crimes "bearing no connection to the war or its participants had become daily affairs." His greatest fear was stumbling into an area of hostilities by accident. Would the route he had chosen get him to his destination safely, he wondered. He had a map, but maps—even those used by Union commanders—were notoriously inaccurate and said to contain "very bad errors."

The picture was further complicated by the way the war was being waged. Whereas in the past battles had been fought on vast open fields and commanders had a panoramic view of the fighting, these were fought from trenches or in wooded areas where the only thing visible was the backs of a few skirmishers. In effect, one observer noted, "the army was fighting blindfolded," and generals knew little more than men they commanded.

Charles realized he would have to pick his way south and hope for the best, but the thought of conducting business under such conditions must have been overwhelming. Business in the region had been described as "dead, dead" by one merchant. "Everything excepting death seems suspended," confirmed another, "and almost every business except the coffin maker has closed."

On the day of Charles's departure, another letter from Amélie arrived lifting his spirits: "My Dear One, everything will work out, so for the love of God—and me—please don't make yourself sick over things you can't control or haven't happened. Be brave and try to have confidence." She even inserted some gentle teasing: "You may be far away but you are not about to escape sermons from your little wife."

Amélie also tried to distract and comfort him with news of home. She described how work in the vineyards was continuing and that *les vignes sont magnifiques*, the vines are magnificent. The only problem, she said, was that herds of wild boar were having a field day in the vineyards and causing damage to the vines. "At night, the peasants go out and raise a hullabaloo and try to beat them away but so far without results."

And then, in a line that surely tugged at Charles's heart, she wrote, "By the way, yesterday was my birthday. I am now thirty-three. I can hardly believe it!"

It was the fourteenth of May, 1861, and the last letter he would receive from her for many months.

||||||||

For the most part, Charles's journey went smoothly, more easily than he had anticipated. The only serious mishap was when his train derailed in Louisville, Kentucky. He was badly shaken but otherwise unhurt.

Two days later, on June 2, he arrived in New Orleans. It was a city he had always loved, one he found "astonishingly seductive" and where he felt completely at home.[5]

Not this time. It felt totally different. The offhand glamour was gone; normal commerce had come to a stop, food was scarce, and there were outbreaks of yellow fever.

Charles checked in with the French consulate, where an old friend, Count Eugène de Méjan, awaited him. Méjan was a seasoned diplomat, a man who knew his way around officialdom and what strings to pull. These days, his main job as French consul was to navigate the dicey and sometimes treacherous road of French-American relations. That job had recently become a nightmare.

When the war started, hundreds of French citizens volunteered to fight, some for the North, many others for the South. Fearing this would compromise France's status as a neutral country, the country's foreign minister tried to stop it, warning that under the Code Napoléon, "If you sign up for an army of another country, you will no longer be considered French."

"It's made little difference," Méjan told Heidsieck. "People are still enlisting." One of them, he said, was the son of French consul of Baton Rouge "who is now a soldier in the Confederate Army."

Drawing attention as well were two grandsons of King Louis Philippe, the last king of France, who were fighting for the other side, the North. Philippe and Robert d'Orléans served under General George B. McClellan, who commanded the Army of the Potomac, the Union's largest army. That they were fighting for a general who was nicknamed "Young Napoléon" had captured the fancy of people back home. Emperor Napoléon III, however, was jealous of their newfound popularity and ordered them back to France. They eventually complied, but not before fighting for more than a year for the Union cause.

Although France was officially neutral, its sympathies leaned toward the South for economic reasons. Cotton kept its mills running, or had until recently. A Union blockade of Southern ports had put the brakes on trade and resulted in a "cotton famine." Not only was France affected, but Great Britain was, too. Textiles were Britain's biggest industry and nearly half a million people were now unemployed.

There were rumblings the two countries might intervene militarily to end the crisis, although France was reluctant to make any moves unless Britain took the lead. Charles hoped it would happen, for his heart was with the South, and that was where most of his American friends lived. "The South is saner and more honest than the North," he told Amélie. "In the North, the war is made by people, les miserables, who are fighting for money. Here, people are fighting for a new nation. If France and Britain combine their navies to break the blockade and establish direct relations with the South, New York, Boston and the other great cities of the North would be lost, and the Union will be dead forever."

Predicting what Napoléon III might do was always iffy. Though he professed to be neutral, it was no secret—especially to Washington—that the emperor had spoken with Confederate emissaries and offered them the use of French shipyards to build warships. He also had said, "If the North wins the war, I'll be happy, but if the South carries it off, I shall be overjoyed."

In Washington's opinion, the emperor was a loose cannon, a dreamer with flights of fancy who acted on impulse and could not be trusted. It was also clear that ever since the Louisiana Purchase in 1803, when his uncle, Napoléon Bonaparte, sold thirteen states' worth of territory to the United States for fifteen million dollars—or about three cents an acre—the emperor had dreamed of regaining France's former colonies in the Americas by installing a puppet government in Mexico. This, he theorized, would block U.S. expansion into Latin America and lay the basis for a French commercial empire that stretched from the Gulf of Mexico to the Pacific Ocean, absorbing possibly even Texas.

He's a "perpetual nightmare," groused Henry Sanford, Washington's minister to Belgium. "The Emperor is at the center of nearly every international problem."

Leery as Washington was of Napoléon III, it was more worried about Great Britain, the world's preeminent military and industrial power. Would it intervene, and if so, on which side? Like the French, hundreds of civilians had already volunteered to fight, some for the Union, some for the Confederacy. Public opinion was sharply divided. "For God's sake, let's keep out of it!" warned British foreign secretary Lord Russell.

Although the country was united in its abhorrence of slavery— *Uncle Tom's Cabin* had been a roaring success in Britain, selling more than a million copies in its first year—most people thought the cotton crisis was a far more urgent problem than the "plight of far-off slaves." Rhymed the satirical journal *Punch*:

Though with the North we sympathize,
It must not be forgotten,
That with the South we've stronger ties,
Which are composed of cotton.

||||||||

Charles Heidsieck felt these problems would probably not affect him. Over the next nine months, he covered hundreds of miles, traveling from one city to another and one plantation to another, meeting old friends and spending time on their estates. In every case, the welcome was warm, but there was also a dark cloud. The gaiety and good times that marked previous visits were gone. With the war, older sons had left to join the Confederate army.

"As for the Negroes," Charles said in a letter to his wife, "they cry when their young masters leave for the war but they continue harvesting the cotton as if nothing has changed."

But the picture *had* changed. On August 6, Washington passed the first Confiscation Act. It authorized the federal government to seize any property being used to aid the Confederacy. "Property" included slaves.

Within a month, on August 30, the Confederate Congress retaliated by passing the Sequestration Act, allowing confiscation of Northern property. (Among the properties seized was Thomas Jefferson's estate, Monticello, then owned by a New Yorker.) Its aim was to strike at Northern financial interests within the Confederacy. Anyone owing money to the North was now required to pay it to the Confederate Treasury instead.

Since he was French "and not a Northerner," Charles hoped the law did not apply to him and that he would be able to approach his customers and collect his money without a problem. As it turned out, there was a problem: no one had any money.

What they did have was cotton, bales and bales of it stacked in warehouses and on docks, going nowhere because of the Union's blockade of Southern ports. Realizing it was worth a fortune in Europe, where looms now sat idle, Heidsieck agreed to accept cotton as payment for his champagne. He would try to get it out of the country, probably from the port city of Mobile, which had not yet been seriously affected by the blockade.

Charles roamed as far north as Virginia and as far west as Kansas Territory to collect it, but getting everything to Mobile was a nightmare. He first had to transport the cotton in rickety carts over bumpy roads before loading it onto rafts down canals and rivers. Passing through Louisiana was the worst part, since bayou country swarmed with rebel guerrillas eager to get their hands on cotton which they then traded for weapons. What cotton they couldn't grab was ordered burned lest it fall into Union hands. Any planter who resisted would be hanged, they warned.

It took weeks for Charles to reach Mobile. His main concern was whether the port would still be open. The Union's naval blockade of the long Southern coastline was still intact, but it was far from perfect. Known as the Anaconda Plan, it stretched like the snake whose name it bore, running nearly four thousand miles, from the mouth of the Rio Grande to the Chesapeake Bay. Its aim was to squeeze the Confederacy until it yielded or expired. Nine out of ten ships, however, were still slipping through, so Charles was reasonably confident he could get his cotton back to France. "If I succeed," he wrote Amélie, "we can double or triple our capital."

With help from influential friends, including the French vice-consul of Mobile, Charles managed to hire two ships. But time was running short, and the Union army was moving closer. It had just captured Charleston; other units were moving toward Mobile and New Orleans. Heidsieck instructed the captains of the two vessels to set off the moment his cotton was loaded, each following a different route in order to avoid Union gunboats. "Even if only one ship makes it," he told his wife, "it will be enough to enable us to pay our bills."

As the first of his sloops set sail, Charles breathed a sigh of relief. Although they were small, the vessels were speedy and highly maneuverable, which made them ideal blockade runners. Heidsieck's second vessel departed two days later.

He watched the calendar faithfully. Two weeks passed. So far so good. The ships would be nearing France by now. That's when the blow fell; one vessel had been intercepted by a Union warship and sunk, its cargo of cotton lost. All his hopes now rested on the second ship.

Summer turned to fall, and the war was heating up. On November 8 a Union frigate, the USS *San Jacinto*, fired two shots across the bow of a British mail ship, the *Trent*, and forced it to stop. Aboard were two Confederate envoys traveling to London: James Mason, former chairman of the U.S. Foreign Relations Committee, and John Slidell, a prominent New Orleans lawyer. Their mission was to persuade the British government to support the South. They were promptly arrested. The incident, known as the Trent Affair, sparked a diplomatic crisis and brought Britain and the United States to the brink of war.

The British minister to Washington, protesting what he said was a violation of Britain's neutrality, sent an urgent dispatch to London saying, "I am so concerned that unless we give our friends here a good lesson this time, we shall have the same problem with them very soon. Warning them that it will mean war unless they surrender will have a good effect on them."

In London, naval strategists immediately began making plans to break the Union's blockade of the South. Its warships would also launch attacks against Union gunboats in the North. In Paris, French officials said they would back Britain in any conflict with America.

President Lincoln, however, did not want to risk war with Britain over this issue. "One war at a time," he told his advisers. Within a few weeks, the crisis was defused when the two Confederate envoys were freed and the actions of the gunboat captain who stopped the *Trent* were disavowed. Britain and France, in turn, reaffirmed their commitment to remain neutral.

Heidsieck was disappointed. He had always believed that intervention by Britain and France would result in a Confederate victory. Nevertheless, he was still confident that the South would win: "I've never seen such devotion to a common cause. It's a curious and amazing spectacle, from young people knitting socks for the soldiers, to the old folks. I am still praying that Europe will eventually intervene for I've never seen anything like it. It's the beginning of a new nation."

And, he might have added, new opportunities for selling champagne. "I am the only representative of a champagne house here. Other houses are going to find themselves in trouble because they don't have anyone here. When the South wins its independence, our champagne house will be at the head of the line!"

Believing rumors that the blockade of Southern ports would be lifted in January, Charles instructed Amélie to have a large quantity of champagne ready to ship the moment it happened: "At least 4,000 baskets. It's also imperative we get the name of our New York agent off the labels. Otherwise the champagne will be rejected by people here. If there is any mark or sign that connects it with the North, people here won't touch it."

He cited Piper, "whom people here no longer want anything to do with." (Charles surely felt some satisfaction, since Piper was where he started his career in champagne before a bitter falling out with his uncle prompted him to quit and start his own champagne house.)

Although the blockade had sharply reduced the amount of champagne coming from France, Charles wasn't terribly concerned. Quite the contrary, in fact. "Our champagne is more popular than ever!" he exclaimed. "We haven't had any to sell for a while because of the blockade and our friends in restaurants have been reduced to serving other champagnes, but that's not a problem. Because they then stick OUR labels on the bottles!"

On November 26 he was overcome by a wave of nostalgia. It was the Heidsiecks' eleventh wedding anniversary. "Note the date of this letter, my darling. It's the first time we've been apart on our anniversary. Certainly our hearts are joined today and across space, but the future which so long ago smiled on us has given way to unbearable loneliness and sadness." Heidsieck signed it, "Your faithful husband and very unhappily yours . . ."

Christmas only added to his depression. That is, until his old friend Eugène de Méjan sent word to come to see him. When he arrived, Méjan handed him a pack of letters, most of them from Amélie. It had been months since he had heard from home. Mail service, like everything else, had been disrupted by the war. Written over a period of months, Amélie's letters had first arrived in New York before being forwarded to the French ambassador in Washington, who then sent them on to New Orleans. Charles was trembling and, at first, too scared to open them. The first letter from Amélie had been written in the spring, seven months earlier.

May 3, 1861—Sorry to hear about the heat. I feel worse and worse that you've been without news from us. I think of the hours you are so far away and hours you are spending alone and so isolated, knowing how our champagne house is in such bad shape.

June 26—It's six in the morning. I've been thinking about the lonely evenings you've told me about in the South and wondered, couldn't my dear Charles write a memoir of his trip, his impressions of such amazing events he's found himself in the middle of? That would be a precious souvenir for me and a great satisfaction for you later.

July 2—According to an American newspaper we received, some champagne houses have contributed money to the army of the North. Because of that, the South has declared these houses traitors and their champagne is now prohibited there. So be careful, my darling, and try to stay neutral.

August 29—The children are doing well, running around with the carefreeness of their age. The future for us depends largely on what's happening with you. God will give us the strength to do what's necessary.

October 3—Everything here is going well. The harvest has begun and the price for grapes is high.

||||||||

It was now January, the start of a new year. Contrary to what Charles expected, the blockade of Southern ports had not been lifted. And there was still no news about his second ship.

It also seemed unlikely that France and England would intervene in the war. Many, like Charles, had long believed that Europe's dependence on Southern cotton would persuade countries to become involved, but that hadn't happened, partly because they had found new sources of cotton in Egypt and Canada. Southern newspapers, however, were still urging planters to "keep every bale of cotton on the plantation. Don't send a single thread until England and France have recognized the Confederacy." Their pleas did little good.

"What a pity," Charles told Amélie. "If the Emperor had taken more initiative, I'm certain that the Confederacy would have given France its entire harvest of cotton as a monopoly for many years. What a coup that would have been! And what a blow that would have been to England!"

As it was, the Civil War was now being fought with new intensity. March and April saw battles erupt at a dizzying pace, battles with names like Pea Ridge, Hampton Roads, Yorktown, and Shi-

"It's War"

loh. The savagery with which they were fought and the amount of blood spilled shook even the most hardened veterans. In another letter to Amélie, Charles wrote: "Reunification is impossible for a sea of blood separates the two countries." He was stunned at how the war had affected people, especially civilians: "The hate that people have and the rage is almost to the point of delirium. Young girls and women are carried away with it more than the men. Young men who haven't signed up for the army might as well give up all hope of marrying because the girls refuse to speak with them."

For the first time, Charles began to think it might be safer if he forgot about his money, dropped everything, and returned to France. The two sides want to "devour each other," he told a friend. "If I do leave, it will have to be from the South because the way North is blocked."

But on April 15 that door began to close as well. That was the day a Union navy force commanded by Flag Officer David Farragut approached the mouth of the Mississippi and laid siege to two forts protecting New Orleans.

The city was the Confederacy's most important port and had been considered invulnerable by Southern military strategists. Believing that any Union assault would come from the north, not the Gulf of Mexico, the Confederate government in Richmond had moved its armies away from New Orleans and concentrated them in northern Mississippi and western Tennessee. It was a fatal mistake.

For ten days, Farragut's fleet of seventeen warships and twenty mortar boats bombarded Forts Jackson and St. Philip before defenders finally surrendered.

Upriver, it was sheer bedlam as residents of New Orleans began destroying anything of value to prevent it from falling into enemy hands. Charles was in the city and described what he saw to Amélie: "Cotton was burned and sugar was dumped into the Mississippi, but the South can sacrifice all its seaports and still continue fighting." Charles still held out hope the South would prevail. "Don't believe everything you read in the newspapers about the North. People here are resisting. If I had ten thousand guns, I could sell them for whatever price I wanted."

The resistance he witnessed was fierce. Fifteen thousand bales of

COM. FARRAGUT'S FLEET, PASSING THE FORTS ON THE MISSISSIPPI, APRIL 24.<sup>th</sup> 1862.
The U.S. Frigate Mississippi destroying the rebel Ram Manassas.

18. Farragut's naval assault on Forts Jackson and St. Philip.
Courtesy of the Historic New Orleans Collection.

cotton blazed along the city's levee. Black smoke billowed up from flame-licked barrels of turpentine and tar. Warehouses were emptied by frenzied workers who hauled cotton and tobacco to the wharf to be heaped on the fires. Shipyards were set ablaze as well along with several dozen seagoing cotton ships and river steamers. Miles of cordwood, cut for steamboat fuel, were ignited, too. Amidst the fire and smoke, there was also looting and mob violence. The poor of the city, including thousands of slaves and indigent whites, salvaged whatever they could, especially sugar, which they gathered up in aprons, pails, or baskets.

On April 25, a week and a half after the invasion began, Farragut's forces entered New Orleans. Six days later, the city, the "jewel of the Confederacy," officially surrendered.

"New Orleans has been taken," a dejected Charles wrote Amélie. "The Confederate flag which was flying is no longer there."

# 9

||||||||||||

## The Beast

Long before falling to Union forces, New Orleans, everybody said, was "the gayest town in America."

It had been that way at least since 1699, when Jean-Baptiste Le Moyne de Bienville landed at the mouth of the Mississippi River on Mardi Gras and celebrated there with his crew, claiming the area for France. Within a few years he would found the city of New Orleans and bring the French tradition of Carnival on Fat Tuesday with him into the New World.

Mardi Gras was undoubtedly a raucous affair in those early years, when the city's population was labeled "the wildest and most undesirable." At any given moment it included deported galley slaves, trappers, gold hunters, and adventurers of all stripes. They lived in "wretched hovels, malaria-infested along with serpents and alligators," according to one history of the city. Even the French colonial governor was overwhelmed. He complained to the royal administration in Paris that it was only sending him "riff raff" to use as soldiers for controlling the city.

By the 1800s, however, parades had begun appearing to mark the last day before Lent imposed its forty days of fasting, repentance, and prayer on the population. The city itself was changing, too. The "hovels" had resolved themselves into graceful buildings inspired by Spanish and French architecture, and a grid pattern was laid out, giving birth to what became known as the French Quarter. In 1857 a secret society of New Orleans businessmen organized itself into the Mistick Krewe of Comus and staged a torch-lit parade complete with floats. The modern Mardi Gras celebration was born.[1]

The party spirit lasted all year, and the music played on even as New Orleans changed hands, passing from French control to Spanish, then back to French again. In a move France would long regret, Napoléon Bonaparte, needing money to finance his campaigns against the British, sold the city along with a huge chunk of North America to the young United States of America in 1803. Americans called the new property it acquired under President Thomas Jefferson the Louisiana Purchase.

What America got in New Orleans was a population so diverse and polyglot you could hear practically every known language on its streets and docks. Nearly every nationality was represented, too, and every skin color showed up in the bars and brothels and fancy restaurants. During Spanish control, free persons of color from the Caribbean islands had been welcomed and settled in the Crescent City. Like nearly everyone else there, they, too, owned slaves. Much of the population was mixed race, the product of a culture that saw wealthy plantation owners openly keep quadroon mistresses and families.

New Orleans accepted it all with a shrug. It even winked at piracy, going so far as to call one Jean Lafitte, the most successful pirate of all, for help in keeping the British out during the War of 1812. The city was well on its way to earning its sobriquet "The Big Easy."

Wealth poured in from enormous, sprawling cotton and sugar plantations lining the Mississippi River and made New Orleans, now with a population of over 150,000, the richest city in America by the mid-1800s. It was said that the greatest concentration of millionaires anywhere in the world existed in the land between New Orleans and Louisiana's capital in Baton Rouge. Those planter-millionaires shipped their products from the big port on the Gulf of Mexico to the entire world, north to New England, east to Europe, and south to Latin America and on to Asia. Then they spent their money freely in New Orleans on horse racing, cards, and luxury goods.

One thing they hung on to was their Francophilia. The free people of color coming in from Haiti and other Caribbean islands merely reinforced that. They, like the Creole population, spoke French. They dined on French cuisine, went to the French opera, wore the latest French fashions, and sent their children to Paris to be educated.

New Orleanians, it seemed, could accept just about everything, but there was one thing they could not and would not tolerate: an outsider telling them what to do or how to live.

Someone like Ben Butler.

||||||||

Benjamin Franklin Butler was one of the most controversial generals of the Civil War. His supporters considered him a genuine hero, a courageous officer who had the guts to make difficult and unpopular decisions. Critics argued exactly the opposite, that he was a coward, scoundrel, and opportunist not to be trusted.

Butler had been a successful lawyer and politician in Massachusetts but never gotten as far as he hoped. One thing always stood in his way: himself.

From his earliest childhood he had been known as "the dirtiest, sauciest, lyingest child" on the block, according to one biographer. "No boy in the country could lie like Ben Butler, and trouble followed him everywhere."

Young Ben was fatherless; John Butler was a privateer who died of yellow fever shortly after his son was born in 1818. To support the family, his mother ran a boardinghouse for millworkers in Lowell, Massachusetts.[2]

Ben was cross-eyed, a "sickly and unattractive" child; by the time he graduated from college he still weighed only ninety-seven pounds. That did not stop him from fighting and challenging anyone who crossed him. At age nine he was expelled from Phillips Exeter Academy because of his brawling. Other schools and other ejections followed. His mother wanted her battling though bright son to prepare for the ministry but Ben preferred the military.

After being rejected twice by West Point, however (he would resent West Pointers all his life), he began reading law and teaching at a school for boys who had been expelled from other schools. It was there, he said, that he learned the value of punishment. "Not one of them went away without a thrashing," he bragged.

Later, as a lawyer, he fought with words as aggressively as with his fists. He was sharp-tongued and thin-skinned. When a newspaper reporter criticized him for "very scaly and disreputable" courtroom trickery, Butler stormed into the reporter's office, called him "a liar and a scoundrel," then tweaked the journalist's nose.

Butler also battled successfully for shorter working hours for factory workers, but then turned around and defended mill owners in another case. Switching sides whenever it suited him became his standard operating procedure. He was a proslavery Democrat when elected to the Massachusetts state legislature but became an antislavery Republican when Lincoln was elected president. He had, his biographer pointed out, an insatiable "hunger for recognition and attention."

That hunger first revealed itself when Butler enlisted in the Massachusetts State Militia in 1830. He was only twenty-one, but thanks to his political connections and knack for knowing which way the political winds were blowing, he rose rapidly to a senior position. By 1855 he'd become a brigadier general, even though he had no military experience.

With the Civil War, his craving for fame and glory came into sharper focus when his state militia helped protect the nation's capital by quelling proslavery riots in nearby Baltimore. Butler was promoted to major general, but it was a hotly debated decision. Yes, critics conceded, he may have helped "save Washington" by putting down riots and keeping rail lines open so reinforcements could reach the city, but he'd also ignored orders to hold fast—and risked pushing Maryland into the arms of the Confederacy. Butler brushed away the criticism. "I have no orders," he said. "I am carrying on the war now on my own hook."

That attitude prompted President Lincoln to suggest that Butler be "delicately removed" and transferred to Fort Monroe, where there would be less opportunity for him to make trouble. The fort, situated on the tip of the Virginia Peninsula, was little more than an

**19.** General Benjamin Butler, ca. 1860. Courtesy of the Historic New Orleans Collection.

eighty-acre field surrounded by low stone walls. Butler might easily have faded into obscurity if it hadn't been for three runaway slaves who were spotted one day creeping along a fence surrounding the fort. Butler took them into custody and put them to work. When the owner, a colonel in the Virginia Artillery, showed up and demanded they be returned in compliance with the Fugitive Slave Act, Butler refused, reminding him that Virginia had just voted to secede. "I am under no constitutional obligations to a foreign country, which Virginia now claims to be," he said. "I shall hold them as contraband of war. You were holding them against the Government: I propose to use them in favor of it."[3]

At first, Lincoln was unsure what to make of Butler's "unilateral policy of emancipation," but it was widely praised in the press and endorsed by the Republican Party, even though Butler was then a Democrat. *Contraband* soon became a euphemism for runaway slaves who sought shelter within Yankee lines. They were not free, however, and Butler was no abolitionist. He considered them "merely property." In a May 1861 letter to the *New York Times* he insisted that the government had the same legal right to enlist runaway slaves as they would "a drove of Confederate mules, or herd of Confederate cattle, which should wander or rush across the Confederate lines into the lines of the U.S. Army." Washington eventually concurred and announced that what Butler did "has been approved."

That June, with his star seemingly on the rise, Butler spotted what he thought was another opportunity to burnish his credentials. With Virginia's secession barely three weeks old, he learned that Union forces were making plans to attack Richmond, the newly declared capital of the Confederacy. The Confederates, however, were also aware of those plans and set up a small garrison known as Big Bethel near Yorktown as a lure to draw the enemy into premature action. Butler took the bait and dispatched two inexperienced units to capture Bethel. Setting off on different roads, the two units became confused, mistook each other for the enemy, and opened fire.

Butler, who chose to stay behind where it was safer, blamed the fiasco on the cowardice of his lieutenants. But no one was fooled, least of all Washington. Butler was relieved as commander of Fort Monroe and replaced by John E. Wool, a semi-retired seventy-two-year-old general whose fighting days were well behind him.

That could easily have spelled the end of Ben Butler's military career had it not been for another military operation in August, this one spearheaded by the Union navy and led by a crusty veteran of vast experience.

Flag Officer Silas H. Stringham entered the U.S. Navy in 1809 when he was only eleven years of age; he was promoted to the rank of midshipman upon turning twelve. He saw action in the War of 1812, the Second Barbary War, and the Mexican-American War. His assignment now was capturing two "sand" forts off Cape Hatteras, North Carolina, that were being used to launch attacks against commercial shipping. To pull it off, however, the Union navy needed ground troops, and it was General Wool's responsibility to supply them. "But I'm too old to lead them into battle," he said. When he offered the role to Butler, Butler jumped at the opportunity. It would be the first joint amphibious operation of the war.

The forts were taken easily, but it was almost a fiasco. On August 28 Stringham's guns opened up on the two forts as more than three hundred soldiers and a contingent of marines rowed through heavy breakers toward land. The boats were swamped and the men barely made it to an island north of Fort Clark. "With powder wet and not a cracker among them," wrote one historian, "they impaled a few wild sheep with their swords, roasted the meat on bayonets, and warmed the leftovers for the following morning's breakfast."

Meanwhile, another company made their way to the mainland only to discover that Fort Clark had been abandoned, its defenders having withdrawn to Fort Hatteras. Stringham then concentrated his guns there and within a day forced the Confederates to surrender. Though much of the bombardment was off target, it was the navy that made victory possible. General Butler, however, was quick to claim most of the credit and ordered a major general's salute fired in honor of "*his* victory," even though he had watched everything from a safe distance offshore.

All that remained was breaking the news to the White House and making an even bigger name for himself. He was determined to get there before Stringham did. After steaming back to Fort Monroe while Stringham "dithered" in North Carolina, Butler bribed a locomotive engineer to make the trip to Washington without his usual train of cars. Arriving late at night, he hurried to the home of

Postmaster-General Montgomery Blair, who lived directly across from the White House. Blair was in his study with an old acquaintance who'd just been appointed assistant secretary of the navy, Gustavus Vasa Fox. When Butler told them about Hatteras, they were delighted and suggested Lincoln be told about it immediately. Here is how Civil War historian Chester G. Hearn described what happened next: "With Butler in tow, Blair and Fox crossed the street and for fifteen minutes hammered on the door of the executive mansion before rousing the sleepy watchman. Lincoln appeared in his nightgown and slippers, looking even taller than he did in public, and Fox announced the victory, Lincoln grabbed the pudgy five-foot naval assistant around the shoulders and whirled him about the room in the strangest victory dance ever witnessed by Butler."

Hatteras was the first joint operation of the war and came as great relief to Lincoln, who was starved for good news after the Union's embarrassing defeat at Bull Run a month earlier.[4] It was also the perfect tonic for Butler, who had "expunged the infamy of Big Bethel" and now found himself in the good graces of the government again.

As he headed home to Lowell, Massachusetts, to await his next assignment, his future could not have looked brighter. He was showered with praise from joyous citizens and not shy in admitting that he loved every bit of it. "I think I at last came to know what hero worship meant," he later recalled.

If Hatteras proved anything, it was that Butler might be useful if another joint expedition arose—as one did the following year when the fleet of Flag Officer David Farragut laid siege to two forts near the mouth of the Mississippi and captured New Orleans.

||||||||

Butler was with Farragut when he steamed up the Mississippi and captured New Orleans on April 25, 1862, after ten days of heavy fighting. Except the "fighting" wasn't over.

Navigating the river and its swiftly changing currents had been a nightmare, and some of Farragut's ships got stuck on sandbars. Upon reaching New Orleans, Farragut discovered why. Instead of using rocks for ballast, Butler had substituted coal, which he intended to

The Beast

sell for his own profit. Farragut exploded: "That's against regulations!" Butler replied with a characteristic dismissal: "I haven't read the damn regulations and what's more, I shan't. And then I shall not know I'm doing anything against them." That was pretty much how he would run New Orleans. No rules would get in his way.[5]

Butler knew nothing about the city, its history, or its people, and had no desire to learn. He was a xenophobe in a city that included forty thousand foreigners, mostly Europeans. He despised Jews and considered African Americans, who made up nearly 50 percent of the population, to be "the inferior race, as God has made it." Though he later modified those views and supported efforts to recruit them for the war, he noted that they "tended to be more subservient than whites because of an inbred disposition to respond to the commands of their masters."

New Orleans was in chaos when Butler took over. Months of war and the Union's naval blockade had cut it off from basic supplies. Trade had been destroyed, and mountains of garbage filled the streets. Cotton and nearly everything else of value had been burned to keep it out of enemy hands. Inflation was so high that a five-cent streetcar ticket became "an acceptable form of exchange." The biggest problem, however, was food: the city was on the brink of starvation.

Butler, nonetheless, settled himself and his wife into the most luxurious spot in town, the St. Charles Hotel. It did not make a good impression on locals, who were already seething with anger over how he had arrived in their city. His entry was like a parade with Butler marching proudly on foot like a conquering hero, followed by an army band playing "Yankee Doodle" and "The Star-Spangled Banner." It was salt in the wound as crowds shouted "Go home, damn Yankees!" and "You'll never leave here alive!" Some onlookers had to be held back at the point of a bayonet.

The new military governor was unfazed and promptly declared martial law. He ordered citizens to turn in their arms, outlawed public assemblies, and closed down newspapers. He also demanded that New Orleanians swear an oath of allegiance to the United States and its Constitution and that ministers and priests pray for President Lincoln during their services. One minister protested, asking,

"Well, General, are you going to shut down the churches?" Butler replied, "No, I am more likely to shut down the ministers." And he did, shipping three of them to a military prison in New York "so that they will at least be out of mischief during the remainder of the war."

Butler was relentless in cracking down on his enemies. Those who refused to swear the oath of allegiance or aided the Confederacy were subject to having their property confiscated. In one case Butler made off with the owner's silverware himself, which earned him the nickname "Spoons." True or not, the episode provided fodder for satirists who caricatured him with spoons protruding from his pockets.

Worse was the name he got after issuing what became known as the "Woman Order," formally known as General Order No. 28.

Ever since their arrival, Union soldiers had been treated with contempt by the ladies of the city, who were armed, as one observer said, "with sharp tongues and full chamber pots." They would cross the street to avoid being on the same sidewalk as the soldiers or would refuse to ride on the same streetcar. Officers were spat on when they went to church and targeted with insulting gestures. The crowning blow came when one woman emptied the contents of her chamber pot on the head of Flag Officer Farragut as he walked under her balcony.

That was too much for General Butler. With Order No. 28, the outraged military governor declared, "As the officers and soldiers of the United States have been subject to repeated insults from the women, (calling themselves ladies) of New Orleans, in return for the most scrupulous non-interference and courtesy on our part, it is ordered that hereafter when any female shall, by word, gesture, or movement, insult or show contempt for any officer or soldier of the United States, she shall be regarded and held liable to be treated as a woman of the town plying her avocation."

News that the "ladies" of New Orleans could be treated like prostitutes exploded across the South. There were huge outcries even from as far away as Great Britain, where the Woman Order was seen as a license for soldiers to rape. But the Order was effective. Insults by word, look, or gesture ended abruptly.

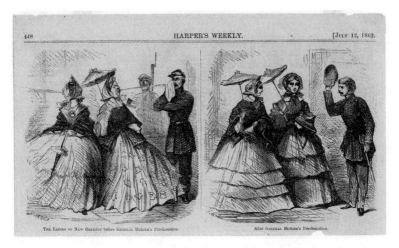

The Ladies of New Orleans before General Butler's Proclamation.         After General Butler's Proclamation.

20. *Harper's Weekly* cartoon showing the effect of Butler's proclamation, July 12, 1862. Courtesy of the Historic New Orleans Collection.

The city, as one newspaper reported, became "quiet as a church." From that day on, however, General Butler had a new name. People now referred to him as "The Beast" or "Beast Butler."

A few enterprising merchants took advantage of the situation by selling chamber pots with an image of Butler's face on the inside. They quickly sold out.

Butler lost no time living up to his nickname. One of his first acts was removing all Confederate flags from the city and replacing them with the Stars and Stripes. The move sparked widespread protests, but it was an incident involving a resident named William Mumford that revealed just how ruthless Butler could be. Just after New Orleans had fallen, Mumford had climbed to the top of the government Mint building where a Union flag had been mounted and tore it down. He then carried it through the streets where it was ripped to shreds by cheering crowds.

Butler was incensed and determined to make an example of Mumford by putting him on trial for treason. Mumford claimed his actions were just something that happened "in the excitement" of the moment. Nevertheless, a military tribunal sentenced him to death. One of Butler's aides warned that if the execution were carried out, the general's life would be in the "utmost danger." Butler

**21.** Caricature of Ben Butler as the "Bluebeard of New Orleans."
Courtesy of the Historic New Orleans Collection.

rejected the warning. "I will be in the utmost danger if I *don't* have him executed," he said. "The question to be determined is whether I command the city or the mob commands it."[6]

Tears and pleas from Mumford's family were to no avail. He was hanged on June 7 in the courtyard of the Mint itself, which, Butler said "was the ideal spot according to Spanish custom."

The execution sparked an avalanche of condemnation.

Butler was vilified in the press with rewards offered for his capture dead or alive. Confederate president Jefferson Davis branded Butler a "felon" and put a ten-thousand-dollar price on his head. "I do order that he shall no longer be considered or treated simply as a public enemy of the Confederate States of America, but as an outlaw and common enemy of mankind, and that, in the event of his capture, the officer in command of the capturing force do cause him to be immediately executed by hanging."

Butler was undeterred. He was determined to impose his will on what he considered a defiant population. "I do not carry on war with rose water," he said. "We were twenty five hundred men in a city of one hundred fifty thousand inhabitants, all hostile, bitter, defiant, explosive . . . a spark only needed for destruction."

He ordered slaves to spy on their masters and insisted that foreigners as well as residents swear the oath of allegiance. He was especially anxious to subdue the foreign consuls, for he was convinced they were actively aiding the Confederacy.

Lincoln seemed to turn a blind eye to events in New Orleans. His priority was winning the war; Butler's shortcomings could be dealt with another day.

And yet Butler did do some good for the city. He worked nonstop and improved conditions for the poor, even dipping into his own pocket to contribute one thousand dollars for a program aimed at their immediate relief. "It's a rich man's war but a poor man's fight," he said.

The general also helped eradicate diseases like yellow fever by imposing quarantines and cleaning up mountains of garbage that had accumulated throughout the city. In a normal year, yellow fever often claimed as much as 10 percent of the city's population. It was something that commanded Butler's attention, for it was the disease responsible for the death of his father when Ben was five months old. After Butler's quarantine was implemented in 1862, only two cases were reported.

Hunger was the most urgent problem, but getting food into the city was complicated. Butler stopped riverboats from plying their usual trade—which often involved transporting weapons and supplies to the Confederacy—and ordered them to start hauling flour, sugar, and other necessities instead. Only those with special passes would be allowed into the city, and none were permitted to carry anything but food. No weapons, no luxury goods, and definitely no passengers.

||||||||

As Butler tightened his grip on New Orleans, Charles Heidsieck continued shuttling between the two cities in an effort to collect payment for his champagne.[7] Little was going right, however, and everything he tried to set in motion seemed to be going nowhere. In a letter to Amélie he grumbled: "Our agent in the North still isn't paying what he owes us. He hasn't put one dollar in my hands! I tried to get back to New York to have it out with him but it's impossible to pass from one section of the country to the other. One needs a special pass to cross military lines."

Charles was also upset about the disappearance of several hundred bottles of champagne he had stored in a Mobile warehouse. He was sure they had been stolen. Irritating him as well was the exchange rate. Clients were now paying with Confederate currency, which was weak to begin with but next to worthless when exchanged for U.S. dollars or French francs. Some had previously paid with cotton, but there was little of that left, since much of it had been burned to prevent it from being seized by Union soldiers. Charles's frustrations were rapidly building to a breaking point. "I don't know if I can stand this much longer. I told you before that everyone here wants to pay but it's so difficult and I don't know what's going to happen. I feel separated from the whole world. It's as if I'm in a tomb. Uncertainty is the worst of it."

Most of that uncertainty surrounded his second ship of cotton and what had become of it. Weeks had passed and there was still no word. Had it escaped the fate of his first vessel, which was sunk by Union gunboats? If not, Heidsieck knew he would be sunk as well. In a fit of frustration, he lashed out at Amélie in a rambling and disjointed letter: "For eleven months I have had nothing from you, no instruction, no news, no guidelines, no encouragement, NOTHING! I'm fighting for self-control so I don't start breaking windows but you should know it's no bed of roses here. I'm not partying all the time as you seem to think."

Amélie had expressed her suspicions during one of Charles's previous voyages when his long absences and the pressures at home boiled over. She was the one who had to deal with the finances, who had to face angry creditors, who had to raise five young children alone—all the while trying to ignore rumors that continued to circulate in American newspapers that her husband had his eye on another woman. Her worries, which she voiced only rarely, fueled Charles's sense of frustration. "The mosquitoes are terrible and the heat is worse than in Paris. Why haven't you been in touch with our ambassador in Washington who's been a client of ours and who is in regular touch with the consuls in Richmond, Charleston and New Orleans?"

As if on cue, Charles was summoned to the French consulate in Mobile two days later and handed a packet of letters. He knew right away who they were from, and his eyes filled with tears. He felt ashamed and was trembling so hard that he could barely read what Amélie had sent.

"My very dear husband," she began, "I know how hard it must be for you, all alone in a country that's on fire. We talk about the war all the time and heard that the South is progressing but it's taking such a long time. Here, everything is fine except for money which is scarce. Everyone is complaining about business. I sold off some stock to a cousin to give us some money to live on but it would be such a joy if you were here for it would give me and children such comfort and confidence."

Charles wasted no time in replying: "I was so happy and almost too scared to read your words because who knew what could have happened in eleven months. I celebrated by emptying some bottles of our champagne. This is one of two letters I am sending you via Havana or Mexico in hopes that one of them will reach you. A thousand kisses my dear soul. God watch over you and send you the happiest moments."

‖‖‖‖‖‖

Spring gave way to summer. It was now July, two months since New Orleans had fallen to Union forces.

Although conditions had improved, major pockets of resistance remained. Many people, including judges, sheriffs, and lawyers, still refused to take the oath of allegiance to the United States as General Butler mandated.

"You have a choice," he warned. "Cooperate or quit." Virtually all resigned. Later, when a newspaper editor asked the general what would happen if he ignored his orders on censorship, Butler replied, "I am the military governor of this state—the supreme power—and you cannot disregard my order, Sir. By God, he that sins against me, sins against the Holy Ghost!"

The biggest sinners, in his opinion, were foreign nationals living in the South who had joined the Confederate army. Numbering in the thousands, they included Germans, British, Irish, and French. Many had volunteered, but many others felt they had no choice, thanks to a decision by Louisiana's governor, Thomas Overton Moore.

After Butler took command of New Orleans, Moore, a slave owner and staunch secessionist, abandoned the capital, Baton Rouge, for Opelousas and Shreveport and began organizing military resistance to the Union and seizing its military posts around the state. Every white male resident of the state, the governor said, foreigner or not, would be drafted into the Confederate army for five years.

When Moore's announcement reached Paris, it set off a firestorm. France's foreign minister protested that the draft violated France's policy of neutrality. But French residents in Louisiana were confused. When they asked the foreign minister if they were obligated to join the Confederacy, he brusquely reminded them, "No! If you

The Beast

sign up for an army of another country, the Code Napoléon means you are no longer French!"[8]

French consul Eugène Méjan was dispatched to Shreveport to work out a solution, but Moore held fast. The draft is final, he said. When Méjan returned to New Orleans, a confused and bewildered Charles Heidsieck was waiting for him. When he asked what all this might mean for him, Méjan said he wasn't sure. "Our government has ordered me to work out a compromise but I don't know where to begin."

Although his business headquarters were in Mobile, Charles spent much of his time in Louisiana, which, he feared, could put him in the crosshairs of any possible draft. When Moore declared that the call-up would begin early the following year, Méjan threw up his hands. "I've tried everything I can think of to work out a compromise but it's useless," he told Heidsieck. "I've stressed to the governor over and over that he can't assimilate our people into his army but it seems like we're getting nowhere."

Eventually, the matter was kicked to the Confederate government in Richmond, where President Davis ordered that the draft be canceled. He also promised to reestablish the privileges of foreign legions or consulates by allowing them to form private militias to protect their citizens and property. In return, those militias were expected to help defend the cities in which they lived. He vowed that the militias would not be used for any other purpose, or, as his secretary of war, Judah Benjamin, put it, "The President believes it would not be good politics to make them serve beyond their own cities."

In other words, Davis did not want to do anything that would jeopardize the chance of France intervening on behalf of the South. Although the French government was holding fast to its policy of neutrality, the Confederate president continued to hope that the emperor would change his mind. "The sword of Napoléon III could still be raised to protect the South," he said hopefully.

For Charles, Davis's decision meant that he could go about his business with no worry about being drafted.

For Butler, however, it was an excuse to renew his war against the foreign consuls, especially the French whom he called "dogs."

In a letter to Méjan, Butler complained bitterly that "very few of the French subjects here have taken the oath of neutrality." At the same time, he noted that "all of the officers of the French Legion, your militia here in New Orleans, have, with your knowledge and assent, taken the oath to support the constitution of the Confederate States!" He also called Méjan's attention to fact that the son of the French consul of Baton Rouge had recently been taken prisoner while fighting for the South.

The general's ire was directed at the British as well, a rancor that had come with his Irish heritage. Butler's family had fought the British for generations. His grandfather had been killed in the French and Indian Wars, and his father had fought for the United States against Great Britain in the War of 1812.

Fueling his xenophobia was the conviction that the British and other foreign consuls were supplying money and arms to the Confederacy. Officially, the job of the consuls was to protect the interests of their countrymen and reflect their country's policy of neutrality, but Butler considered it a sham and went after them with a vengeance.

At the Dutch consulate he seized $800,000 hidden in the consul's vault which he said was to be used for buying arms for the Confederacy. He then sent his secret police to the offices of a French shipper to confiscate $400,000 in silver coins which he suspected were being used for the same purpose. After meeting with the British consul, Butler discovered that sixty members of the British Guard, the militia protecting the consulate, had sent their weapons and uniforms to the rebels. For this "flagrant violation of neutrality," Butler ordered every guardsman who could not immediately produce his gun and uniform to leave New Orleans in twenty-four hours.

But it was the *Magnolia* incident that convinced the general, perhaps more than anything else, that the Europeans were up to no good and could not be trusted. The *Magnolia* was a Confederate steamer that was captured when it attempted to break through the Union's blockade. When Butler's soldiers climbed aboard they discovered a letter revealing that the Spanish consul in New Orleans was to collect a 5 percent share from the profits of a proposed sale of eighty thousand muskets to the Confederacy.

Butler's crackdown on the consuls illustrated how precarious the situation had become for foreigners. That included Heidsieck, who was now staying with a friend in Mobile, still outside Union control, and traveling to New Orleans when possible to check for correspondence and to collect for sales of his champagne. He still had a substantial amount outstanding. In early July, when he wrote to Amélie, it was clear he knew he was in danger.

July 5—Just to let you know I'm still alive and taking care of some urgent business, collecting twenty five thousand francs and a few ious that I've been promised. I've signed on as a bartender on a steamer that travels regularly between Mobile and New Orleans to bring flour to residents of New Orleans. We are traveling under a flag of neutrality but absolute prudence commands all my acts. I can't say anything about what goes on. I'm here in New Orleans for just a few hours. It goes without saying that all our papers are checked, and we are able to go into the city only under strict surveillance. Every letter I write will probably be read so I must be careful. I don't want to compromise myself or anyone else. Now I must close for I don't want to be late getting back on the steamer. P.S. You must not under any circumstances send any more champagne here unless you have other news from me.

July 8—I'm here again under neutral status. Again I was a barman on a steamer, but it's the only way I can get news from you and take care of business. It's neither possible nor prudent to give you any details.

July 11—This is my third trip and it's becoming more and more dangerous. I'm searched when I come in and searched when I leave.

What Charles did not tell Amélie was that he was traveling on a steamer that was prohibited from taking passengers. It was authorized to carry only flour and other essentials to New Orleans. Charles, however, had managed to get around the restriction by persuading the captain to hire him as a *garçon de buvette*, or bartender, which technically made him part of the crew. He explained to the captain how dire his financial situation was and that coming aboard was the only way he could get back and forth between the two cities to wind up his business in the United States before heading back to France. He described how urgent it was, that his family desperately needed him, and that he himself was terribly homesick. The captain finally yielded.

About the only thing that encouraged him was the way the war was going. Momentum had shifted in favor of the South after Confederate forces managed to beat back attempts by the Union to capture Richmond, capital of the Confederacy. It was, he told Amélie on July 11, just the "tonic" he needed: "Based on everything I'm seeing, and for reasons that are too long to explain, I think the South is going to carry this off and become rich. If that happens, if the South triumphs, we will be rich, too. We will be absolute masters of the market."

||||||||

But Charles wasn't about to wait. He was determined to finish his work and get out of the country as fast as possible. Having already made three trips between Mobile and New Orleans, he resolved to make only two more to collect letters and money and then leave . . . by catching a blockade runner to Havana or Mexico and finding a ship that would get him back to Europe.

The fourth trip went smoothly, which gave him hopes that the final one would be no different.

On July 27, the day of his departure from Mobile, friends accompanied Charles to the boat to say good-bye and wish him well. As he was about to board the *Natchez*, the consul of Mobile asked him to carry a diplomatic pouch to his counterpart in New Orleans. Inside was an envelope bound tightly with string and sealed by the minister of foreign affairs in Paris. The consul explained that he'd been holding the pouch for some time because he had been unable to forward it. Charles agreed to serve as a courier, and the consul gave him an authorizing letter.

Four days later, after an uneventful trip, he arrived in New Orleans. That's when everything began to go wrong. Charles was told by an officer that he could not leave the ship without first proving his nationality and justifying the aim of his trip. Charles

The Beast

showed him his passport and explained why he had come to New Orleans. It did no good. Security had been tightened, the officer said, adding that Charles and the rest of the crew would have to spend the night on the dock until their papers could be verified.

Next morning, Charles was ordered to report to General Headquarters and the man in charge, Benjamin Butler. He was surprised and somewhat concerned. Like everyone, he had heard of "The Beast" and was wary of what he'd be facing. Then again, he reassured himself that he had his passport and other supporting documents. As a precaution, however, he asked that the French consul be notified immediately.

When Charles arrived at headquarters, he was escorted into a large room guarded by a line of soldiers. A short time later, he was led into Butler's office. The general was at his desk and clearly in a foul mood. There were no introductions or polite greetings. "Start explaining yourself!" Butler bellowed.

According to notes of the interrogation that Charles recorded immediately afterwards, he introduced himself, saying he was a champagne merchant and wanted to pick up personal and business letters from the French consulate. "Here is my passport and other papers, sir." Butler glanced at them and threw them back. "Those are worthless and you, as far as I'm concerned, are a filthy liar!"

Charles was stunned; it took him several seconds before he could respond. Finally, he said, "I resent your odious insult and insinuation, sir."

"Well then," snapped Butler, "how does it happen that you came here under false pretenses, disguised as a bartender and traveling on a vessel which you *knew* was prohibited from carrying passengers?"

Charles replied that he was not a passenger, that he was part of the crew and traveling for business. His job of bartender on the boat was "the closest possible approximation" to his actual line of work. "I am, as I said, a champagne salesman."

That drew a sarcastic response from Butler. "A bartender in the South is one of the most menial employments and is usually, on board steamers, entrusted to a Negro steward. Is not a gentleman, such as you consider yourself, *disguised* when he takes upon himself such employment?" Before Charles could reply, the general added this insult: "How is it possible that anyone with good taste, much less the crew of a small steamboat, could drink enough of even so poor a wine as 'Heidsieck champagne' to make it profitable?"

Charles bristled, but Butler quickly changed the subject. He was staring at the diplomatic pouch Charles was holding. "Do you know what that pouch contains?" he asked. Heidsieck said he did not.

"Hand it over," Butler demanded.

Charles refused. "I am charged to hand it personally to the French consul for whom it's intended and to no one else. The consul has been notified of my arrival."

"I'm the boss here, and I want that pouch!"

Charles shook his head. "Sir, you have no authority to demand that. I must protest in the name of France and my rights as a French citizen!"

"Protest all you want!" Butler growled. "You are nothing but a French dog and you will pay dearly for your resistance! Now, for the last time, give me that pouch!"

"Never."

"You're risking your life."

"I can't . . ."

Turning to soldiers who were standing nearby, Butler shouted, "Seize this man and keep him under guard!" Butler then grabbed the pouch and was about to cut it open when Méjan arrived. Charles quickly explained what was happening. "Don't worry," the diplomat said. "I'm sure it's all a frightful misunderstanding. I'll talk to the General, explain the situation and have it quickly cleared up."

Méjan entered Butler's office where almost immediately a "terrible outburst" erupted. The French diplomat emerged minutes later looking shaken. "I asked General Butler to return the dispatches and let you go, but he refused. I explained that the consul in Mobile had authorized you to carry the pouch and showed the General a letter stating that, but he wouldn't listen. He was furious and threatening, cursing France and the French with all the resources of his vocabulary. One of the things he said was, 'I've got one Frenchman and he'll pay for the rest.'"

"I'm not sure what's best to do at this point," Méjan said. "The General clearly detests me but let me try one more time to reason with him."

Entering Butler's office again, the consul pleaded with him to return the dispatches and let Heidsieck go. Once again, Butler refused.

"In that case, sir, I shall immediately lodge a formal protest with Washington. I will also notify my own government and Emperor Napoléon III himself about what you are doing."

Butler exploded. Rising from his chair, he yelled, "I don't give a shit about France or its emperor! What's more, I'm arresting Heidsieck and sending him to Fort Jackson with the next shipment of prisoners."

Méjan was horrified. Heidsieck, he said, was "not acclimated" to the kind of conditions he would face at Fort Jackson. "By sending him there you are committing murder in cold blood!"

Butler was unmoved. "He's got three days to get his affairs in order. Now send him back in here. I'm not finished with him."

Charles knew he was in trouble the moment he saw the consul come out of Butler's office. "It's worse than I could have imagined," Méjan said, shaking his head. "I'll explain everything, but first he wants to see you again."

Charles reentered Butler's office. Once more, the general was seated at his desk, but this time he was holding a knife. He had sliced open the diplomatic pouch and broken the seal on the envelope of dispatches. He was now was cutting away the strings.

"Sir, I strongly protest," Charles said. "Isn't this to be done only in the presence of the consul, Monsieur de Méjan?" Butler ignored the question and began spreading the dispatches across his desk.

"Your name is Charles Heidsieck?"

"Yes, General. I'm Charles Heidsieck, a Frenchman from Reims. I'm a businessman, I sell champagne." *But he knows all this, he knows who I am, what is this leading up to,* Charles wondered.

"You were a bartender on a steamer called the *Natchez* when you traveled here?"

"Certainly, General. It was my right. I had my passport and the necessary visas to come and go as I wished. I obeyed all the rules and haven't broken any laws that I know of."

Butler shook his head, then pointed to the dispatches on his desk. "Those are what you were carrying?"

"Yes, sir."

"Do you know what's in them?"

"*Mon Générale*, not at all."

Butler began sifting through the documents. "This is a scandal, a complete scandal!" he growled. "You're no courier. You and your government are serving as a postal service for those damned rebels!"

Before Charles could reply, Butler growled, "I'm placing you under arrest for crossing military lines under false pretenses.[9] You will be imprisoned in Fort Jackson until I decide what to do with you." Charles was stupefied. As he was ushered out of the office, Butler wadded the now empty envelope into a ball and hurled it toward the door. Charles picked it up and stuffed it into his pocket, keeping it as evidence that Butler had violated diplomatic protocols.

Méjan was waiting when he came out. "Look my friend, I know you are brave but your life is in danger. Fort Jackson is the worst place in Louisiana. When I spoke with the General earlier, I tried to explain that you are not acclimated to such conditions and that sending you there amounts to cold-blooded murder. He said he didn't give a damn."

Fort Jackson had been one of two forts protecting the entrance to New Orleans that Union forces captured three months earlier. It was now a prison perched on a swampy part of the Mississippi Delta and surrounded by snakes and alligators.

Charles shuddered as Méjan described what lay ahead. "If you have anything you want sent to your children, your family, I'll take care of it. But try not to lose heart. In me, you have a defender and friend. I shall not cease working to obtain justice and liberty for you."

Charles scribbled a few words of "farewell" to his wife and told her how much he loved her, then drafted messages to Emperor Napoléon III and members of the French Parliament. He also wrote to the cardinal and archbishop of Reims as well as the mayor of Reims. Méjan took the letters and left.

That afternoon, Charles's transfer to Fort Jackson was confirmed. It would take place in three days. Until then, he would be kept under

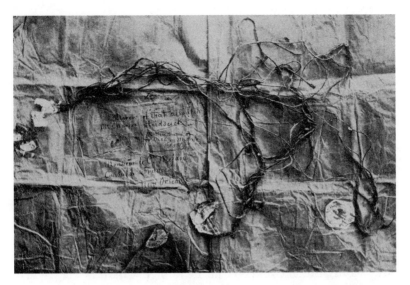

22. Heidsieck's diplomatic pouch, which was seized by General Butler.
Courtesy of Champagne Charles Heidsieck.

close guard in the city's Customs House, a massive granite building that had been used by the Confederacy for manufacturing gun
carriages but was now a prison holding two thousand Confederate
soldiers—and Charles Heidsieck.

News of his arrest and impending imprisonment quickly spread.
A number of French residents petitioned Butler "as an act of grace"
to release him and let him return home. Some offered bribes, substantial sums of money. All were turned away.

Butler, meanwhile, continued pouring over the dispatches Charles
had been carrying. What he found left no doubt in his mind that
Charles was a spy for the Confederacy and should be hanged. In a
letter to Washington, Butler claimed there were documents containing "treasonable information" from the French, Swiss, Spanish,
Prussian, and Belgian consuls. There were also a "great number of
letters to private persons, mostly rebels, or worse, intermeddling
foreigners, containing contraband intelligence."

Butler informed his superiors that he had placed Heidsieck under
arrest for espionage and would be imprisoning him in Fort Jackson
until he could be put on trial.

According to the Union army's definition, which was based on international law, a spy was "a person who secretly, in disguise or under false pretense, seeks information with the intention of communicating it to the enemy" in wartime. That, in Butler's opinion, described Charles perfectly. Death by hanging was the traditional punishment.

Espionage, however, was not a crime under the *civilian* laws of either the Union or the Confederacy. As a result, captured spies could only be tried and punished by *military* tribunals. Complicating matters was that neither the North nor the South had a single spy agency devoted to the collection and analysis of intelligence information. This left it to individual officers like General Butler to determine what facts were relevant and what should be done. In other words, Butler could do what he wanted. Charles's fate seemed all but sealed.

Butler knew that the South, especially in the first year of the war, had the advantage of recruiting spies because of the large number of Confederate sympathizers in Washington. The most valuable were those who were socially connected, and no one, Butler realized, was more connected than Charles Heidsieck, the man known as "Champagne Charlie." His name had been made famous in the newspapers. It was instantly recognized in New York social circles, at political receptions in Washington, and by business figures and foreign diplomats in the South.

And so, Butler began building his case against Charles, one he was determined to end with the Frenchman's execution.

|||||||

Charles passed most of the time before his transfer to Fort Jackson by writing letters and recording what he remembered of his interrogation. "I am repeating word for word everything that passed between the General and me. I am perfectly sure of my memory and the accuracy of my notes, but what I cannot fully convey is the manner and unspeakable tone of my interrogator."

On the evening before his departure to Fort Jackson, Charles asked to see a priest. The soldier guarding him said he was prohibited from letting anyone see him. "I have strict orders," he said, "but I also know you to be an honorable man. If you give me your word and promise to return within two hours, I'll turn you over to a Catholic soldier, an Irishman, who will accompany you to a church." Charles gave his promise.

Charles had a deep faith, but if he hoped to find comfort by seeing a priest, he may have been disappointed. When the priest heard what was happening, he was horrified and all but confirmed what Méjan had said, that Charles might not survive. He gave Charles extreme unction, the final anointing administered to those on the verge of death.

Later, as Charles and the soldier headed back to General Headquarters, the soldier stopped. "I need a favor," he said. "My son is dying of croup and I live just over there. In the name of *your* children, will you wait for me here and not try to escape while I see if mine is still alive?" Charles was touched by the soldier's concern and said he would wait.

But as the guard disappeared down a narrow neighboring street, Charles knew this was his chance. It would be so easy to escape, just a short walk of two hundred yards. That's how far away the port was. As he stood up and could see ships belonging to some of his friends, freedom beckoned. Charles knew they would be only too willing to hide him and spirit him away. But he had given his word; he'd promised he would wait until the guard returned. Charles sat back down.

A short time later the guard was back, and he was smiling. His son was still alive, he said, and might even survive. Charles congratulated him warmly, and he and the guard returned to the Customs House. They arrived within two hours.

Even knowing he had kept his promise, sleep that night proved elusive. He knew that when the sun rose, he would be hauled to prison.

# 10

||||||||||||

## Into the Jaws

As a convoy bearing Charles and seventy-three other prisoners neared Fort Jackson, words of his friend Eugène Méjan flashed through his mind: "It's the worst place in Louisiana."

Charles shuddered. After all he had been through, was this what it came down to? Was this how it ended? He'd been told what the prison was like and what he would likely face, but it still came as a shock.[1]

It was August 6, 1862. It had taken more than two days for the convoy to make the sixty-mile journey from New Orleans to Fort Jackson, a bombed-out Confederate stronghold that had recently been converted into a Union prison.

Fort Jackson was one of the newer prison camps to be established for incarcerating prisoners of war. More than 150 would be erected before the war was over, all of them characterized by filth, disease, starvation, and death. They went by such names as Alton, Point Lookout, Belle Isle, and Elmira—or "Hellmira," as inmates called it because of its staggering death rate. Conditions for both sides were "disgraceful and morally outrageous," said one historian. "Half-crazed prisoners frequently beat or killed one another while fighting for near-starvation food rations."

So appalling were conditions that even poet Walt Whitman was driven to comment about "the measureless torments of the helpless young men, with all their humiliations, hunger, cold, filth and despair, their hope utterly given out."

More than fifty-six thousand soldiers would die in the prison camps, a number equivalent to 10 percent of those who would be killed in the war. The most notorious prison was Andersonville, a sprawling hellhole in Georgia crammed with eight times the number of prisoners it was meant to hold. In the fourteen months of its existence, nearly a third of the forty-five thousand Union soldiers held there would die.

One who survived, but just barely, was Robert H. Kellogg. He was only twenty years old when he walked through the gates.[2] "As we entered the place," he wrote, "a spectacle met our eyes that almost froze our blood with horror . . . before us were forms that had once been active and erect—stalwart men, now nothing but mere walking skeletons, covered with filth and vermin. . . . Many of our men exclaimed with earnestness, 'Can this be hell?'"

Similar fears gripped Charles as he and the other prisoners were removed from the convoy and marched toward the entrance of Fort Jackson.

The fort was perched on the southwestern bank of the Mississippi and surrounded by what was euphemistically called a "wet ditch." In other words, a moat. It was carved out of the river and populated with "natural wardens"—snakes and alligators.

The star-shaped fort had other natural defenses as well. Its location at a bend in the river meant the current there could suddenly become a raging torrent, making it impossible to navigate or cross.

Compounding the misery for prisoners was the subtropical climate. With more than sixty-five inches of rain falling each year, mosquitoes infested the area; yellow fever and other diseases were rampant. There were floods as well, from December through May, along with dense fogs that created a sense of profound isolation. After that it became even worse, for that was when the hurricane season began, bringing with it tidal surges that often swamped the fort.

Fort Jackson, built in 1822 and named after President Andrew Jackson, had been a key component in the defense of New Orleans. Its red brick walls towered twenty-five feet above the ground and were twenty feet thick. Two "curtains" of gun emplacements had adorned the walls, each with eight guns pointed at the Mississippi River. In the center of the fort was a barracks for five hundred men that was considered bombproof.

But that was before. Now it was in shambles. Shelling by Union forces had left gaping holes and wide cracks in the walls, along with a roof partially collapsed. Even before that, however, conditions were so deplorable that Confederate soldiers defending the fort mutinied against their officers.

Charles and the other prisoners were herded inside and confined to an enclosed area reeking with mold and stifling humidity. The floor, little more than pounded earth, was inundated with water from heavy rains and flooding; mud was everywhere. Charles was assigned to a space on a higher portion of the floor, but it was only marginally drier than the rest of the area. He began scooping out mud with a pail left for a latrine before dropping his mattress onto the ground. That was when he spotted a white-haired old man, just across from him, lying prostrate and unmoving in the muck. Heidsieck approached and, with help, carried him to the spot he had just cleared. He then settled himself into the old man's space and tried to clear his mind.

Night came swiftly, along with thoughts of home, of Amélie and his children. The grapes would be nearly ripe by now, and it wouldn't be long before the harvest. How he longed to be there. Lying on his mattress, Heidsieck gazed at the stars visible through holes in the barrack's roof. In the distance he heard the sound of a flute, an Irish melody called "The Last Rose of Summer" from the opera *Martha*. *Balm for a tired spirit*, he thought before finally drifting into sleep.

The next morning when he awoke, Charles discovered the old man across from him had died.

|||||||||

It was now the hurricane season, and with it came torrential rains, high tides, and something perhaps even more terrifying—alligators. On scraps of paper and a pen he obtained from one of the guards, Charles wrote down what it was like: "Their close presence was highly disagreeable when the river rose to the height of the windows which were devoid of frame or glass. Placing their paws on the sill of these openings, the hideous beasts thrust in their menacing heads and opened their enormous mouths, showing every intention of invading the casements."

Gone now was Charles's earlier lighthearted comments about hunting alligators while touring the South and how killing them was "easy." This time he was armed only with stones and bricks that he and the other prisoners threw into the mouths of the beasts. "The jaws then closed, the redoubtable rows of teeth clacking together, the head disappeared and a splashing sound announced the retreat of the enemy."

Fearing such attacks could come at any time, the prisoners began stockpiling more stones and bricks to defend themselves. Charles's accuracy so impressed his cellmates that they gave him the "ammunition" and told him to fire away.

Alligators, however, weren't the only enemy. There was also disease borne by insects and filthy water. Many prisoners became seriously ill.

Food was another problem. There was an adequate ration, but it was barely edible. Everything, including meat, was raw, and all was dumped into a single bucket. Everyone had to eat with their hands.

But here, thought Charles, was an opportunity. He asked to see the officer in charge and offered to cook for everyone, prisoners and guards alike. It would give him something to do rather than sit and wait for alligators to attack, he explained, as well as improve living conditions for one and all at the fort. When the officer agreed, Charles set about scavenging bits and pieces to build a primitive stove and turn himself into a chef. What he prepared was nothing fancy, he admitted, but it was at least palatable.

Meanwhile, the days rolled on, one unbearably like another. There'd been no news from anyone, not from home or any of his friends. *Have I been forgotten? Does anyone even know I'm still alive?*, he wondered. He thought about the letters he'd sent to officials before his imprisonment. *Had they gotten through?*

When opportunities arose he also wrote letters from prison to anyone he could think of—family, friends, church leaders, govern-

Into the Jaws

ment officials—pleading his innocence and stressing the urgency of the situation, but there were never any assurances the letters would get through. They were essentially the same. "Of what am I guilty? Nothing! I was in the right and obeyed all the rules and regulations. Nevertheless, I was grossly insulted by General Butler who used brutal force trying to break me. Have I given up? No, but each hour is precious, there's no time to lose. I am confined in a cell, inundated with water and mud and infected by deadly diseases. Unless you move quickly, I will be reduced to nothing more than a cadaver, useless to my family and useless to myself."

In fact, officials *were* moving quickly. His incarceration had sparked a furious letter-writing campaign on his behalf involving friends, French government officials, the mayor of Reims, and the city's archbishop. Even before Charles had left New Orleans, Consul Méjan had already fired off two letters to General Butler urging him to reexamine the case. That Charles was a spy, a courier for the Confederacy, is completely unfounded, he argued. "Heidsieck was as ignorant of what the diplomatic pouch contained as I was," he said, "and would never have come to New Orleans if he had any fears for his safety."[3]

A few days after Méjan's letters, Jules Treilhard, the first secretary of France's legation in Washington, wrote to Secretary of State William Seward. "SIR: A Frenchman, belonging to one of the most respectable commercial houses in Champagne, Mr. Chs. Heidsieck, has been lately arrested by orders of Major-General Butler, and shut up in Fort Jackson. He has not been informed of the motives of his arrest; has not been subjected to any interrogatories, and has not been confronted by any witnesses accusing him."

Treilhard echoed Méjan and insisted that Heidsieck was not a spy:

Mr. Heidsieck traveled to New Orleans only to obtain tidings from his family and this without any concealment of the packet of letters he was carrying to the consul of New Orleans. He was as completely ignorant of their contents as Mr. Méjan himself. He is now imprisoned at one of the most unhealthy places in Louisiana where the life of an unacclimated stranger may, at this season above all, be greatly endangered. In the name of justice and humanity, as well as in the name of good relations between our countries, I ask you to do all you can to secure Mr. Heidsieck's immediate release.

Treilhard's letter struck a nerve. Two days later, on August 23, the commanding general of the Union armies, Major General Henry Halleck, weighed in. Halleck, no fan of Butler's, ordered the military governor to conduct an "immediate investigation" into the charges against Charles and explain why the Frenchman had been arrested.

A month would pass before Butler replied, but Charles's plight had caught Washington's attention. It also caught the attention of France's emperor and empress thanks to Amélie, who reached out to the royal couple on behalf of her husband. To the empress she described how Charles had been imprisoned and "condemned to a thousand sufferings. Oh, I beg of you with tears in my eyes, to ease my pain and bring my husband back to me."

To the emperor she wrote: "We were once one of the most prosperous houses in Champagne but we have been plunged into bankruptcy. Our entire family, one of the most honorable in the city, now faces ruin and desolation." She described the brutal interrogation Charles experienced at the hands of General Butler and how Butler had "grossly insulted the French nation and Your Majesty by saying he didn't 'give a shit about you or our country.' I hope you can help us for my pain is profound."

||||||||

Charles, however, was unaware of what was happening. Confined with hundreds of other prisoners in squalid conditions, he was cut off from nearly everything. Often, his mind would drift to other times, to when life was so much different—the parties and receptions he attended where he was the guest of honor, the newspapers that tracked his every move and hailed him as "Champagne Charlie," the hunting expeditions followed by glorious sunsets and camping out under the stars. It was a different world then; it felt like a lifetime ago.

One day, two visitors appeared from that "other world." They were friends from New Orleans who had talked their way past the guards at the front gate. But Charles's joy in seeing them was short lived, for they brought terrible news. His second shipload of cotton, the one he was depending on to save his business after the first one was sunk, had been intercepted by Union gunboats and burned. Everything aboard was lost.

Charles felt crushed, utterly defeated. His friends tried to cheer him, to give him some reason for hope. Everyone, they said, including Napoléon III, was writing letters and exerting pressure on the Lincoln administration to secure his freedom. "Hold on. Don't give up," they pleaded. "Something will work out." They assured him his family was well.

Then, from the handle of a cane, one of his friends pulled out a tightly rolled piece of paper. "Here, write to your family but do it quickly," he said. "It's the best thing you can do for them. We'll make sure they receive it."

Charles began writing. "My dear Amélie, in a week, I will have been in prison three months." The date was October 18, 1862. He described the wretched conditions, how he and other prisoners had been squeezed into a filthy space thirty feet long and twelve feet wide and forced to eat and drink from a dirty trough.

He then revealed something that must have come as a shock to Amélie: Butler had offered to free him. The offer, he said, occurred about a week after his imprisonment and was made on the condition that he leave the country immediately. "I refused. It's not only liberty I want; I want justice. I hope you understand and are not upset with me. I want Butler to apologize for his insults; I want him to acknowledge that as a citizen of a neutral country, I have the right to travel freely and conduct my business as is necessary." That business, he told Amélie, was far from finished. He still had funds to collect from those who owed him money and had promised to pay: "I still don't understand why I am here or what I have done wrong. I feel as if I am the victim of a ferocious beast. My suffering and morale are indescribable and I see nothing ahead that will change it."

That October, Fort Jackson was decimated by an outbreak of yellow fever. Everyone, including Charles, was evacuated to another

**23.** Fort Pickens in 1861, shortly before Heidsieck arrived.
*Harper's Weekly*, February 23, 1861.

prison, Fort Pickens, a heavily fortified structure on an island in Pensacola Bay just off the western end of the Florida Panhandle.

Although the fort was situated in a dry, sandy area and provided an escape from yellow fever, other maladies, including pinkeye and sunstroke, took their toll on the prisoners. Charles, already weakened and depressed, became seriously ill.

On October 9, Fort Pickens was attacked by a Confederate force of one thousand men. The Confederates were eventually driven back, but their assault on the stronghold left those inside in even worse condition.

|||||||||

In New Orleans, General Butler had just finished his report to General Halleck explaining why he had arrested Charles. His explanation was far from complete and in some instances completely false or misleading: "Soon after my coming to this city, it became a matter of necessity to allow a boat to ply between this city and Mobile, for the purpose of bringing flour.... It was one of the expressed and published conditions that no information or passengers should be conveyed between the two places. To evade and violate this condition, Charles Heidsieck was permitted to smuggle himself on board the boat, in the pretended capacity of barkeeper or under-steward,

Into the Jaws

and made several trips between the cities, carrying hundreds of letters and papers and bearing communications between rebels and their sympathizers."

"Smuggled" aboard? In fact, records show the captain gave him permission to come aboard, which the captain later confirmed.

"Disguised" as a barkeeper? That was untrue as well. On the manifest, Heidsieck clearly stated his own name and occupation and explained that "barkeeper" was simply the closest job to his regular one.

Butler told Halleck that Charles carried letters and papers for the "rebels and their sympathizers," implying that he was a spy.[4] He did not point out that Charles had *not* tried to conceal the letters, nor did he reveal that Charles stated emphatically he had no knowledge of what they contained. The general also failed to mention that the vice-consul of Mobile had written to him explaining why he had given Charles the diplomatic pouch in the first place: that because of the war, it was only way and quickest way to get the dispatches to the consul in New Orleans.

One of Butler's chief accusations was that Heidsieck "was carrying on a contraband trade in wines." That was false. Charles indeed was transporting a large quantity of champagne, but it was part of a transaction his sales agent in New York had made *three years earlier*. Charles was merely delivering the champagne to the customer who had bought it.

In concluding his report to Halleck, Butler said that after he arrested Charles, "I offered to discharge him upon the condition that he should immediately leave for France, whose protection he has claimed, which I trust that every other man who behaves as he does will do." Butler did not bother mentioning that Charles still had important business to finish or that Charles rejected the offer because he wanted "justice" and an "apology" as well as an explanation of why he had been imprisoned.

||||||||

By the time Butler's report reached Halleck's desk in Washington, no one was even thinking about the Frenchman. Everyone's attention was consumed by the war.

The Union, in late August, suffered a crushing defeat at the Second Battle of Bull Run. At the same time, Native American uprisings were erupting in the West.

Then came September 17, the deadliest day of the war. The North called it the Battle of Antietam, after a creek that ran through a Maryland farm field. The South referred to it as the Battle of Sharpsburg.

With the outcome of the war far from certain, General Robert E. Lee was convinced that the time had come to take the war to the North, that a victory in Maryland—which was still part of the Union but contained vast numbers of Confederate sympathizers—might prod the state to join the Confederacy. If that happened, the road to taking Washington DC would be significantly widened.

Another dynamic was in play as well. From the day the war started, Confederate leaders like President Jefferson Davis believed that Europe's dependence on cotton would persuade it to join the war on the side of the South. That hadn't happened, partly because France and Great Britain feared the South would lose. But the battle ahead could change that, Davis thought. One more victory might impress the two countries with a sense of the South's military power and persuade them to recognize the Confederacy.

It didn't happen. After twelve hours of intense, often close-range fighting, twenty-three thousand Union and Confederate soldiers lay dead, wounded, or missing. It was the bloodiest single-day battle in American history. Both sides were shaken by the losses. Although the battle was largely a stalemate, the Union claimed victory when Lee's Army of Northern Virginia retreated first.

Five days later, on September 22, President Abraham Lincoln, feeling empowered by at least the semblance of victory, warned in a preliminary Emancipation Proclamation that he intended to free Southern slaves if the Confederacy continued its rebellion. (He did not issue the final proclamation until January 1 the following year.)

The Battle of Antietam/Sharpsburg effectively ended whatever hopes Confederate leaders had that France and Great Britain would intervene.

As for what became known as the Heidsieck Incident, the entire matter might well have been forgotten had it not been for a letter General Butler discovered while going through the dispatches Charles had been carrying. It was a letter from the French foreign minister advising the Confederacy that it would soon receive a shipment of cloth and other material for making military uniforms.

When news of the letter reached Paris, it set off an uproar. Questions flew fast and furiously in the French Parliament as members of all political parties demanded to know how the foreign minister could have been so careless as to let such a sensitive document fall into Union hands. "You have put the life of a French citizen at risk!" one politician charged. The minister apologized and promised to make amends, saying he would pay out of his own pocket "a sizeable indemnity" to Charles and his family for their suffering.[5]

The matter was far from settled, however, for it soon sparked a bitter row between the United States and France. Washington, ever mindful of France's sympathies toward the South, accused the French government of violating its pledge to remain neutral. France, in turn, protested the "theft" of the diplomatic pouch and demanded that "its bearer, Charles-Camille Heidsieck, be freed."

Recriminations flew back and forth. When France insisted that the United States pay damages to Charles for his suffering, Washington countered that France reimburse Americans in France who suffered in the Revolution of 1848.

With civil war raging and its outcome far from certain, many Americans, both inside the government and out, had become weary and fed up of the incessant feuding, not only with France but with other countries like Britain and Spain, which also were supposed to be neutral.

In a lengthy essay titled "Our Foreign Relations," *Harper's Weekly* wrote: "Nations, like corporations, are soulless and selfish; they generally take advantage of their rivals' troubles to assail them. A couple of years ago, no European nation cared to join issue with this country. Now that we are in trouble France, Spain and England are all quarreling with us."

Spain, the journal said, was claiming damages for the burning in Spanish waters of an Anglo-Confederate steamer. Britain, in turn, was letting its shipyards be used for building warships for the Confederate navy. In Bermuda and the Bahamas, the governors of those British colonies were granting "official protection to blockade-runners and rebel privateers" while refusing to provide coal and other supplies to Union vessels. When Washington protests, *Harper's Weekly* added, "the British Government replies that it is without power to carry out its own neutrality laws."

The problem was that everyone had different interpretations of what neutrality meant. Even though Queen Victoria insisted that Britain would adhere strictly to the laws of neutrality, Chancellor of the Exchequer William Gladstone argued that did not mean English shipyards could not be used for building Confederate warships and blockade runners. Although he was against slavery, his sympathies were with the South for economic reasons. What he feared was that the North would try to reunite the country by force, thus jeopardizing Britain's lucrative trade with the Confederacy.

His argument for allowing English shipyards to be used for building ships for the South focused mainly on the construction of the CSS *Alabama* at the Lairds Dockyards near Liverpool. Under the law, he said, it is permissible to build a ship designed as an unarmed vessel—provided it isn't armed until *after* it sails into international waters.[6]

That is what happened with the *Alabama* when it was launched on July 29, 1862. Manned with an English crew and Confederate officers, the armor-plated steamer immediately set course for the Azores. Only after reaching the islands but still in international waters was it outfitted with torpedoes, heavy cannons, and other guns. Described as a "commerce raider," the *Alabama*, powered by both wind and steam, preyed successfully on Union merchant and navy vessels for two years, sinking more than sixty. Washington lodged protest after protest, but it did little good.

"There is no use whining about the injustice involved in this state of our foreign relations," *Harper's* said. "The experience of the past year has proved that Europe would be well pleased to have the powerful republic of the United States divided into two feeble, jarring and jealous halves. And that experience further shows that until we have suppressed the rebellion we shall be in no condition to undertake a war with even the feeblest of foreign powers. Whatever mischief these foreign enemies of our country may contrive we can only, as the boys say, grin and bear it."

As for the case of Charles Heidsieck, *Harper's* added: "If therefore, France insists on reparation for the eminently just and proper arrest of the spy Heidsieck, and for the equally righteous penalties inflicted on other French rebel sympathizers at New Orleans, we must grant it. . . . We cannot fight Europe and the rebels together. We must square accounts with the latter first. Then we may have the leisure to deal with foreigners."

||||||||

That October, toward the end of his fourth month of captivity, Charles was approached by a noncommissioned officer to whom he had given French lessons. The officer said he had just learned that General Butler had received word from Washington that Heidsieck should be freed. The officer added that when Butler opened the communication he flew into a rage, declaring it to be "false" before tearing it up.

A few days later another document arrived, and this one was impossible to ignore. It was dated October 20 and signed by the general in chief himself, Henry Halleck. "GENERAL BUTLER: The Secretary of War directs that you modify your decision in regard to the release of Mr. Heidsieck, and instead of requiring him to depart from the United States you will make the release upon the condition that he will not again enter the lines of the insurgents."

If Butler was angry before, it was nothing compared to how he felt now. He was trapped; he had to comply. There was no avoiding it.

This time, when Charles was notified of the new conditions for his release he accepted them.

On November 16 the gates of Fort Pickens swung open and he emerged a free man . . . seriously ill and barely able to walk.

Spurring Washington's decision to order Charles's release may have been an article that appeared in French newspapers just the day before. It was about a proposal by Emperor Napoléon III for a six-month armistice in the Civil War. The armistice would be overseen by France, Britain, and Russia and require that "Southern ports be open to the commerce of the world." This, the emperor emphasized, "would put a stop to the effusion of blood, and hostilities would probably never be resumed. We can urge it on the high grounds of humanity and the interests of the whole civilized world. If it be refused by the North, it will afford good reason for recognition, and perhaps for more active intervention."

It had been assumed for some time that the odds of French intervention were virtually zero, but Washington wasn't about to take any chances, not with someone like Napoléon III whose actions were so unpredictable. How much of factor it may have played in resolving the Heidsieck Incident is unclear, but Charles was freed the very next day.

And much to Washington's relief, the emperor's proposal for an armistice was shot down by Britain and Russia.

"Beast Butler," however, was seething. He could not believe what just happened, that he'd been ordered to release Charles without even a trial. "I arrested him as a spy—I confined him as a spy—I should have tried him as a spy, and hanged him upon conviction as a spy, [and that is what would have happened] if I had not been interfered with by the government at Washington."[7]

# 11

IIIIIIIIIIII

## "We Are Not in Venice"

The gaunt, frail figure who emerged from Fort Jackson was not "Champagne Charlie." He was no longer the dashing young Frenchman who had captured America's attention with his *joie de vivre* and helped make champagne its most celebrated drink. At forty years of age, he was suddenly an old man, fragile, broken in spirit and barely able to comprehend that his long ordeal was finally over.[1]

Gone was his health, gone was his livelihood. He had no money. All he had were the clothes on his back, the prison garb he was given when he first arrived at Fort Jackson. The champagne house he had worked so hard to make one of the best was now bankrupt. When friends first saw him after his nearly four months in prison, they were stunned. "He is hardly recognizable," one said. "His wife must be warned so as not to be too shocked when she sees him."

Charles was transported to New Orleans, where he would spend the next three months trying to recover and searching for a way to get back to New York while being cared for by friends. He was severely depressed. Being free again seemed to make little or no difference. Marie, the oldest of his eight children, would later observe that during those first days after being released he was virtually numb to the "joys of his freedom." "Everything is lost, my fortune, my honor," he told his mother and sister. In a letter written the day he was finally freed, the pain and anguish of what he had gone through came gushing out:

I didn't know what to do. I was desperate, I wanted to scream. When they put me in prison, I was sure I didn't have any time to live, that I was going to die. At night, I couldn't sleep. I would bite my mattress or stuff a blanket in my mouth so people near me couldn't hear me crying. The tears I should now shed are for friends who have helped me and supported you through all this time. Although I am now powerless, my conscience is clear. I am humbled but not humiliated. I hope that with a little help and time and the love of my wife and children, I will be able to restore my honor and reputation and wipe away the slurs that have been made on my name, the good name my father gave me and the one I want to leave to my children.

But in Reims, Heidsieck's "good name" was taking a beating. Angry creditors were no longer simply pounding on the door of his champagne house demanding to be paid; they were practically breaking it down, filing lawsuits and taking other legal action. For Amélie, the champagne house they had built and cherished felt almost like prison. There seemed to be no escape, no one to turn to. Even old friends who had tried to help the family financially were turning away.

"Dearest Amélie," wrote one, "I am very sorry to say to you that I have received from some people in Lyon the bitterest complaints about your financial administration. They were threatening to sue you, to get their money. . . . Now you know that I cannot stand any loss without serious consequences for my family, especially in my old age! Should you compromise me for any reason, it would be my death!"

In New Orleans, rumors were swirling that General Butler was about to be recalled. Washington was fed up with complaints about corruption and the general's "talent" for self-enrichment. Everyone remembered what he did during the assault on New Orleans when he switched rocks for coal as ballast on Farragut's freighters, then shipped the coal north and sold it for a princely sum. Flour, salt, sugar, liquor, tar, turpentine . . . it didn't matter. Whatever he could get his hands on and sell for a profit, be it to the North or South, he did, ignoring regulations that prohibited trade across enemy lines. When New Orleans needed meat, he gave his brother Andrew a

Union pass to go into Confederate Texas to round up a herd of cattle. When the Union army announced it needed caps for its soldiers, Butler arranged to buy a huge quantity at low price then charged the government a much higher one. He was formally accused of "corruption in making contract for army caps" but justified his actions by claiming he used his own money to buy the goods. "If you can do better elsewhere, then do so," he said. They couldn't, and they already had the caps, so nothing came of the charges.

It was much the same when it came to cotton. Even though trade across Union lines was illegal, Butler's campaign for "opening a free trade in cotton with the insurgent states" proved enormously popular, especially among textile owners and workers in New England, who had suffered greatly from the loss of Southern cotton. Butler and his brother quickly amassed huge fortunes thanks to speculators who bribed their way through treasury officials and army officers to make deals with planters and brokers, trading salt and gold for cotton and sugar. Both sides frequently used French agents as go-betweens to preserve the fiction of trading with a neutral.

What was surprising is that President Lincoln went along with it. Although many Northerners outside of the textile industry objected to supporting the enemy's economy by trading for Confederate cotton, Lincoln believed that "appealing to the self-interest of Southern planters would divide their loyalties" and hasten the day toward peace. But as one observer noted, Lincoln failed to "realize at first . . . what vast corruption went hand in hand with his plans."

Much of that corruption revolved around Butler's brother Andrew, who acted as the general's agent and helped set in motion the one scheme that probably caught the attention of Charles Heidsieck. It involved the sale of liquor. When a certain Union commander complained about his troops getting drunk after payday, General Butler seized the moment to forbid liquor sales in New Orleans. Andrew, who was known as "the Colonel" even though he'd been refused the commission, then made the rounds of all the liquor stores, buying up their stock of "intoxicants" at sharply discounted prices. As soon as he finished clearing them of all their booze, the general lifted the ban. Andrew then sold the liquor back at inflated prices. The brothers made an enormous profit.

No matter how it looked, no matter how spurious such dealings were, Butler never felt the need to apologize or make excuses. He never tried to justify or explain his actions, whether it involved liquor, silver spoons, cotton, or coal. After the war there were allegations that Butler had looted gold from a New Orleans bank. He brushed it off, saying his Massachusetts constituents would not hold such actions against him. "The people would think I was a fool for not having taken twice as much," he said.

Of all his escapades, one of the more amazing involved a schooner loaded with one thousand sacks of salt destined for the Confederacy. The boat had been detained by Union treasury agents on Lake Pontchartrain, a brackish estuary off the northern shore of New Orleans. When Butler was notified, he feigned indignation that anyone would try to smuggle salt to the rebels and ordered the vessel released. Besides, he said, the detention had been a mistake because the captain and shipper were carrying permits (from his office). He then ordered that the salt, which customs agents had seized, be returned.[2]

Butler had no authority to do that, but by the time anyone raised the point it was too late; the boat with its cargo of salt was long gone. Treasury agents later learned that six hundred sacks of salt, costing two dollars each, had been carried across Lake Pontchartrain. Four hundred were sold to the Confederate army for twenty-five dollars a sack; the other two hundred were peddled to civilians for thirty-six dollars a sack with the profits to you-know-who.

And that was just the beginning. Before long, ten thousand sacks of salt had made their way across the lake. A Union surgeon who remained behind enemy lines to care for wounded soldiers spilled the beans, or salt as it were. Quite by accident, he happened to spot a huge pile of sacks filled with salt next to the railroad. When he asked a Confederate officer where they came from, the officer replied, "We bought that salt from General Butler."

Butler's assets, when he assumed command of New Orleans, were estimated at $150,000. Four months later, as rumors of his departure began circulating, they had soared to three million.

If "The Beast" was about to be relieved of his command, no one was happier to say "good bye and good riddance" than the foreign consuls.[3] They'd been on Butler's hit list almost from the day he took charge of the city. He was sure they were helping the Confederacy and was determined to stop them, levying heavy fines and threatening imprisonment. He also staged raids, confiscating money, weapons and other material such as morphine, and gunpowder before they could be transferred to the rebels. Protests from foreign capitals "created more than a flutter in the State Department where Secretary Seward, just convalescing from the migraine of the *Trent* affair, had no wish to offer Europe—which was officially neutral—another cause for intervention in the Civil War."

Seward promptly appointed a special commissioner to look into the problem. The problem, the commissioner ruled, was mostly Butler. Eleven of thirteen cases Butler submitted to him were overturned. In one case more than 160 kegs of silver the general had confiscated were returned to the Dutch consul. In another, dozens of barrels of sugar that the Greek consul allegedly planned to sell to the rebels were also returned. A heavy fine levied against a British firm for running the blockade to supply rifles to the Confederates was remitted as well. The commissioner also ordered Butler to give back $405,000 he had impounded from Heidsieck's friend, French consul Méjan.

This last case, however, revealed how duplicitous the situation was. That money later went from Méjan to a French concern in Havana as payment for supplying clothing to the Confederate army.

In a letter to Secretary of War Edwin Stanton, Butler said that the commissioner's actions had done more "to strengthen the hand of secession" than anything else he had witnessed. Of his own actions, especially against those "who supplied arms to traitors," he suggested that, if anything, he had been too soft. "They should have been *hanged*," he said, "but they were only fined."

In response, the commissioner charged that Butler's behavior had been guided by "fitful, unregulated, unrestrained, promptings of military power."

Although Butler was well aware that he had made many enemies, it still came as a shock when, in mid-December, he learned that he was being recalled. When he asked for a reason, no one would say. Not Stanton, not Seward, not even Lincoln offered an explanation, but there was no question that foreign pressure had been brought to bear.

In a farewell address to the citizens of New Orleans published in one of the newspapers, Butler said he was not bitter. "I found you captured, but not surrendered; conquered but not orderly; relieved from the presence of any army but incapable of taking care of yourselves. I restored order, punished crime, opened commerce, brought provisions to your starving people, and gave you quiet protection, such as you have not enjoyed for many years."

On the eve of his departure from the Crescent City, he received an anonymous letter threatening assassination if he appeared in public. Butler dismissed it. He and his wife had planned an evening out and were determined to see it through by going to the Varieties Theater where the comedy *Honeymoon* was playing. The situation was tense, but the moment the couple appeared in their box a most surprising thing happened: the actors stopped the play and the entire audience burst into applause.[4]

Even more astonishing was what happened the next day when the Butlers proceeded to the wharf to board the ship that would take them back to Boston. Hundreds of people, mostly from the poor and working class of the city, were there to say good-bye. They remembered how Butler had helped them. A correspondent for Boston's *Journal* wrote: "I could not repress the conviction that General Butler, with all his harshness and severity toward the rich and rebellious, had won the love and esteem of the downtrodden and suffering masses in this city."

||||||||

Butler's exit could hardly have escaped the notice of Charles Heidsieck, even though he was still weak and in poor condition. After four months of imprisonment, he was trying to recover his health enough so he could do the same for his champagne business. Two letters from Amélie, written months earlier and forwarded by the French ambassador in Washington, arrived and brought him renewed determination.

One was an urgent plea Amélie had written to the French ambassador asking for assistance in getting news about her husband: "I know he was going south and that he had his passport but I've been completely deprived of news from him and I'm filled with worry. Having seen in the newspapers that you were in Richmond, perhaps you can find out something from the consul there. I'm writing to you as a wife and mother. I'm also attaching a letter for Charles." Her letter to Charles, dated January 21, 1862, read:

> My dearest Charles, I'm not sure if this will reach you with every-thing changing, but it's been so long since I've heard from you. I know you are isolated and that the country is in flames. What a ter-rible test the good Lord is sending us. Here, business is going more or less badly, but the children are fine. Marie is doing well in school and has been promoted. Louise is in school also but not doing very much. Our Charles is now as tall as Marie, and his work in school is okay, except in science which is very slow. But his character and behavior are really good. He is so sweet and gentle and his sisters love him dearly. Pauline is my companion, my little shadow, and we're inseparable. Emilie, our baby, is a real character, gay and mis-chievous. She speaks a little but understands everything. When I have them all around me, we are a happy band and I am so happy, but without you my heart remains sad. The children think of their father often, even Pauline who says, "My father is in America!" They think of you morning and night.

Amélie's words came as much-needed comfort to Charles and helped spur him to what needed to be done next. In response to the French ambassador, he wrote that he hoped to come to Wash-ington in the next two or three months, "as soon as I can manage a sea voyage."

The escalating war had made travel overland impossible. All nor-mal routes were blocked as both armies moved supplies and brought in reinforcements. On December 13 the Union suffered a crushing defeat in Fredericksburg, Virginia, losing nearly thirteen thousand men, seven thousand more than the Confederacy. The toll almost equaled the number killed at Antietam in September. "If there is a worse place than Hell, I am in it," said President Lincoln as the two sides continued to inflict staggering losses on each other.

Winter was usually a time for armies to recoup and catch their breath, but the fighting now was at such a fever pitch that battles were practically nonstop. Vicksburg, Chancellorsville, and Gettysburg lay ahead. "We are now in the darkest hour of our political existence," said Confederate president Jefferson Davis.

Charles had often said he was sure the South would win—or hoped it would. Unlike Northerners, he told Amélie, Southerners were dedicated, "fighting for a cause and a new nation, not money." A Charlotte, North Carolina, newspaper, the *Evening Bulletin*, had described how "the young ladies of the Female Institute at Clinton, Mississippi . . . sent to the Confederate Quartermaster at Jackson 50 pairs of socks, all knit by the fair hands of that institution." Everyone, Charles stressed, was committed.

Now, however, his confidence wavered. No matter how much he loved the South, he realized the war could go either way. The best thing he could do was to get back to France as soon as possible.

The struggle to recoup his losses seemed as if it had been going on forever. He'd fought with a sales agent who had cheated him, traveled hundreds of miles in an effort to collect the lost money, only to end up languishing in a prison surrounded by snakes and alligators. Now he was spent, but his exhaustion wasn't only physical. He was worn out and worn down.

On March 21 Charles boarded a steamship and set off for New York. A New Orleans newspaper reported that he would soon receive one hundred thousand dollars from the French government to make up for his suffering. France's foreign minister said he, too, would pay Heidsieck a substantial sum out of his own pocket, an apology for the letter he wrote saying France was making uniforms for the Confederacy and which convinced General Butler that Heidsieck was a spy. None of the money was ever received, but even it had been it would only be a drop in the bucket. Charles's account in France was overdrawn by nearly two million francs, and bills were still piling up.

A mountain of correspondence greeted Charles when he arrived in New York. There were letters from his wife as well as drawings from his children. There was also a visitor waiting for him. It was Adolphe Prevost, the judge from the bankruptcy court in Reims.[5] His appearance only added to Charles's apprehension. *Am I about to be fined? Or possibly jailed?* He knew lawsuits had been accumulating for months as creditors went to court in an effort to get their money.

His plight was also noticed in American newspapers. One reported that Emperor Napoléon III had taken a personal hand in the matter by sending a warship to pick up Heidsieck. Its mission, the writer said, was to demolish the "*Bastille*" in which Heidsieck had been imprisoned and return the Frenchman to the arms of "*la belle France*." The writer added: "It appears plain enough why the French should desire the reclamation and return of this wandering son. But we doubt whether Heidsieck wants to be 'reclaimed.' Can anyone think of being delivered up to the volubility of a lot of angry French creditors without horror! Incarceration is bliss in comparison."[6]

Charles's financial situation was indeed dire, but the bankruptcy judge was surprisingly reassuring when he told Charles that he would not be charged with any crime for failing to pay his debts. "You did not act in bad faith," Judge Provost said. "Only the war and the consequences of it are responsible for the current situation. You will, however, have to pay something but how much is something for the liquidators to decide."

Charles was now officially bankrupt. Although his name had been legally cleared of anything criminal, it did little to alleviate his despair and sense of loss. Other family members shared that feeling and worried what would happen when he finally returned home to Reims. "The swords are out for Charles, and friends have fallen away," Amélie told her sister-in-law Emilie Henriot. She described how "humiliating" bankruptcy had been for everyone and how she had to let staff go in order to make ends meet, "but I will still do my best to hold my head high."

For Charles there were more headaches ahead. He still had to face his duplicitous sales agent, Theodore Bayaud, and prevail on him once again to pay for his champagne. A representative from the bankruptcy court had already met with Bayaud in an effort to persuade him to pay but, with no legal jurisdiction in America, had failed. Heidsieck was no more successful. Bayaud was still holding fast and refusing to settle his accounts. He continued to argue that he didn't have to pay a penny because of the war.

As his frustrations mounted, Charles lashed out at those closest to him. In a letter to his family he accused his brother-in-law Ernest, who oversaw work in the vineyards, of "egoism, stupidity and a lack of delicacy," of spending too much money and going ahead with projects that were unwarranted, projects that Charles himself had nixed before going to America. He complained to Amélie that her letters sometimes sounded like they'd been written by someone else "instead of my wife." And he was irritated to constantly hear how tough things were in Reims. "I can't just come running back to France every time there's a problem," he said. "There are problems here, too!"

Charles's outburst revealed the terrible strain he was under, his feeling of helplessness after months of imprisonment, and his fear of what lay ahead. But his words stung. They cut deeply into the hearts of those who loved him, especially Amélie, who wrote:

> All of this makes me really sad to see you so tormented, and I hope this letter isn't going to give you any regrets or make you not want to come home. I accept your reproaches but let's not undermine our faith in each other. . . . You said that I don't sound like your wife when I write to you, that I sound like someone else. I don't mean to but it's been nearly two years since we've been together. Please know that I am still your loving and adoring wife and that I have been doing everything I can to keep our champagne house together. I have reached out to friends but many have stepped away. . . . I should also tell you that my parents have sold their family house in Ludes. It was with great sadness that they did this for they, like all of us, remember the vacations we took there, the sweetness of family reunions and how the children were always happy, but they sold it to keep our business going.

"We Are Not in Venice"

Adieu, my friend, from your little wife who loves you and embraces you with all her heart.

In a separate letter, Ernest's wife, Emilie, pleaded with her brother-in-law to be more understanding about what the family was facing:

You're a good man with a sincere heart, but you have changed. I can understand your anger up to a certain point but isn't there more in your heart for us? Oh my poor Charles, you must have really suffered to be so hard on us. But we've suffered as well. . . . As for Ernest, you must recognize how much he's done. I swear to God he's done everything possible, everything YOU would have done, to keep our business standing, but the rug has been pulled out from under us. Obstacles have grown up in your absence and only your presence will take care of them. The public is judging you harshly. I can send you my thoughts but I can't speak for the public or bill collectors who have been so unforgiving. . . . You still have a hard road to travel, a mountain that you've got to get over. Find within yourself the courage you need. It's easy enough for me to write it but you can do this!

In a few weeks, you will be with us again, back in your hometown. I cannot tell you what a great joy it will be after such a long absence. It might be a little sad for you but you will find hearts that are waiting for you and yearning to show their devotion and affection. In time and together, I think we can put everything together again.

P.S. Please write to Ernest. He has heard nothing from you for two years. News that you've been liberated has completely energized him.

If Charles was upset with how he was being judged by the public, he was probably even more troubled by what he was reading almost daily in New York's newspapers. Papers that once treated him like a conquering hero and reported in lavish detail his every move now struck a dramatically different tone.

"Alas! how have the mighty fallen!" exclaimed *Wilkes' Spirit of the Times*. "The eminent wine merchant, the mighty buffalo hunter of the prairies, with an elegant double gun (which he brought back but didn't fetch the buffalo), the honored guest of every 'saloon' in the nation, whose name is a household word in every restaurant throughout the land, arrested at last, shut up in a common jail, awaiting a disgraceful dismissal from our country and an ignominious return to his own."

Charles's arrest by General Butler prompted many to wonder if the Frenchman they thought they knew and admired might be someone different . . . namely, a spy for the Confederacy. As *The American Gentleman's Newspaper* put it, "The way of the transgressor is hard, the walks of iniquity will surely lead to crime, treason, bankruptcy, and poverty, and Charles finds at the end of those pleasant walks a cul-de-sac punishment. He had received from this nation nothing but kindness and benefits heaped overflowingly upon him, but in an evil hour perverseness and ingratitude found him a willing instrument for traitors' hands, led him cheerfully to a traitor's work, and leaves him to a traitor's fate."

Criticism was relentless as reporters who once idolized him seemed to go out of their way to bring Charles down. "Everything is gone," one wrote. "Even his name, once . . . sublime in the wine market, will fall to the inheritance of counterfeiters, no longer to be the synonym of generous sparkling juice, but to be shunned as the sign of bogus imitation. Poor Charles!"

The fact that many of the newspapers attacking Charles were also pro-Butler only made matters worse. "He's the only General we've got!" one paper said. Another paper, *Harper's Weekly*, was effusive in its praise for what Butler had done in New Orleans and said that his arrest of Heidsieck was fully warranted. It described how Charles had worked as a barkeeper on a steamer between Mobile and New Orleans "and in that capacity served as a rebel spy and mail carrier; for which crime he was very properly sent to prison by General Butler."

Charles was at a loss. Pleas for understanding—of innocence—seemed to make no difference. In a letter to Amélie he wrote: "The wrong they've done to my business and reputation is aggravated day after day by the things they are saying. Some have referred to me as the enemy. It's all terribly misleading and unfair. If my clients here in New York believe what they are reading, they can't help but think I'm the enemy."

And then came a news item that nearly did Heidsieck in: "The Beast" himself was in town.

Butler had arrived in New York just days after Heidsieck. He was there to attend a public dinner in his honor at the Academy of Music. The affair was being staged by an abolitionist organization called the Loyal League to show its appreciation for his "distinguished services" during the war. According to the *New York Times*: "The academy was crowded to its utmost capacity. The boxes, dress circle and balcony fairly blazed with the beauty and fashion of the city, while the deep aisles of the parquet and the more remote recesses of the theatre were relieved from the somber colors of male attire by the waving plumes, the ruddy ribbons, and the glittering jewels of New York's fairest ladies."

Not all the publicity was in Butler's favor, however. A satirical magazine, *La Crosse Democrat,* came out with a tongue-in-cheek article titled "The Life and Public Services of Benjamin F. Butler." But it was a cartoon on the magazine's cover that must have driven the general mad. The cartoon portrayed him as a chained mastiff in an iron collar. "BEAST" was written on the mastiff's forehead, and the animal was making a vain effort to bite a little Frenchman who danced away while making a certain gesture.

Butler's hatred of Heidsieck was still white hot, and the cartoon only fueled it. Friends warned Heidsieck he should get out of the country as soon as possible, that they had heard the general had hired "some brigands" to murder him. Heidsieck merely shrugged. With everything he was facing, it seemed like nothing. "We are not in Venice," he said.

A few days later, standing in the corridor of his hotel, a bullet whistled past his ear.[7] He did not need another warning. Heidsieck booked himself on the next ship back to France.

# 12

||||||||||

# The Homecoming

Everything has to be perfect, Amélie Heidsieck thought to herself. She'd rented a comfortable hotel room, she'd brought her prettiest dress, and she'd collected daughter Marie from her nearby boarding school. Now all she had to do was wait—something she'd been doing for more than two years. Waiting for Charles.

It was August 1, 1863, and tomorrow the wait would be over. That was when Charles said his ship would be arriving in Le Havre. From there, he said, he would head straight to Paris and to her.

There were butterflies in Amélie's stomach, and she couldn't sit still. Just one more thing, she thought. Was it flowers for the room or a fresh baguette? He might really appreciate that after all the complaints he'd made about the quality of bread in the United States. She told Marie she would be right back.

Within a few minutes there was a knock on the door. *Maman* must have forgotten something, Marie thought. But when she opened the door, there stood her father. Even thin as he was, even haggard as he looked, even though she had last seen him when she was only seven years old, she knew immediately who it was. "Papa," she said, and as Marie was later to write, she fell into his arms.

When Amélie returned minutes later, Charles's shirtfront was damp. Marie's tears or Charles's, she didn't know, but Marie was hanging on to her father as though she would never let him go.[1]

And then, so was Amélie.

Good weather, Charles said; they docked early.

Very soon reality would intrude and the scramble to put things together would begin in earnest, but for the moment all that was forgotten—all the financial struggles, the months in prison, the days and nights of uncertainty, the loneliness and worry. They were together again; once more they were a family.

But no one was under any illusions. The worst was still ahead. Charles may have returned, but he and the rest of the family would soon be facing the criticisms and snubs from people they had considered friends. Some crossed the street to avoid them, as Amélie had written when Charles was still in the United States. Many others gossiped behind their backs. He's a spy, some whispered, and spies are sneaky, disloyal, untrustworthy. He bragged about all the champagne he was selling . . . and now he claims he can't pay his bills?

It was humiliating. Even though the bankruptcy court had cleared Charles of any wrongdoing, it did little to assuage the rumors that were swirling.

In making its ruling, the court said its decision "rested a great deal on the morality, regularity and precautions surrounding the actions of the bankruptee. The response prepared and written by Charles Heidsieck is a monument of prudence. There was no speculation, no bad faith in any instance. . . . Only the war and its consequences are responsible for this situation."

Not only was Charles innocent, the court said; he'd also been, until his imprisonment, a successful businessman developing a thriving enterprise that was on track to grow, "an achievement due primarily to the personality of Charles Heidsieck." If poor decisions had been made, they had been made in his absence and without his knowledge.

Nevertheless, the judge said he could not absolve Charles of the entire debt; he would still have to pay a percentage of what was owed, the amount to be determined later. That amount, however, could be staggering. The overdraft on one of Heidsieck's accounts was more than three million dollars.

Although the court's judgment may have felt like a vindication for his family, making them feel as though they could now hold up their heads again, it was not enough for Charles. He vowed to repay every last *sou*, every last cent, of what he owed, no matter how long it took. That was, he said, the only way he could truly recover his honor.

And the only way to do that, he realized, was to start from scratch, rebuild his champagne house *and* try to restore peace in the family. The latter would be especially difficult. Poor decisions by his partner and brother-in-law Ernest had proved particularly upsetting. One of those decisions involved hiring an agent to oversee sales in California. When Ernest first pitched the idea, Charles said it was unnecessary and would be too expensive, and had specifically vetoed it before leaving for the United States. Ernest went ahead and hired an agent anyway.

The two brothers-in-law were now barely on speaking terms. Charles knew, however, that he would somehow have to find a way to put aside his anger and make peace with Ernest if progress were to be made.

It was the women in the family who took the lead, especially Amélie, who had assumed more and more responsibility in both business and family matters during Charles's absence. She knew what was at stake and keenly felt how fine the line was between business and family.

Ernest's wife, Emilie, was involved, too. She had written to Charles while he was recovering in New York, addressing him as "dear friend" and begging him to understand her husband's position. "Please write to Ernest," she pleaded. "He hasn't heard a word from you in two years and has had to shoulder everything alone." Even sales and marketing, which Charles normally handled, suddenly became Ernest's responsibility, an area completely outside his experience.

His responsibilities were winemaking, tending the vineyard, determining when to harvest and which grapes to use in making champagne.

Normally, Charles would have been at his side throughout the entire process, but Charles was gone, and it was left to Ernest to figure everything out. *Shall I use 100 percent Pinot Noir? Or should I add a bit of Pinot Meunier and Chardonnay for complexity and extra richness? What's it going to take to keep our style, our quality?* A bottle of champagne was not made with one wine from one vineyard; it was a blend of as many as thirty or forty "base wines," still wines made from grapes that were picked before they were fully ripe. The goal was to make the final product, or *cuvée*, better than the individual wines themselves. Putting the parts together, the *assemblage*, was an intensive exercise that required a discriminating palate and great powers of concentration. Amélie's input would have been invaluable, since her tasting abilities were as refined as Ernest's, and he knew Charles respected her taste. But she, too, had extra responsibilities, namely, five children to raise alone and a mountain of bills to attack. Her time to help Ernest was extremely limited.

Now, she added another urgent task: bringing her husband and her brother back together for the sake of the business and the family. To accomplish that, she and Emilie began writing calming, affectionate letters to one another, even though they lived only a few kilometers apart. With as many as eight to ten mail deliveries every day, letters could reach their destination within hours of being posted, so exchanges became almost real-time conversations.

Both women were aware their husbands would be peering over their shoulders as they wrote. In their letters, they cited the need for understanding and compassion, as well as a fresh start. They reminded each other of the deep affection that held the large, interconnected family together. They knew or at least prayed that the entire family would support them financially and emotionally.

Gradually, tempers cooled. Charles and Ernest reached an agreement that, as their wives had suggested, drew in people from the extended family. Edouard Werlé, head of Veuve Clicquot and also mayor of Reims and a cousin by marriage, was among the first to pledge financial support. He was joined by another cousin by marriage, Louis Roederer, head of Louis Roederer Champagne, and then others. With them and with substantial financial input from the Henriots and Heidsiecks—Charles's mother sold her *hôtel particulier* and moved to a smaller residence to add to the capital—Champagne Charles Heidsieck was reborn.

Benefiting from family loans, Charles and Ernest contributed equal amounts to the company's capitalization and reinstated the division of labor they previously had: Charles as business manager and salesman, the face of the champagne house, and Ernest in charge of the vineyards and winemaking. They also agreed to being responsible for equal amounts of the debts the court ordered them to repay. Only Charles, however, committed to reimbursing the debts in full.

Once again, he registered the marque for the new company in his own name. An earlier court battle with Piper-Heidsieck had confirmed the right to use it for his business. More importantly, it was the name people knew, one customers were familiar with and which had won a large number of devotees in Europe and America—where many now simply ordered "a bottle of Charles."

Charles saw his new company, Charles Heidsieck & Cie., as an opportunity for both redemption and success, and it seemed to generate a "rebirth" in him as well, overriding any lingering effects of the trauma he'd suffered in America.

In the spring of 1864 he began plotting a demanding schedule of travel through Europe, a schedule that would keep him on the road for six months of the year. He appeared so energetic to others that people said it was as though he had found a fountain of youth.

But it was an energy born of desperation. This was his one and only chance to rebuild his business, and he was determined to make it work. From his time in America he knew exactly what it would take: himself. It would require his personality, his being there in person, getting his name in front of people, and lots of publicity. He would also have to answer questions, over and over again—about his imprisonment, his bankruptcy, and what was happening with the business. People had to see him and read about him to stir their interest and convince them to spend their money on his champagne. They had to know he was really back and that he could be trusted.

It would be a wearying, exhausting trip. He would crisscross Europe to consolidate what he had done before, traveling to Belgium, the Netherlands, Great Britain, and Scandinavia, developing new contacts to make his champagne an even greater success.

Something more was driving him as well: stories about his father, stories he had heard ever since he was a toddler. Charles-Henri had died when Charles-Camille was only two years old, but the stories

**24.** Heidsieck at home in Reims, 1864, posing in the shirt he wore in prison.
Courtesy of Champagne Charles Heidsieck.

had embedded themselves in his psyche, almost like fairy tales. Now, after his financial difficulties, they weighed heavily on him.

"You had a father to be proud of," his German uncles admonished him, "and if you emulate his way of thinking and doing things, you will surely find your own road to success."

His mother, too, stressed his father's achievements and had said she remained unmarried after her husband's death because "no sacrifice was too great for you. . . . I would do anything for your honor."

And no one, it seemed, tired of telling him the story of his father's spectacular achievements in Moscow. It was a story that had almost attained the status of a myth: a young and dashing Charles-Henri on a white stallion charging his way across wartorn Europe to reach the Russian city before Napoléon and his powerful Grande Armée could fight their way there, and then how Charles-Henri alone had sold thousands of bottles of Heidsieck champagne to the celebrating Russians. As a boy Charles-Camille pictured his handsome, charismatic father standing up in his stirrups shouting and waving a bottle of champagne to the cheering and, of course, adoring crowds.

Now with a new company and vast responsibilities on his shoulders, Charles decided to take on the added challenge those stories presented to him. Although he had been home less than a year and was still feeling the effects of imprisonment, he decided this was the moment to go to Russia. But as much as he wanted to "emulate" his father, that story had become something of a burden, one he constantly felt compelled to measure himself against. It was late summer, time, he decided, to put that burden behind him.

Some of his competitors were already in Russia, including his distant cousin Louis Roederer, who had helped him financially. Roederer, in fact, had found Russia's thirst for champagne to be so enormous that he was devoting a third of his production to that market. Veuve Clicquot and Mumm were selling substantial amounts there as well.

Much of the attraction revolved around one person: Czar Alexander II. It was he who had embarked on a program of liberalization by eliminating serfdom and modernizing the judicial system using the French legal organization as a model. He also expanded educational opportunities and allowed the press more freedom.[2]

What intrigued Charles, however, was that Alexander had shown himself to be a serious fan of sparkling wine. "Among all the czars, Alexander II was one of the greatest *amateurs* (lovers) of the wine of Champagne," one historian wrote. A writer who spent time at the court in St. Petersburg recounted how the czar would move from table to table during banquets, sit down for a moment or two, and "wet his lips" with champagne at each stop.

Because he was the czar, however, Alexander insisted that the champagne he drank be the very best and clearly distinct from what anyone else could get, no matter who they were or how much they could pay. Roederer found a way to stroke the czar's ego and, at the same time, help allay his fears of being poisoned. Those fears were very real, as there had been several attempts on his life.

Consequently, the Russian leader demanded that his champagne bottles be made clear instead of the typical dark green so he could see the bubbles and detect anything inside that might be irregular. He also ordered that the bottom of his bottles be flat to guard against any explosive that someone might try to hide in the punt (the indentation at the base).

To that effect, Roederer created a clear crystal bottle that was used for Alexander's champagne and *only* for his. The czar was well pleased, but he went even further to ensure his champagne remained uncontaminated and uniquely his by sending his personal *maître de chais*, or cellar master, to Reims each year to oversee the making of champagne for the Imperial Court. All these precautions may have made the czar seem paranoid, but his fears of being murdered would prove justified when he was killed by a bomb thrown at him in 1879.

That was fifteen years in the future, however. For now the combination of Russia's showing a more open face to the world, a champagne-loving czar on the throne, and his resurrected company on an upward trajectory all served to reinforce Charles's determination to penetrate the Russian market.

But there would be no white horse for this particular Heidsieck venture. Charles would ride the "iron horse" on a rail journey of sixty hours, a route that would follow much of his father's path through a huge swath of Germany—Hamburg, Bielefeld, Lübeck, Dresden, Berlin—and then to St. Petersburg. In St. Petersburg he had an appointment to meet a certain Monsieur Voigt, someone who, it was said, knew everyone who was anyone in Russia and knew how to get things done in that massive country.

The meeting was everything Charles hoped it would be, and he immediately hired Voigt as his agent. Voigt, for his part, wasted no time in proving that he did indeed know Russia and the Russians. He hustled Charles into a round of meetings with wine merchants and key people in Russian society, then on to tasting sessions and dinners. Charles wrote home that he rarely got to bed before two in the morning, and many nights not before five. Some nights he got as little as three hours of sleep before the meals, meetings, and tastings began again.

"The Russians are awake and lively night and day, and they never stop drinking," Charles wrote to Amélie. "At one dinner with only five people, they drank fifteen bottles of champagne, not to mention Sherry, Bordeaux and some Port."

It was a grueling schedule, and Charles admitted it was almost more than he could take. "I'm not a young man anymore," he lamented to Amélie. He was forty-two at the time.

Nonetheless, he was fascinated by what he saw in St. Petersburg. The display of luxury, the sumptuous private palaces, all of which seemed to be open to everyone and with people passing through them at all hours—he took it all in.

When Charles moved on to Moscow, he was startled and thrilled to meet people who actually remembered his father's arrival there fifty years before and were eager to tell him about it. Hearing the story from firsthand witnesses must have made his father come alive to him in a vibrant way. Such encounters, even more than the success of his champagne, made him feel the long voyage and the tiring hours of wining and dining had been worthwhile.

Now, for the first time since his return from America, Charles could relax. With the long trip to Russia he not only had renewed old contacts and built new ones; he'd also found a new strength and confidence in his abilities, as well as increased certainty about the future success of his business. It helped that 1864 had been a wonderful year for champagne. A wet spring followed by warm, sunny weather for most of the summer had ensured that the fall harvest would be bountiful and "above average."

It was time to go home again, help with the harvest, and, more importantly, do what he'd longed to do while imprisoned: get to know his family again. He and Amélie already had five growing children, and soon there would be more . . . three others, a second son and two more girls, would be added.

||||||||

In America, President Lincoln had just been reelected to a second term. Although the Civil War continued to rage, the country was about to celebrate its second official Thanksgiving, a holiday the president had declared the year before after a decisive victory by Union forces at Gettysburg. "It has pleased Almighty God to prolong our national life another year," he began his declaration. Most signs now pointed to the North's winning the war and eventual reunification of the republic.

All that, however, had become merely a distant rumble for Heidsieck. Hopes of getting the reparations promised him by the U.S. government had faded into the background. Washington had rejected his demand of two thousand dollars for each day of his imprisonment. Even his own government had failed to come through.

Although Charles swore he would never make another trip to America, friends there still kept in touch, sending him the latest news and their sympathies for what he had suffered. "Monsieur Heidsieck, dear friend, we've read of your numerous sufferings and ordeals with much sad interest. Surely no one is more fit to offer sympathy than those who have suffered themselves. You know us to be warm Confederates. We've felt nothing but hardship and experienced every kind of insult from the hands of our conquerors."

The letter was from a young girl named Maggie, the daughter of a family friend, who was sent to a convent school in Columbia, South Carolina. On February 17, 1865, the city was captured and burned by forces under General William Tecumseh Sherman. "We became aware of the presence of this modern Attila by the roar of the cannon and explosion of shells. His overwhelming numbers easily defeated our small forces."

Maggie's letter was a passionate outpouring of emotion, a searing reminder of what war was like that ran more than twenty pages and was painful for Charles to read as he learned what had happened to his friends.

Sherman's crushing campaign through Georgia and the Carolinas was aimed at frightening the civilian population into abandoning the Confederate cause. He had just torched Atlanta, although controversy exists over how much of the city he burned. Retreating Confederates apparently set fire to warehouses to deprive the Federals of valuable supplies and equipment, and those fires quickly spread. However, Sherman did order the destruction of Atlanta's business district and, following that, made good on his promise to Lincoln to "make Georgia howl" by staging his famous "March to the Sea." He made no apologies. "War is cruelty," he said. "There is no reforming it. The crueler it is, the sooner it will be over."

Maggie's state was a target of particular interest, since it had been the first to secede. Its fall, Sherman believed, would have a devastating effect on Southern morale . . . and it did.

In her letter to Charles, Maggie described the "downfall of our noble struggle." She told how soldiers "cursed us as they set fire to our convent and other buildings. I hope you will not think me egotistical when I say that Sherman and his band of fiends do not deserve to bear the title of soldiers."

The heart of Columbia was reduced to rubble, she said. Houses that still stood displayed white flags as a token of surrender and a plea for protection.

Streets were deserted save for Yankees and Negroes who were using their lately acquired freedom to point out to the soldiers where their former masters' valuables were. Night was falling on the city but darkness was not allowed to hide these deeds of villainy. They had plundered all day and all night they were to burn. We saw one row of houses and then another consumed by the devouring elements. No humanity was shown. Can you believe me that our convent was

fired and ransacked like the other buildings? Even after solemn prom-
ises from Sherman himself to the Mother Superior to assure her and
us of our safety.

Maggie said she and a hundred of her schoolmates were forced
to flee and spend the night in a graveyard "among the peaceful dead,
preferable company to the living who were bent on our destruction.
I was exhausted but glad to be resting my head on a tombstone, all
the while the fires raging . . . frozen screams of despair from those
watching their houses burn . . . unexploded shells now ignited and
bursting . . . drunken soldiers yelling demanding our bodies. It was
a place of torment. All that was needed to make it perfect was Beel-
zebub and his followers."

Next morning, Maggie said, General Sherman, mounted on a
horse, appeared at the gate of the cemetery. "Sherman came in person to apologize to the Mother Superior with his cap on his head
and the stink of a cigar in his mouth. He was beating his boots with
his riding whip as he endeavored to apologize for the burning of
our convent and said his orders were that it should be spared. She
replied, 'General Sherman, apologies are in vain.'"

When Sherman finally left, he gave them a month's provision of
hardtack and coffee "but no water for washing or drinking and no
food." What Maggie could not have predicted was that in less than
two months the war would be over.

In closing, she only expressed hope that she and Charles might
meet again if he returned to America. "I still have the shawl you
bought for Amélie which you asked me to hold," she said, before
signing off, "From your little friend, Maggie."

||||||||

Although Charles's imprisonment had erased any desire to return
to America, one item of news must have brought out a tiny, satisfied smile. It concerned President Lincoln's second inaugural ball
of March 6, 1865.[3]

For several days, thousands of people had been streaming into
the nation's capital for the grand event. Two days earlier, with the

war in its final stages, they listened as the president gave what is considered the greatest inaugural speech in history. "With malice toward none; with charity for all . . . let us strive to finish the work we are in."

But then came "a night for the history books" as revelers converged on what poet Walt Whitman called "the noblest of Washington's buildings," the Patent Office Building, to celebrate the inaugural. Tickets cost ten dollars each and were good for three. One man and a lady on each arm. By the time the ball was in full swing, four thousand celebrants had filled the top-floor hall, dancing quadrilles, waltzes and Virginia reels. At 10:30 p.m. President Lincoln and his wife arrived, their presence filling the hall with even more energy. The party, however, had only begun.

At the stroke of midnight, the doors were thrown open to an elaborate buffet. Oysters, roast beef, veal, turkey, venison, smoked ham, lobster salad, and a lavish display of cakes and tarts were spread across the table more than two hundred feet long. The centerpiece was the Capitol Building in pastry. There was also a pastry sculpture of Fort Sumter surrounded by ironclads.

To help lubricate the affair, three champagnes along with "Old Sherry" and "Old Madeira" were listed on the menu. The champagnes were De St. Marceaux & Co., G. H. Mumm, and Champagne Charles Heidsieck. Good salesman that he was, Charles must have been thrilled with the free publicity, but considering what eventually happened, he would not have had any regrets about missing the party.

The affair soon became a shambles as famished partygoers charged the buffet table and made a mess of it. "In less than an hour, the table was a wreck . . . positively frightful to behold," reported the *New York Times*, as men carted away trays piled high with food for their friends, determined to get their ten dollars' worth, it seemed, but slopping stews and jellies along the way. According to the *Washington Evening Star*, "The floor of the supper room was soon sticky, pasty and oily with wasted confections, mashed cakes, and debris of fowl and meats." All of this was lost on the president and his wife, who had dined earlier and were long gone by the time the affair devolved into chaos that included several food fights.

Back in Reims, Charles was enmeshed in different kind of struggle. Problems with his brother-in-law were turning out to be more difficult to resolve than anticipated. Ernest, he thought, had grown lazy, or maybe was just tired. Whatever it was, he needed watching; the new business could not be allowed to get off track. It had to be perfectly managed, and the quality of champagne had to remain at the highest level. But with all the travel he faced, Charles needed someone he could trust to monitor both Ernest and the business. There was only one person who was qualified to do that: Amélie.[4]

Through the years he had seen for himself that what his mother had said about Amélie before their marriage was true: she was both intelligent and astute. She knew her younger brother well and also understood what Charles wanted and was working for. Having lived and breathed the champagne business her entire life, she could easily step in as Charles's surrogate and be his eyes and ears.

What's more, he trusted her palate. He frequently made use of her tasting notes on various champagne vintages when talking with merchants on his travels. Amélie included them in long, detailed letters about both family and business. Much as he valued and depended on them, there were times he may have wished for less. "Quit bothering me, and just take care of business," Charles wrote during one of his journeys. "I know what I have to do. I'm on the spot and am the best judge of where I have to go."

Charles's concerns about his champagne and Ernest's attention to its quality were merited, according to an American customs official who arrived in Reims in 1865 to oversee the duty charged on champagne exported to the United States. Robert Tomes was not only a diplomat but also a champagne connoisseur with strong opinions about the sparkling wine. "Though it may be conceded that most of the champagne directly imported into this country [America] from Rheims [*sic*] . . . is genuine," Tomes wrote, "it can be by no means allowed that it is of the highest quality of wine. I have in fact the testimony of all the chief exporters of champagne, to prove that the wine sent to the United States, though 'good and wholesome,' is of inferior quality to that generally sent elsewhere, and always to that kept at home."

Tomes got his own proof of that soon after he arrived in Champagne when he dined with several champagne makers. "I had hardly turned off the first glass, when I remarked a flavor of which my palate, though not unused to the best of Heidsieck, Mumm, and Moët and Chandon, in America, had been hitherto unconscious. It was the first time in my life that I had enjoyed a glass of champagne, as wine."

Tomes noted that champagnes sent to the United States were too sweet, fit only "for the gulping crowd." Heidsieck's champagne was included in that group. He also observed that Piper-Heidsieck was cornering the American market with "its superior commercial judgment."

Charles must have fulminated hearing that, and it's quite possible he complained to Tomes in person, since Tomes reported that his official duties brought him into "direct and constant association with the wine manufacturers."

Tomes's comments about the quality of champagne going to America did not change Charles's mind about going there himself. He remained adamant about never returning and would rely solely on his agents to take care of business rather than risk another prolonged absence. His primary mission now was trying to pay off creditors and support his family. When days of depression and overwhelming worry swept over him, he said he tried to put them into "the little box" inside himself and keep working. It was on those days that his daughter Marie would try to comfort him by singing an Irish melody called "The Last Rose of Summer" from the opera *Martha*. It was the song Charles had heard in the distance on his first night in prison, the song that had finally helped him drift off to sleep. Now it became almost a talisman for him.

If there was any relief for Charles, any bright spot in his business, it came from Mother Nature. Each year since his return from America, the harvest had consistently been above average; grapes were good and plentiful, producing hundreds of thousands of bottles of champagne.

None of those harvests was better than that of the year the Civil War ended, and "proved" what an ancient peasants' legend said: that God sends a terrible harvest to mark the start of war, and a beautiful one to herald its end. The harvest of 1865 sent Robert Tomes into raptures:

> The summer and autumn of the year 1865 were the most remarkable seasons ever known to the "oldest inhabitant" of temperate Europe. Days of bright suns and clear skies followed each other in almost constant succession. . . . The hot and clear weather continuing without abatement throughout the summer, the grapes were ready to be plucked at the end of August . . . some three weeks earlier than usual. Everyone was in a joyous humor, and talked of the abundance and excellence of the crop. . . . It is as if every man had drawn a prize in a lottery which often gives nothing but blanks.[5]

Tomes tasted the "sweet and luscious grapes" and found he was not the only one enjoying them. "Honey-sucking bees in swarming multitudes seemed so sated with sweetness that they had become too kindly to wound, or so intoxicated" they no longer had the inclination to sting.

So it was in 1865, a legendary year that people in France would talk about for generations and where sales of champagne to the United States would skyrocket with the end of the Civil War.

||||||||

That war, the costliest and deadliest ever fought on American soil, all but ended when General Robert E. Lee surrendered at Appomattox on April 9. Five days later, President Lincoln was assassinated at Ford's Theatre.

Later that year also, the long struggle for emancipation gained a victory when the Thirteenth Amendment to the U.S. Constitution was ratified, ending slavery and indentured servitude.

But America was far from unified or at peace with itself. Less than a week after the amendment's ratification, a group of disaffected Confederate officers founded the Ku Klux Klan to resist Reconstruction. In North Bend, Ohio, America's first train robbery took place. And in

Springfield, Missouri, the first "fast draw shootout" occurred when Wild Bill Hickok shot and killed Little Dave Tutt over a poker debt.

The Wild West had begun, and even Mother Nature was in on the action. A severe earthquake shook the San Francisco Bay area, while in Oregon, a forest fire consumed nearly one million acres of timber.

That year also saw a brief notice in the *New York Times* dated February 22, 1865. It was in a column headlined "DIED" and read as follows: "BAYAUD —At Sterling City, Colorado Territory, on Wednesday, January 18, of congestion of the lungs, THOMAS J. BAYAUD, of this city. His remains will be brought here for internment. Notice of the funeral thereafter." Bayaud? Charles Heidsieck certainly knew a Theodore Bayaud, but Thomas? Had Charles thought about it, he might have recalled meeting Thomas a few years earlier when he confronted Theodore about payments for champagne. With so many issues facing him, however, it's more likely Charles had all but forgotten Thomas.

Thomas, though, had not forgotten him.

# 13

||||||||||||

# The Man Who Never Forgot

Of Denver's founding, someone said, "It was as if the angels were carrying a city to a proper place and accidentally dropped it here."[1]

There was nothing inevitable about Denver. It was never a sure thing. It could easily have become a ghost town just like so many other places in Colorado. "The difference was the people involved," said one resident, "the people who worked to keep the town alive. There were a lot of ambitious people who laid the groundwork for the Denver of today."

One of them was Thomas Bayaud.

|||||||||

Bayaud had been dreaming of adventure and exciting challenges, but commitments to the family's import-export business kept him tied to New York. With his brother Theodore ready to take over company operations, Thomas could, at long last, set out. It was 1857 when he packed up and headed off for new life in America's West.

Somewhere along the way—it may have been near Buffalo—Bayaud joined a group escorting a wagon train bound for what was then Kansas Territory. When they reached the South Platte River at the base of the Rocky Mountains, he and the settlers drew lots for parcels of land along the river. Their new home was a scruffy mining camp called Denver City.

25. Thomas Bayaud, 1859. Courtesy of History Colorado.

Like so many others heading west, Thomas contracted a serious case of "gold fever." There had been a recent discovery of the precious metal in the Rockies, and cries of "Pike's Peak or Bust" were still bouncing off the mountainsides.

Calling Denver City a "city," however, was a little more than a reflection of wishful thinking by the gold prospectors. The "city" was nothing but a collection of tents, teepees, shacks, and shanties, as well as a few crudely constructed log cabins strung out along the banks of the South Platte and its tributary Cherry Creek. "A rough

The Man Who Never Forgot

and tumble place filled with many shady characters," remarked one observer. The editor of the newly created *Rocky Mountain News* called them "bummers" and said gamblers, prostitutes, and saloon keepers arrived in droves to "mine" the miners.

There were also Native Americans. The Cherokee, in fact, had discovered gold in the South Platte River years earlier, but they had seen no need to spread the information. Cheyenne and Arapaho also camped by the river annually and probably were aware of the gold. The chief of the Arapaho, Little Raven, was, at first, welcoming to the white men who seemed to arrive like a sudden fall of snow. He was even willing to share his camp with them. It was a decision he would live to regret when, six years later, the settlers massacred more than 150 of his people at Sand Creek.

None of the tribes, however, was prepared for what was about to befall their land and lives when a certain white man from Georgia brought his Cherokee wife home for a visit in July of 1858.

William Greeneberry Russell was one of the original Forty-Niners who had worked the goldfields of California. When he heard rumors of gold closer to his wife's home, he decided to try his luck there . . . and struck pay dirt. Word leaked out that he and his companions had spotted bits of gold in Little Dry Creek, one of the other tributaries of the South Platte. News of their discovery spread like wildfire and sent everyone into a frenzy. The mere whisper of the word "gold" could set off a stampede, one person noted, and stampede they did. By fall hundreds of prospectors had joined in, and when spring came in 1859, thousands more were panning for gold there and on other streams feeding into the South Platte River.

In those few months, Denver City, a ragtag town of about three hundred people, had become a throbbing mining camp of one hundred thousand or more. With no organized government, it was a place of "vendettas and vigilantism," one person said. William Hepworth Dixon, an Englishman who visited, wrote that in Denver "a man's life is of no more worth than a dog's." But he also acknowledged that people there had "perseverance, generosity and enterprise."

*What could be better,* Bayaud thought. *This is perfect! It's everything I pictured the West to be.* And so it was, in the summer of 1859, that

Thomas decided this was where he would end his westward journey, settle down, and turn his dreams into reality. Everyone, it seemed, was obsessed with striking it rich, and Bayaud was no different.

Staking a claim, be it for panning or hard-rock mining, was easy enough, but it was a rough-and-tumble affair. It involved, unsurprisingly, a wooden or iron stake with one's name scribbled on it, a so-called "monument," stuck in the ground at the northeast corner of the claim area. Claim jumpers found them easy to uproot or move; as often happened, a miner would return after a night at one of Denver's round-the-clock saloons (there would soon be more than four hundred of them in the city) to find his claim usurped or planted somewhere else. It was a risky system, but every starry-eyed hopeful who came to Denver to seek his fortune seemed to think the risk was worth it.

And still they came, the hopeful, the desperate, the daring, "traveling on foot, in covered wagons, by horseback and even pushing their belongings in wheelbarrows."

Thomas was in the middle of it all. He staked claims in Gregory Gulch along Cherry Creek close to where it joined the South Platte. Thousands joined him, jockeying for lots and scrambling for claims. The Gulch had been named for John Gregory, who discovered a gold-bearing vein there earlier that year. Within months of his "find," the Gulch became known as "the Richest Square Mile on Earth." It also was perhaps one of the most colorful ones, because one of Bayaud's neighbors was Mrs. Frank Duffield, a.k.a. Poker Alice, the cigar-smoking card player and brothel owner.

It is unclear how well Bayaud did as a prospector, or if his claims paid off as well as he hoped, but it quickly became apparent that Thomas had not left behind the business skills he'd acquired in New York. Miners needed equipment, he realized, and places to live. Not to mention ways to let off steam and have a good time. He was soon running a general store, a wholesale liquor store, and a hardware store. He also owned a sawmill and served as a representative for a timber company.

One of the other "Argonauts"—early settlers of Denver—said of Bayaud, "I regard him as one of the best of the remarkably large number of very bright men who were brought to Denver by a love of adventure in those early days."

Bayaud certainly wasted no time in proving he was indeed one of the brightest, because within four months of his settling in an ad appeared in the *Rocky Mountain News* announcing the arrival of a shipment of "Imported Wines & Liquors" from "bonded warehouses" in New York. Among the "delights being offered to the Pike's Peak Public" was "Champaign [*sic*], the veritable Charles Heidsieck." The ad had been placed by Bayaud's family's business in New York, calling attention to the wide variety of merchandise that was, of course, available in Thomas's store. There were even chandeliers and Havana cigars for any successful miners. As for Heidsieck's champagne, it had already made a splash back east, and there was no reason to believe it would be any less of a sensation here.

But Thomas was not ignoring other business interests. In September of 1859 he presented a plan to Denver City officials for building a timber span bridge over the South Platte. It would be situated at the foot of Fifteenth Street and, when completed, be a welcome time saver for people who often had long waits for a ferry to get across. Officials approved Thomas's plan and awarded him a twenty-five-hundred-dollar contract.

Problems and financial disagreements soon arose, however. When spring arrived and work on the bridge had yet to begin, city officials, fearing the whole project might collapse, sent a friend of Bayaud's, Sam Curtis, to talk with him and get things moving. Curtis told a historian in 1901: "I was on a committee to settle with T. J. Bayaud for building a bridge over the South Platte River at the foot of Fifteenth street. After many evenings, and drinking many of his whiskey punches, we finally reached a settlement, paying him largely in town lots which passed into the hands of Charles Heidsieck."

The settlement, Curtis said, also covered Bayaud's expenses, a long list that included "whisky one dollar, coffee and beans eleven dollars and twelve cents for the men" working on the bridge.

The bridge, when it was finally completed, was an impressive structure, but its existence was short lived. A historian of Denver recounted its fate:

From the beginning of things here in 1858 until May, 1864, historic Cherry Creek had been an inoffensive little stream in certain seasons of the years, and an invisible one in the other seasons with its broad sandy bed hot and dry. After midnight (May 19, 1864) the creek suddenly became an angry, roaring torrent that exercised its long-reserved powers of devastation without warning. Wreckage piling against the creek bridges, low, wooden affairs, had early in the proceedings loosened them from their bearings and away they had gone. The South Platte had risen to an unprecedented stage, flooding far beyond its nominal limits, and had quickly demolished the bridge at the foot of Eleventh street and another at the foot of Fifteenth.

Despite the problems, Bayaud was prospering and continuing to astutely acquire bits and pieces of land for himself and as an agent for others. Records show he already owned at least seven houses in Denver City, more than one hundred lots of land, and another one hundred acres along the South Platte on the edge of town. It appears at least one or two of the lots were purchased for his brother Theodore, who was Charles Heidsieck's sales agent.

In early 1860 Thomas decided to return to New York for a short visit. Charles also happened to be there. He had just received a letter from Amélie saying that Theodore was still not paying for champagne being shipped to him on consignment. It involved thousands of bottles and several hundred thousand dollars.

When Charles confronted him, Theodore offered one excuse after another. It was clear he was selling the champagne, because the agency was prospering and Bayaud was regularly ordering more. He just wasn't paying for it or, when he did, was paying less than the amount owed.[2]

Angry words flew back and forth, and Thomas must have heard some of it, for his presence was noted by Heidsieck, who made a brief mention to Amélie that Thomas was back "from a town named Dewer [sic]." The two had first met eight years earlier when Charles hired the Bayaud agency to represent his champagne company in America. They crossed paths again in New York in 1857 when Charles first confronted Theodore about irregular payments.

On both occasions, Charles and Thomas talked about the West and the thrill of seeking new adventures. At the time, Thomas was still trying to make up his mind whether to leave the family business and seek his fortune out West. Charles encouraged him to do so, to take a chance just as he had done in 1852 when against all advice he set off alone to the New World to introduce Americans to champagne.

Thomas never forgot what Charles told him. Nor did he forget what Theodore had done. At one point, according to Heidsieck's descendants, Thomas told Charles he was appalled at how his younger brother had cheated him and that if there was a way to make it up to Charles, he would.

||||||||

Although he had become a successful entrepreneur in Denver, Thomas Bayaud was concerned about much more than business. He was deeply religious and, according to one of his friends, "the most devoted and consistent follower of Christ that I know."

Soon after opening his liquor store, he turned an upstairs room into a meeting place for Episcopalians. With no minister, Thomas himself often conducted the services. When a minister was finally brought to Denver and parishioners were ready to build a church, Thomas helped finance it and became a member of the first vestry selected to manage affairs of the congregation. The name they chose for the new church was appropriate: St. John's in the Wilderness.

Thomas was an enthusiastic member and directed a boys' choir. He also gave the boys French lessons to make sure their pronunciation in French hymns was correct. "He was no fool," said one observer, "and definitely understood what it was like to be a young boy in the free and easy West so he paid them each a nickel for every choir rehearsal they attended."

Meanwhile, Thomas's instincts about his new hometown were proving correct. Although placer gold, the gold that was panned, had played out, causing many of the early arrivals to move on to more promising areas, hard-rock mining had begun as individuals and more and more companies burrowed into the mountains following veins of gold ore. With it came an increased demand for the supplies Thomas and others were selling.

The raucous little mining camp, still considered part of Kansas Territory, was rapidly turning itself into a supply hub for the entire area and into a real city with schools, hotels, churches, and shops. After first losing much of its population, as most mining camps did, Denver City was now, in the wake of the Civil War, attracting increasing numbers of people. Many were disaffected Southerners searching for new lives in the wide-open West, where starting over seemed as easy as just getting to town.

Among them was the man famous for advising, "Go West, young man, go West and grow up with the country." Horace Greeley arrived the same year Bayaud did, in 1859, to check out the goldfields on his tour of the West.

Many who went west did so in response to advertisements placed in newspapers "back east." Those ads stressed "the idealistic purity of the country" with its "vast expanse of unclaimed land ripe for the taking. Readers are assured that life out west will be far easier than the drudgery of farm life on the crowded east coast." The ads also declared that "recently arrived immigrants will find gold ready to be plucked from the ground or water, fertile land begging to be tilled and planted, and a temperate wilderness empty of human habitation and ready to be civilized by white Americans."

No mention was made of the Native Americans already inhabiting the land, more than a thousand of whom were at that point camped in the area. On February 18, 1861, the federal government "removed" that concern when it made it legal for towns to register themselves on what was called Indian land. The Indians were paid $1.25 per acre. Ten days later the U.S. Congress officially created Colorado Territory, the first step on the way to statehood, which would happen fifteen years later.

For nearly all of those who answered the newspaper advertisements or came in response to their own dreams, disillusion awaited. Only a very few struck it rich, and most found the work as hard as or even more demanding and dangerous than what they had left. They stood all day in freezing water panning for flakes of gold or trying to carve and drill tunnels into rock-hard mountains. And if that didn't keep them busy enough, they often fought with other would-be miners for stakes. Gold, they discovered, was not just lying around waiting for them to "pluck it."

Thomas Bayaud was instead "plucking" wealth from the land in a different way by accumulating property in Denver City and its surrounding area. Records at the Colorado Historical Society show that already by the end of March 1860, when he had been in Denver for less than a year, he owned land there valued then at more than forty-five thousand dollars, equivalent to nearly one and a half million dollars today. Over the next four years, his property empire and businesses continued to grow.

||||||||

On January 17, 1865, Bayaud took his horse from the stable and left Denver to check on his gold-mining claims around Cherry Creek. It was an icy day, and apparently his horse slipped and fell, throwing Thomas to the ground. Thomas was pinned under the horse and unable to get free. When he was found, he already was suffering from a severe cold that quickly turned into pneumonia. He was carried to the nearby home of a priest, where he died the next day. He was forty-nine years old.[3]

In Musquito, a gold-mining camp at the foot of the Rockies, the following note, dated January 21, was posted in a news sheet by one of its editors: "I have to chronicle a sad event that occurred in our town on Wednesday, the 18th; I refer to the death of Mr. Thos. J. Bayaud, who came to this place on Monday evening, and on the way contracted a heavy cold, which became rapidly worse until Wednesday morning, at nine o'clock, when he expired. Deceased was not known personally to our citizens, yet his reputation had arrived before him, and here all feel deeply the loss of a worthy, active, an energetic man, stricken down in the prime of life and usefulness."

Bayaud's funeral was held at St. John's in the Wilderness, the church he helped found, and was conducted by Father Kehler, the Episcopalian priest he brought to Denver. Hundreds turned out to mourn a man who had brought so much to the community. A street in Denver would be named in his honor.

After the funeral, Thomas's body was returned to New York for burial in the Bayaud family plot in Greenwood Cemetery in Brooklyn. He had never married or had children.

What he left behind, however, was a legacy that would dramatically change the life of a certain Frenchman and his family forever.

# 14

||||||||||

## "War Seems to Follow Me"

The years passed slowly . . . sometimes painfully. Charles worked continuously to build his new champagne house. There were still mind-numbing bills to pay off from his earlier business, and creditors to ward off who came at him like a swarm of angry bees. The bankruptcy court's ruling, while clearing Charles of any malicious intent or criminal wrongdoing, still meant that a large part of his company's profits were blocked and had to go directly to creditors.

Although Charles had worked to assure each creditor that they would be paid in full, not everyone was pacified. Payments were too slow, some complained. Lawsuits piled up, and he often found himself in court.

In the midst of all this Charles received some startling news. He had inherited land in Denver, Colorado, that was part of an estate belonging to one Thomas Bayaud, who had died. Charles had only a fleeting memory of Thomas, but recalled meeting him briefly in New York when he was there to iron out problems with his sales agent, who was Thomas's brother. Thomas had become upset when he learned that his brother was cheating Heidsieck, and he had promised to make it up to Charles if he ever could. If this were so, Charles realized it could be a way out of his financial nightmare. He quickly notified his creditors that he might be able to pay them sooner than expected.[1]

But there was a catch: Charles would have to go in person to lay claim to the property. Either that or send someone else with power of attorney to act in his behalf. Reluctant to leave a business that was just beginning to find its feet, but also fearful of returning to a country where he had been imprisoned, Charles sent a friend who volunteered to go in his place.

Within a few months, the friend was back saying that the whole thing was "a myth." There is no land in Denver, he said. The friend then began spreading the word that Charles had fabricated the entire story. When Charles proclaimed his innocence, many people refused to believe him. According to his oldest daughter, Marie, "Even people considered very intelligent began to question whether there was a place called Denver."

Once again, Charles found his integrity being questioned and his name being dragged through the mud. There seemed to be little he could do about it. He was convinced his "friend" had lied about the situation and had managed to get the property for himself before selling it and pocketing the money. There was no way of proving it, however. Buying and selling land in the West had always been a dicey proposition, he was told. Gold claims were often vandalized, and deeds could change hands with a simple signature.

With his claims of innocence met with skepticism and outright disbelief by people in Reims, Charles became tight-lipped. He would never talk about Denver again and never divulged who his so-called friend was. He vowed never to speak the man's name again.

||||||||

Charles's plight contrasted sharply with the larger picture in Champagne. Thanks to that extraordinary harvest in 1865, these were good times for most champagne producers. They were barely able to keep up with demand from customers both at home and abroad. After seeing sales plummet more than half during the Civil War, production levels were not only back to normal; they were climbing.

The financial success of champagne was reflected in Reims itself, where sweeping urban-renewal plans had been launched. As one American visitor described it, "Public promenades have been taste-

"War Seems to Follow Me"

fully laid out," though some of the walks are new and "uncomfortably gravelly" with not much shade to protect them yet. The visitor noted, however, that there were "tall and wide-spreading oaks and elms" along the broad avenue leading to the Aisne canal, a vital link to the Rivers Marne and Seine that enabled champagne makers to get their bottles to the coast for shipment abroad and further afield in France. Under the direction of Reims's mayor, Edouard Werlé, who also headed Veuve Clicquot, the avenue to the canal had been widened and lengthened to make access to loading docks easier and more convenient.

At the same time, special attention was given to preserving the older and more historical parts of Reims. One item saved was an ancient carving on the front of the Maison Rouge Hotel. It read: "In the year 1429, at the consecration of Charles VII, in this hostelry named then the Striped Ass, the father and mother of Joan of Arc were lodged, and their expenses paid by the city council." Even then, politicians could not resist the urge to brag.

But there was one thing missing in Reims, and that was any discussion of politics. "Louis Napoléon has put his firm finger on every lip," said Robert Tomes, the U.S. customs officer who had come to France to oversee the duty charged on champagne exported to America. "No one dares whisper the words *liberté, fraternité, egalité,* or hum the faintest stave of the Marseillaise." Tomes conceded, however, that the prosperity Napoléon III's reign had brought to the city meant that "there did not seem to be a man who was inclined, even if he dared, to doubt the benefits of imperial absolutism."[2]

Yet it was becoming clear there were problems waiting to disrupt the effervescent times. For all the emperor had done to modernize French industry and help Champagne by expanding the nation's railway system and improving its banking operations, there were too many stories of scandals and government corruption tainting his reign.

During Carnival in Paris one year, he'd been seen stumbling around, his eyes glazed from opiates, his speech slurred. According to witnesses, the emperor was "surrounded by drunken officers and prostitutes dancing the cancan." The party, they said, "finally ended at dawn with everyone collapsing in a rack of champagne bottles."

Like his uncle before him, Napoléon III had surrounded himself with ministers and other officials chosen more for their loyalty to the Bonapartes than to the welfare of the country. To ensure that loyalty, he showered them with extravagant gifts (his favorite general received four thousand dollars' worth of chocolates) and paid them huge bribes. He skimmed millions from the national treasury, setting up secret accounts to funnel money to his family and mistress. Mindful that French regimes rarely lasted more than twenty years, the emperor also kept seventy-five million dollars on deposit for himself in a London investment bank.

But that was a mere sideline compared to other miscues. His attempt in 1862 to gain a foothold in the Americas by setting up a puppet empire in Mexico had proved disastrous. Worse was what happened eight years later when he foolishly declared war on Prussia, the most powerful of the German states.[3]

It was a minor diplomatic flap that sparked it. Spain had deposed its Bourbon queen, a descendant of France's Louis XIV, and decided to replace her with a nephew of King Wilhelm I of Prussia. France protested, and Wilhelm decided not to push for installing his nephew on the throne. But the Prussian king said he still reserved the right for someone else in his family to inherit the throne.

There the matter might have ended had not Otto von Bismarck interfered. Bismarck was the Prussian chancellor and the real power behind the throne. He had been looking for a way to unite Germany's states under Prussian domination, and suddenly he saw how it to do it. Intercepting Wilhelm's written response to Napoléon III, he reportedly reworded it to make it sound as if the king was insulting France. An indignant Napoléon III, on July 19, 1870, took the bait and did just what Bismarck hoped: he declared war and dispatched troops to the Franco-German border. In a flash, the German states also did what Bismarck hoped and joined together to fight a common enemy. The Franco-Prussian War, also known as the War of 1870, had begun.

In Paris, crowds at train stations chanted "Rout the German blockheads" and held out bottles of wine to the departing troops. In Champagne, producers, including Charles Heidsieck, rushed to find ways to protect millions of bottles of champagne. Many built fake walls to conceal as much as possible. They took an old saying as a warning: "The German hates the Frenchman but loves his wine."

Two weeks after Napoléon III's declaration of war, several hundred thousand Prussian troops, along with thousands of reservists from throughout Germany, poured across the border, overrunning Alsace-Lorraine and nearly everything that stood in their way. Only one thing slowed them down: the weather. Heavy rains turned the chalky landscape into a morass of sticky, gray muck. Wagons sank to their axles as horses strained at their harnesses.

In the vineyards the picture was just as grim. This should have been the hottest, driest time of the year, but instead it saw vignerons doing everything they could to save their battered, water-logged vines. Lost on no one was the fact that the weather had changed the moment the invasion began. Once again, that ancient legend was proving true: God sends a bad harvest to mark the beginning of war.

The Franco-Prussian War would be the bloodiest of the century. New weapons made killing faster and easier. The French had the *mitrailleuse*, the world's first machine gun, which they nicknamed "the coffee-grinder." Their foes called it "the hell machine." Lethal as the *mitrailleuse* was, it was no match for Prussia's long-range guns.

As each attempt by the French to attack or counterattack was thrown back, Napoléon III, against all advice, announced he was taking personal command and moved his armies to Sedan near the Belgian border, little more than sixty miles from Reims. It was a terrible mistake. Sedan was surrounded by high bluffs; all the Germans had to do was bring up their artillery. There was no way for Napoléon III and his hundred thousand men to retreat or escape. "We've caught them in a mousetrap," said one delighted Prussian officer.

One of the French emperor's generals had a different view: "Here we are in a chamber pot, about to be shitted on."

On September 1 the German big guns opened up, raining twenty thousand shells on French forces and creating "a ring of fire the likes of which had never been seen," recounted one soldier.

The next day, a tearful Napoléon III surrendered his sword to King Wilhelm who had arrived to watch the battle. Thirty-eight thousand French troops had been killed, wounded, or taken prisoner.

The German onslaught had only begun, however. Paris was the primary target, and the route to get there ran straight through Reims. The thought of this made Charles shudder. The prospect of being caught in another war, especially one that pitted his country against Germany, his father's homeland, was almost more than he could bear.

Not only had his father been born and raised in Germany; Charles himself had studied there. It was almost a second home to him. Through the years he had relied on his German uncles for advice, and he remained close to them and their families. In addition, since his return from America it had become more important to him commercially; he had steadily been building up his business throughout the German states. But now, he realized, all that could be lost. He'd barely survived one war, and facing another was inconceivable.

In despair, Charles sat down at his desk and composed a sad and worried note to Amélie: "War seems to follow me."

# 15

IIIIIIIIIIII

## The Denver Miracle

It was cold, bitterly cold, the coldest winter Champagne had known in decades. "It's worse than that winter of 1859 in Boston," Charles thought. Snow had piled up in the streets and on roofs of houses; icicles hanging from the eaves curtained the windows. Even fires blazing all day in the fireplaces barely took the edge off the freezing temperatures.

Making life even more miserable was the presence of an occupying army. The Prussians had moved into Reims four months earlier, on September 3, 1870, after handing Emperor Napoléon III a devastating defeat and taking him prisoner in nearby Sedan. The Second Empire and all of its early optimism were dead; a sense of helplessness and hopelessness had settled over Champagne.[1]

Paris, too, was feeling the terrible cold as a new government attempted to hold out against the Prussians. Food and other essentials had been cut off by Bismarck's armies, which now surrounded the city. One sculptor helping man the city's defenses created a statue in snow and ice of *Resistance*, a naked young woman sitting atop a cannon with her arms determinedly folded. Freezing conditions kept the statue intact for days, long enough for an engraving of it to be done and distributed. Men guarding the city would fall asleep and never wake up—frozen to death.

Reports came in to Reims about near-starvation conditions in

LA RESISTANCE.

FIGURE OF "RESISTANCE," EXECUTED IN SNOW ON BASTION NO. 85.

26. The ice maiden giving a frosty reception to the Prussians. Authors' collection.

the besieged capital as residents resorted to eating dogs, cats, and even rats. Parisian officials ordered the slaughter of animals from the city's zoo to provide food for the desperate population. "It is devilishly cold here and no means of making a fire," the painter Édouard Manet wrote. "The coal is, of course, kept for cooking. And what cooking!" One only had to look at the *carte*, the menu, at the Café Voisin, just months earlier a symbol of the city's glamorous life. It refused to surrender to the harsh conditions and instead produced a Christmas dinner that included elephant consommé, bear chops, and marinated kangaroo. Its *pièce de resistance* was *chat flanqué par rats*, cat garnished with rats.

There was, however, no shortage of champagne for the dinner. Dozens of bottles of it and other wines were pulled out of Voisin's well-stocked cellars to wash down the exotic fare.

That was small consolation to champagne producers like Charles Heidsieck. France's economy was in tatters, and sales had plummeted 50 percent as transport came to a standstill. At the same time, the *crayères*, where millions of bottles were stored, were being emptied by thirsty Prussian soldiers who had no trouble ignoring orders to leave the cellars alone.

The Denver Miracle

The thirst of the troops was so pronounced that even an experienced career soldier like General Philip Sheridan was astounded. He was well aware of the adage, "Soldiers drink," but what he saw amazed even him. President Ulysses S. Grant had sent Sheridan to France as an observer during the Franco-Prussian War. The Civil War commander followed the Prussians as they marched the sixty miles from where Napoléon III had surrendered in Sedan to Reims. "Almost every foot of the way was strewn with fragments of glass from champagne bottles, emptied then broken by the troops," he wrote. "The road was literally paved with glass, and the amount of wine consumed (none was wasted) must have been enormous."

During earlier wars and occupations, some champagne makers like Jean-Rémy Moët and the widow Clicquot had resigned themselves to such losses. "Let them drink," they said. "They'll become our best customers afterwards." Charles wasn't sure he could wait that long. He'd managed to get his new company, Charles Heidsieck et Cie, off the ground, but he'd barely made a dent in paying off his debts, and more bills were coming in every day.

The picture, however, was about to become more dire. France's new government vowed to continue the war, and Bismarck's patience was running out. Three days after the New Year began, his armies surrounding Paris opened up, raining artillery shells and incendiaries on the city. Nothing was spared. Not homes, not schools, not churches, not even hospitals. Bismarck warned that he would occupy the entire country unless the French surrendered.

With their forces in disarray and plagued by mass desertions, the French government finally gave in and agreed to an armistice, which was signed on January 26. Although it would take four more months to hammer out a peace treaty that would essentially give the Prussians everything they wanted—Alsace-Lorraine and a war indemnity worth billions of dollars—the war was effectively over. Troops, however, would continue to occupy Champagne, including Reims, for another two years until France had paid the indemnity in full.

Part of that indemnity would fall directly on the champagne houses in what was called a *prélèvement libératoire*, a direct levy on the houses. Pol Roger had to pay three thousand francs, or just over eleven thousand dollars. De Venoge was levied nineteen thousand francs, or more than seventy-two thousand dollars. Moët & Chandon, the largest of the producers, was hit for thirty-eight thousand francs, which today would be almost $145,000. Figures for many houses, including Charles Heidsieck's, are missing.

In a sense, Champagne was being held hostage until the indemnity was paid. To make sure that happened, the Prussian commander of Champagne, the Grand Duke Mecklembourg-Schwerin, posted the following notice: "Troops are under orders to in no way to interfere with the harvest. The transport of wine barrels including those that are empty will not be stopped, nor interfered with in any part of territory of Champagne. All unauthorized entry into the vines, any damage will be severely punished according to the laws of war."

Soldiers, however, frequently found ways to get around the orders. For the people of Champagne, the misery seemed never-ending. Not only had their region borne the brunt of the occupation, but its economy was practically dead. Transportation remained crippled, crops had rotted on the vines, and more than two and a half million bottles of champagne had been pillaged. Reims itself had been turned into a Prussian administrative center with the occupying troops continuing to patrol the streets. It was a constant and bitter reminder of all that had been lost.

Heidsieck's losses mirrored those of other houses. Big or little, they all presented an irresistible target for Prussian soldiers who quartered themselves comfortably in the cellars and helped themselves to as much champagne as they wished.

||||||||

Charles's office in the heart of Reims was cold on that January day of 1871, and it was already growing dark. Amélie, the children and home beckoned, so he was reluctant to answer when someone knocked on his door.

"An urgent message for you," said the visitor, handing Heidsieck a piece of paper. It read almost like a formal summons: "L'Abbé Raverdy, grand vicaire de l'Evêque du Colorado, informe Monsieur Heidsieck qu'il est pour quelques jours à Bourgogne dans sa famille, et qu'il se met à sa disposition pour lui donner sur ses importantes propriétés de Denver, les détails les plus complets et les plus intéressants" (Father Raverdy, grand vicar to the bishop of Colorado, informs Mr. Heidsieck that for a few days he will be at his family's home in the village of Bourgogne, and will be available to give him complete and interesting details about his important properties in Denver).[2]

Charles was puzzled. *Property? What property? I don't own anything in Denver.* He told the messenger he didn't know a Father Raverdy, then tipped him and sent him on his way.

Charles had forgotten the message until he got home and felt the piece of paper in his pocket. He pulled it out and read it again. The priest was asking him to come see him in his hometown, Bourgogne, now known as Bourgogne-Fresne, about twelve kilometers from Reims. Bourgogne—the town of Bourgogne—suddenly rang a bell in Charles's memory. His mother had told him about a friend, an abbot who had once been the village priest. She had been involved in raising money for the church, and the abbot told her about a talented and intelligent young man who was hoping to go to seminary. That man's name was Jean-Baptiste Raverdy.

*But Denver?* This was not the first time Heidsieck had been notified that he had inherited land there. Five years earlier he'd been told that one of Denver's early settlers had left him his property. It didn't make any sense to Heidsieck. *Why would someone I don't know be giving me his land?* Although it sounded bizarre, Heidsieck sent a friend to check it out. When the friend returned, he told Charles that there was nothing there, that it was all a myth. It had left Heidsieck bitter and suspicious of any more "gifts." In the years that followed, he tried to put all thoughts of an inheritance out of his mind.

But now they came rushing back. Could there actually be something there? Something of value? Word from a priest, a man of God, made it seem possible. Why would such a man lie? With his debts still pressing, Charles's hopes began to rise again. According to his oldest daughter, Marie, who meticulously recorded every detail of the event in an unpublished manuscript, her father was "burning with impatience" to find out and decided to go immediately to Bourgogne and talk with Raverdy.

The weather, however, remained terrible. Temperatures had plummeted; Marie recorded that they were "glacial." Snowdrifts were piled high, and roads were impassable. Not a single coach was running, and Heidsieck was unable to find coachman willing to tackle the trip. He finally convinced the owner of a small inn to let him borrow his big, skinny trotter and a broken-down, two-wheeled buggy which Marie labeled a *tape-cul*, a rattletrap or a bone-shaker. Rough ride or not, when her father asked if she would like to come along she was not least bit deterred and "accepted with enthusiasm." The two bundled themselves up and took off for Bourgogne "in our picturesque carriage through an all-white, snow-covered countryside."

Raverdy's family home was a small, low-ceilinged cottage with an enormous fireplace and a few pieces of furniture. Everything, from andirons in the fireplace to a round table in the center of the room, showed they been well cared for and were polished to a brilliant shine, Marie noted.

Father Raverdy, she said, was tall and appeared "rigid and cold, a direct man who came right to the point." She and her father had barely removed their coats when the priest unfolded a map of Denver which he spread on the table and "his fingers began walking from one place to another, while explaining precisely the situation of each lot."

"Eighty lots here have been lost, but a hundred here can certainly be saved. Those along the Platte River have little value at the moment, but they could well acquire some. Here their value is considerable." (Father Revardy's fingers settled on the center of the city.) "On these over here we have a church and a school, and on the other one, the Methodists have their chapel. There they are building substantial houses, so you have rents to collect. These you probably should sell because I fear they may be expropriated."

Raverdy went on for half an hour, leaving both Charles and Marie dazed by what he was telling them. All of the property, the priest said, was the "legacy" of Thomas Bayaud, the older brother of Heidsieck's sales agent in New York. He related how Thomas had died in the winter of 1865 after being thrown from his horse and trapped in the snow before eventually succumbing to pneumonia.

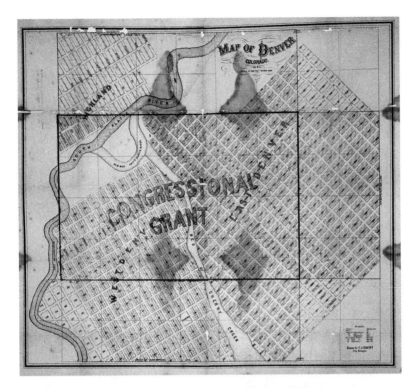

27. Map of Denver, 1865. Courtesy of History Colorado.

For Charles there was a momentary flashback as he remembered meeting Thomas in New York. He'd felt an immediate kinship with him, because the two were much alike in their desire for new adventures, Charles by trying to do business in America, Thomas by hoping to start a new life for himself out west. Charles had encouraged Thomas to follow his dreams, but that had been the end of it. Never did he imagine that Thomas would think of him again, certainly not this way, bequeathing him an enormous amount of land in one of the richest parts of the West.

Thunderstruck, it took Charles several minutes to compose himself. Then the questions came pouring out. "Are you sure about this? Why did Thomas do this? Is this his way of making up for what his brother did to me? How did you become involved? Did you know Bayaud, talk to him? If so, what did he say?"

28. Father Jean-Baptiste Raverdy. Courtesy of History Colorado.

Father Raverdy listened patiently and tried to respond to Charles's questions, but was reserved in his answers.

Yes, he said, he did know Bayaud, but he declined to say how he met him or how he became involved. Raverdy admitted there was no mention of Charles in Bayaud's will but that the land, "Thomas's legacy," as he called it, was his way of compensating Heidsieck for the harm his brother had done. Raverdy could not explain how eighty of the lots Charles inherited had been "lost"; he did not know if they had been taken over by squatters or been stolen by Heidsieck's "friend" five years earlier.

What the priest *did* say was something more important: that Heidsieck now owned a substantial amount of land in one of the richest parts of the West . . . *and* that he, Raverdy, was willing to serve as Heidsieck's legal representative and administer the inheritance. He would be Heidsieck's eyes and ears.

That was something he was well placed to do.

||||||||

Raverdy arrived in America fresh from his seminary education in France where he had been recruited as a missionary by the vicar general of the Archdiocese of Santa Fe. When he left for the New World, Raverdy was a deacon of the Catholic Church but not yet a priest. He would be ordained in America. He spoke no English, but his management skills were already evident to the coterie of French priests who made up the recently established Archdiocese of New Mexico.[3]

Raverdy was twenty-nine when the archbishop of Santa Fe decided to send him to tend the spiritual needs of Catholics arriving in Colorado, which was part of the New Mexico archdiocese. He was accompanied by another Frenchman, Father Joseph Projectus Machebeuf. The two arrived in Denver City on October 29, 1860, just as the Pike's Peak Gold Rush was cresting. They were surprised by what they saw. "We found not a city," Machebeuf wrote, "but the little village of Denver, made up of low frame stores, log cabins, tents and Indian wigwams on the banks of the Platte."

Raverdy was soon dispatched to an even more desolate place called Mountain City, later known as Central City, to become the first pastor of the new mining settlement. It was a wild time, with thousands of prospectors rushing to the area and competing for stakes in nearby Gregory Gulch, site of the area's first gold strike. One of those prospectors was Thomas Bayaud.

Meanwhile, Father Machebeuf had been traveling the goldfields, energetically buying up property for future Catholic churches or schools in any community he thought might become permanent. He was, it seems, a little too energetic. To finance his purchases, he borrowed money often at usurious rates. To make matters worse, many of his properties were in settlements that ended up becoming ghost towns.

The Vatican was not pleased, and it was left to Father Raverdy to clean up the situation. Raverdy was in charge of all property the Catholic Church owned or managed in the huge diocese of Colorado. In that capacity he would have poured through hundreds of deeds and documents, not only of the Catholic Church but of others as well, and been struck by how erratic and irregular the registration system was. Deeds often had words and names changed and numbers crossed out, or they were blotted with so much ink that they were virtually unreadable.

That may explain how those eighty lots Heidsieck inherited had been "lost" and how the "friend" he dispatched to Denver five years earlier had made off with land that belonged to Charles.

Heidsieck's knowledge of Denver was next to nothing before he met Raverdy. He thought the name was "Dewer" and was unsure which side of the Mississippi it was on. Raverdy did his best to fill him in, explaining that buying and selling property was risky business. Government oversight was "limp and inefficient," with land frequently being transferred from one person to another with a simple "X" or signature. It was made even more complicated by the fact that many of the gold prospectors flooding into the region came to escape checkered pasts and frequently changed their names. There were hundreds of "John Smiths" and "Jack Jones."

Although Denver had been consolidated as a city in its own right, it was nominally subject to the "jumbled laws of the strife-torn Kansas Territory, but without any way to enforce them," said one early historian of Colorado. "People were a law unto themselves."

"Frenzy and insanity" was how another observer described Denver's first years. "The country was literally swarming with people who crawled over the mountains, through the canons [sic], and up the gulches, nearly everywhere, searching for signs of gold." Newspapers reported that "people bet on everything, from dogfights to snowfall and gambled with mining stock, real estate, railroads and banknotes."

It was said that Denverites "lived solely on excitement and speculation," including occasional gunfights. The first shootout happened as winter descended in 1859, and concerned "accumulated disagreements" between two men who met on the east side of Cherry Creek with Colt revolvers. It ended quickly when one of the gunfighters was wounded in the abdomen—not seriously, but it ended the fight.

The second duel reflected not only the boredom of the winter months but also growing tensions in the country as civil war approached. On March 6, 1860, some of the early settlers of Denver sat down to an elegant dinner, during which one of them, Doctor J. S. Stone, "a man of extreme Southern views," took offense at something Mr. L. W. Bliss, "an anti-slavery man," said, and threw a glass of champagne in his face. The following day the two of them met to settle their differences near the Fifteenth Street bridge Thomas Bayaud was building. They were armed with shotguns. At thirty paces, as a crowd looked on, they turned and opened fire. Stone was shot in the groin and only died months later "after great suffering."

Those long winter months were hard on everyone, Raverdy told Heidsieck. When mines played out and people had no means of support, nearly everyone, including the city fathers, amused themselves with card games, using town lots and other parcels of land as poker chips. "They won and lost whole parcels of downtown Denver in a single evening."

One historian of Denver, writing in 1901, described the picture this way: "In the midst of all this ceaseless activity, honest toil, and worthy endeavor, were scores of human leeches and parasites, robbers, gamblers, desperadoes, petty thieves, and poor wrecks of womanhood. Like buzzards which detect their unsavory food from afar, these outcasts had come in flocks in the spring months of 1860."

That was just a year after Thomas Bayaud arrived, Raverdy said, but Denver stayed that way through most of the decade. Many people gave up and left, but those who stayed had no work and spent most of their time drinking or fighting. Fires, floods, and contaminated water led to a major epidemic.

In 1865, a few months after Thomas's death, lawlessness rose to new levels with attacks on supply trains. At the same time, profiteering sent prices skyrocketing. There was even a plague of grasshoppers of biblical proportions that decimated all vegetation in the area.

In the end, real estate prices plunged so low that entire blocks of Denver changed hands in poker games. There would soon be a dramatic turnaround, however.

Denver induced the railroads to build a spur that would connect the city to the brand-new transcontinental railroad. In May of 1870, one year after the Golden Spike was hammered in at Promontory Summit in Utah to join the Central Pacific Railroad coming from Sacramento to the Union Pacific coming from Omaha, the first locomotive chugged into Denver. A huge crowd was on hand to witness the occasion, including Native Americans, fur traders, and miners. Many of the spectators had never seen an iron horse before. This one carried one-day-old Omaha newspapers, two-day-old Chicago papers, and "two hundred whooping Masons."

The train's arrival marked the end of Denver's pioneering days and the birth of what would soon be the fastest-growing city in the West.

But there's a little more to the story. Miners from nearby Georgetown wanted to outdo the "Golden Spike" event in Utah and announced they were donating a silver spike, one of pure silver, to Denver to celebrate completion of the tracks. At least that was their intention. A fellow named Billy Barton and his friends said they would deliver the spike to the Colorado governor, who was presiding over the welcoming ceremony. On the way, however, Barton and his buddies passed through the town of Golden and stopped to quench their thirst. They got royally drunk and ran out of money. To keep on drinking, they pawned the spike.

Meanwhile, in Denver, Governor John Evans kept looking at the clock. The hour was late. Spectators were growing impatient, but there was still no silver spike. In desperation, when no one was looking, Evans grabbed a regular spike, wrapped it in white paper and held it up for the crowd to see. Everyone cheered. After the spike was cere-

29. Denver, ca. 1862. Courtesy of History Colorado.

moniously hammered in and the people had departed, Evans went back and retrieved the silver spike from the pawn shop. He kept it in his desk drawer as a souvenir.

||||||||

Within the first month of the railroad's arrival, more than a thousand visitors and tourists had been attracted to Denver, and over the next ten years it brought in at least one hundred new residents every day.

By 1880 the population of Denver was eight times what it was in 1870. Land values had soared, too. As Heidsieck struggled to grasp the magnitude of what had been given to him, he realized he now owned nearly a third, possibly closer to half, of Denver, the fastest-growing city in the West. With help from Father Raverdy, whose experience would enable him to sell that land at the right time and for the right price, Heidsieck knew then that he would finally be able to honor the debts he had vowed to pay. It wouldn't be easy and it wouldn't happen overnight, but for the first time since he'd been plunged into bankruptcy—for the first time since he'd been released from prison nearly a decade ago—he was finally able to take a deep breath.

He called it the "Denver Miracle."

# EPILOGUE

The "Denver Miracle" changed everything for Charles-Camille Heidsieck, and yet it changed nothing . . . at least not at first. The mountain of debt he faced when he was released from prison—equivalent to more than $12.5 million today—kept growing as interest accumulated, even as he chipped away at the principal.

The Denver inheritance would not be a magic wand that could wipe out all the debts with one wave.

In the months following his meeting with Father Raverdy, Charles was back on the road selling champagne to England, Germany, the Netherlands—nearly every country in Europe. He still had not fully recovered his health after his imprisonment, and the nonstop work quickly took its toll.

Raverdy, too, was working. With legal authorization from Heidsieck, he began sorting out deeds and clearing title to properties that were now Heidsieck's but which had been left in legal tangles for years. Gradually they began disposing of the properties. Not all of the sales records have survived, but in 1880, ten years after "the miracle," we know that ten of Heidsieck's lots were sold for 450,000 French francs, or about $1,750 today.

Denver, meanwhile, was exploding. It was fast becoming a major city where property values were skyrocketing. Lots worth a few hundred dollars when Thomas Bayaud acquired them were now changing hands for millions of dollars. Yet, that mountain of debt Charles faced was still there.

Also there was Ernest, his partner and brother-in-law. Things had gone from bad to worse and when their contract expired in 1876 the partnership was dissolved. It was a contentious "divorce," leading to lawsuits and a family rift in which many members never spoke to each other again.[1]

Charles labored on for another ten years, but in 1886 he admitted he was too tired to go on, that it was time to retire. His oldest son, Charles-Eugène, had been working at the company for several years and agreed to take over. Charles's younger son Henri would also join the company once he finished his education.

From the moment of his retirement, Charles-Camille never returned to the offices of the champagne house he had built. "I go out for a walk but when I get to the corner where the office is, I stop and turn around," he said. His sons were doing extremely well, he explained, so why should he get in the way.

Seven years later, on February 3, 1893, Charles-Camille Heidsieck passed away. He was seventy-one. Amélie and the children were with him when he died and promised to honor his dying wish: to finish paying off the debt.

It would be 1901, another eight years, before they were able to do that, nearly forty years after Charles had walked out of prison and into bankruptcy.

"Even miracles take a little time," Pablo Casals once said.

|||||||||

In 1895, two years after Charles's death, Charles-Eugène decided to do something his father had never done: visit the site of the "miracle." He traveled to Denver and toured the properties that had enabled their champagne house to survive. The amount of land and its value amazed him. It also amazed the *Rocky Mountain News* in 1949 when it published an article about Heidsieck's inheritance. The list of lots ran more than a page in the city's register, the paper said, and were now worth hundreds of millions of dollars.

The same year Charles-Eugène visited Denver, the spirit of Charles-

Camille proved it had lost none of its magic. Paul Mestrozzi, head of the royal military orchestra of the Austro-Hungarian Empire, wrote a new waltz that his orchestra premiered before Emperor Franz Joseph I at a lavish ball on January 26. It was "The Charles Heidsieck Waltz." The emperor was known to be a lover of champagne, but he also loved the waltz, for it later moved on to Paris and was performed at the most popular music hall of its day, La Scala.

If Charles-Camille had still been alive, he would have been thoroughly tickled before sweeping Amélie up for one more circle around the dance floor.

His panache was still flourishing in 1922 when his grandson Jean-Charles set off for America "to find out what's going on." What was going on was Prohibition. It had become law of the land but Jean-Charles wasn't fazed. "What a great opportunity!" he exclaimed. Like his grandfather, he was colorful and willing to take risks. Of all the champagne producers who did business during Prohibition, no one did it better than Jean-Charles.

Wasting no time, he began moving massive amounts of champagne into America, shipping it first to places like the Bahamas, where booze was still legal and where smugglers then took over, or moving it through Canada, across the Great Lakes, and into Detroit, where it was sold to people including Al Capone. In Canada, Jean-Charles was almost shot when "three goons pointed guns at my head." In Mexico he had drinks with a bootlegger who placed an order for twenty thousand cases of champagne. If the cops or Coast Guard was near, the bottles, which were wrapped in waterproof tar paper, were left on sandbars or simply dumped into the ocean, where they could be picked up later.

In 1959 a young couple digging for clams off Cape Cod saw several bottles bobbing in the water. The labels were gone, but when the bottles were opened, the brand on the corks read, "Charles Heidsieck, Extra Dry, 1920." There were still bubbles, and the champagne was still good.

Thanks to Jean-Charles, the Heidsieck champagne house sold more bubbly to the United States during the thirteen years of Prohibition than ever before.

In a way, Prohibition was a major force in creating a truly international market for champagne. Producers had to send their champagne through numerous other countries, such as Canada, Mexico, Panama, and the Bahamas. According to a study by Perrier-Jouët, the ingeniousness of the smugglers "knew no limits" and was a major factor in boosting champagne's popularity in the New World.[2]

That same study, which was commissioned in the year 2000, would surely have brought a smile to Charles-Camille Heidsieck's face, for it justified his faith in America and the way he did business. He once claimed, "There is no country where one can make one's fortune so easily on the condition that one has a product that pleases and sells well." Actually, it involved much more than that.

Perrier-Jouët had long believed that its champagne was just as good as Heidsieck's, and it was frustrated that it wasn't selling as well. To find out why, it hired an association of historians to study the problem. In their report they got right to the point. One name is key for understanding the American market, they said, and that name is Charles-Camille Heidsieck. "Rarely does personal history become so entangled in a country's history. Rarely does one person set the tone, the pattern for success as strongly as Heidsieck did."

That tone, the historians stressed, was set by his being there *in person*, by being in direct contact with customers and establishing personal relationships. Heidsieck was the only head of a major champagne house to do that. He was the one newspaper reporters followed, that people in restaurants sang songs about when ordering "a bottle of Charles." He was the one invited to parties and fancy receptions where government officials and other dignitaries—even the president of the United States—lined up to shake his hand. Other champagne houses, by contrast, including Perrier-Jouët, simply relied on agents and lower-level officials to conduct their business . . . and it made all the difference.

"The sale of champagne there certainly depended on the history of America," the historians said, "but also on the men chosen by each brand to assure its success and sale overseas. The example set by Charles Heidsieck is essential for comprehending the American market."

Incredibly, the study may never have been read. It was set aside when Perrier-Jouët underwent a change in ownership. It sat in a drawer, essentially forgotten, until an archivist discovered it two decades later. The study's conclusions, however, were as relevant as ever. Heidsieck's daring venture in the United States helped open the door for other *grandes marques*. "He set the example . . . his was the name others followed," the archivist said.

Today the United States is one of the world's largest consumers of champagne, second only to Great Britain in terms of the number of bottles imported. By another measure, however, it ranks first, since Americans are the biggest spenders, choosing to buy the more expensive, higher-quality brands . . . a success story that was foretold more than a century earlier when the champagne firm of G. H. Mumm created an ad showing Uncle Sam pouring champagne into his hat and proudly declaring, "I am the winner!"

Meanwhile, champagne's universal popularity has prompted dozens of other countries to get into the sparkling wine business, such as Italy with Prosecco and Spain with Cava. The world, it seems, is awash with bubbles. A number of Champagne houses, including Moët, Mumm, and Taittinger, now make sparkling wine in the United States. Law prohibits them from calling it champagne, so their bubbly is labeled simply as "sparkling wine, *methode champenoise*."

Whatever these sparklers are called, those who market them are still influenced by the steps taken by a young Frenchman who set off for America in 1852. "Champagne Charlie understood the importance of the personal touch and still today in the world of fine bubbles this touch is as important as ever," said Eileen Crane, former winemaker and director of Domaine Carneros, Champagne Taittinger's Napa Valley winery. "Great champagnes and other sparkling wines are so often enjoyed on milestones. They become part of our memories, our histories. Wines without bubbles can be fine but great bubbles become part of the joy of who we are. So we need a personal connection to the champagne we choose, the kind of connection Champagne Charlie established two hundred years ago."

Although these are good times in the champagne industry, everyone is aware of what Heidsieck himself knew: that good times do

## La Consommation du Champagne en Amérique

Extrait de
**" BONFORT'S WINE & SPIRIT CIRCULAR "**
NEW-YORK, 10 Janvier 1899

TABLEAU de l'importation du Vin de CHAMPAGNE
à New-York et plusieurs autres ports de l'Amérique
du Nord (*) en 1898.

| MARQUES | CAISSES de 12 bouteilles 1898 |
|---|---|
| G.-H. MUMM et Cⁱᵉ | 86.855 |
| Moet et Chandon | 34.206 |
| Pommery et Greno (**) | 28.318 |
| Heidsieck et Cⁱᵉ | 13.808 |
| Vᵛᵉ Clicquot | 11.669 |
| Ruinart Père et Fils | 10.271 |
| Louis Roederer | 9.095 |
| Perrier-Jouët | 8.535 |
| Piper-Heidsieck | 8.022 |
| Ernest Irroy et Cⁱᵉ | 3.585 |
| Bouché Fils et Cⁱᵉ | 2.147 |
| Duc de Montebello | 1.765 |
| Charles Heidsieck | 1.708 |
| Divers | 7.780 |
| Total | 227.761 |

(*) Sous réserve des envois que la douane n'aurait pas signalés.
(**) Les États-Unis seuls non compris le Canada.

Dessin de A. Willette.

L'Oncle Sam. — « Je t'ai vaincue, ma fille, et je suis crâneur parce que je bois
du Champagne G.-H. Mumm, tous les ans, comme s'il en pleuvait! »

**30.** A grinning Uncle Sam celebrates victory, 1898. He is saying to the young woman:
"I won you over, girl! And I'm proud because I drink Mumm champagne every day,
like it's raining." Courtesy of Champagne G. H. Mumm.

not roll on forever. "We're always looking over our shoulder to see what's coming," one producer told us. "No matter how good things are now, we're always looking toward the next crisis."

Today that crisis is climate change. Although there could be unexpected hailstorms or downpours or even blizzards, weather used to follow a pattern so predictable that producers hardly had to consult a calendar. Not now. "It hails when it never used to hail, rains in the summer when it used to be dry, is dry in the winter when it used to rain," moaned one grower.

In Champagne, record-breaking heat waves have recently sent temperatures soaring as high as 43 degrees Celsius—about 110 degrees Fahrenheit—something that would have stunned Charles Heidsieck. In 2019 the heat forced producers to jettison substantial portions of their harvest, because grapes were actually burned by the sun and thoroughly dried out. Harvests now routinely take place two weeks earlier than in the past, in August instead of September. Warmer temperatures have also spurred new diseases and seen vine pests reproduce at a faster rate, with four cycles a year rather than two.

The change in climate has forced growers to rethink nearly everything they do, even the way they plant their vines. No longer do they worry about spreading vines further apart to maximize the amount of sun their grapes get. Now, in an almost total reversal, hillsides with less exposure to sunlight are producing well-ripened grapes. And new locations are tempting producers, as well—England and even parts of Scandinavia.

It is a different battle, one Charles-Camille Heidsieck might not recognize, but the goal is still the same: to make quality wine, no matter what difficulties and struggles are thrown at them. Conflict is something the Champenois know well and know how to deal with. It is something they expect. It is what makes each glass of champagne feel like a victory.

That fatalistic feeling permeates Champagne—an inheritance from being the most blood-soaked region in all of Europe, perhaps in the world. The fatalism has soaked deep into the soil, been absorbed by the vines. It is in the *terroir* of the province. Nothing there has escaped war's savagery—not vineyards, not villages and cities . . .

Not even the dead.

When World War I unleashed its worst on the royal city of Reims, front lines came within three kilometers of the *caves* of Champagne Charles Heidsieck. Charles-Eugène Heidsieck, then head of the firm, moved himself, his workers, and their families underground into those *caves* in the fall of 1914. Most of them would live there until the end of the war, more than four years later. Above them German guns bombarded the city for more than a thousand straight days.

The cemetery where Charles-Camille Heidsieck was buried was not spared.[3] It was caught in what one witness described as "a hurricane of fire." Graves were blown open while private chapels, memorials, and tombstones were scattered across the land like beads from a broken necklace.

Lost in the destruction was Heidsieck's final resting place. War had indeed followed him, as he once said.

Even to his grave.

His remains were never recovered, but pieces of his tombstone were found . . . with this inscription: "He Has Left His Name to His Children as an Inheritance of Honor."

# ACKNOWLEDGMENTS

Champagne is a drink that almost demands to be shared, which may explain why we encountered so much generosity of time, spirit, and expertise while working on this book. Here are the people we'd like to thank:

Marie-France Beck "introduced" us to Champagne Charlie several years ago when we wrote *Champagne: How the World's Most Glamorous Wine Triumphed over War and Hard Times*. It was also she who introduced us to Mathieu Heidsieck and Sophie-Charlotte Husson, who opened their home and the Heidsieck family archives to us.

Dr. Daniel Sutherland responded to our Christmas Eve request like a genuine Santa Claus. Dan proved himself to be an astute historian and scholar as he carefully guided us through the Civil War even as other demands on his time were far more pressing. But he went much further and truly became a friend, bridging time zones and distances to help us in myriad ways through months of work.

Stephen Leroux, head of Champagne Charles Heidsieck, and his team provided us with documents and other materials as well as a few glasses of marvelous champagne.

James Gabler, a true gentleman whose work on Thomas Jefferson's travels and wines is a tour de force, graciously shared his notes and thoughts with us.

Eileen Crane, who headed Domaine Carneros for more than forty years, took time to give us a master class in bubbles in America.

Michelle DeFeo, president of Laurent-Perrier U.S., helped us understand the challenges the industry faces.

Stephanie Scherer's diligent research into nineteenth-century American newspapers turned up valuable nuggets for us.

Stephan Kraxner, an archivist for Pernod-Ricard, discovered a real treasure for us buried in a desk drawer: a long-forgotten study revealing how Champagne Charlie was regarded by his competitors.

We're also grateful to Colorado History, especially Bethany Williams and Jori Johnson at the Stephen H. Hart Research Center, who excavated file after file to come up with invaluable records for us and did so with incredible goodwill and speed.

We thank Brigitte Batonet, a stalwart at the Comité Interprofessionnel du Vin de Champagne, a master of details about champagne with a memory to match;

Norman Doyle, whose paper for the San Francisco Civil War Round Table zeroed in on important questions about Champagne Charlie; and

Dr. Evelyne LeJeune Resnick and Françoise Lafon, on whose friendships we imposed for help with nineteenth-century French.

Archivists who went far beyond duty for us include Alyssa Bentz, corporate historian for Wells Fargo, who not only gave us information on the Concord Coach but also pointed us to the French Gold Ingots Lottery; Rebecca Smith at the Williams Research Center of the Historic New Orleans Collection; Frédéric Mongin at the Bibliothèque Carnegie de Reims; and Isabelle Pierre, the Heritage Manager of Veuve Clicquot, Krug and Ruinart.

We also thank the team at Potomac Books, including our editor, Tom Swanson, and his assistant, Taylor Rothgeb, who was unstinting in her helpfulness and overall niceness.

Our agents Peter and Amy Bernstein proved they are among the best in the business.

But what really helped was being able to lean on old friends for advice and comfort, such as our former agent Robert Shepard, who nudged us to pursue the Champagne Charlie story before he went off to law school; Randy Resnick, who got us through countless technical glitches as only a patient friend can; Nick Prince, who helped bring back South African memories to us; and Gerry Holmes and Jennifer Ludden at NPR, two people who are always there when we need them.

We thank them all.

But especially we thank our daughters and grandson, who put up with our neglect and distraction as we worked on Champagne Charlie. They are the real sparkle in our lives.

# NOTES

## Introduction

1. Photo and account of Scott dinner are from the company archives of Champagne Charles Heidsieck. Suggested further reading is Scott's diary at Scott Polar Research Institute at University of Cambridge in England.

2. Damage in Champagne from World War I described in Forbes, *Champagne*, 182–83, 188.

3. Sales figures for champagne are based on records from Comité Interprofessionel du Vin de Champagne.

## 1. The First Sip

1. Details of the "first sip" are from the Mount Vernon Ladies Association of the Union (MVLA) from research prepared by Mary V. Thompson, January 7, 2000. Jefferson's order of champagne for Washington is from Gabler, *Passions*, 170.

2. Washington's purchases and Hunter's visit to Mount Vernon recounted by MVLA.

3. King Louis XV shipping regulations in Forbes, *Champagne*, 132–34.

4. Use of coal in furnaces for glassmaking is from Larkin and Hughes, *Stuart Royal Proclamations, Vol. 1.*

5. Jefferson's preference for champagne without bubbles from Gabler, *Passions*, 153.

6. Fears that sparkling champagne might disappear are explained by Bonal, *Le livre d'or du Champagne*, "XVIII Century Success and Widespread Consumption."

7. Sparkling champagne never brought to a good table, Gabler, *Passions*, 184.

8. Franklin's life in Paris is re-created from materials at the Benjamin Franklin Historical Society and from Gabler, *Passions*, 17–18.

9. Importance of wool as an industry in Champagne from Merriman, *Margins of City Life*, 183.

10. Importance of speaking a foreign language described by Tomes, *Champagne Country*, 91. For his work as a consular official in Champagne, see page 90.

11. Florent-Louis Heidsieck's work in a textile factory in Berlin from Charles-Henri Heidsieck, "Overview of Heidsieck Family," 4.

## 2. Young Charles

1. Description of Reims and preparations for coronation from Merriman, *Margins of City Life*, 177–81. See also Byrne, "Best Laid Plans."

2. Description of Charles growing up and his father's trip to Russia from Charles-Henri Heidsieck, "Overview of Heidsieck Family," 9; and Glatre and Roubinet, *Charles Heidsieck*, 10–13.

3. The bulk of this chapter is based on letters and documents from Charles-Henri Heidsieck, "Overview of Heidsieck Family," 12–13; and Marcel and Patrick Heidsieck, *Vie de Charles Heidsieck*, xii, 5–14.

## 3. Discovery of the New World

1. Descriptions of Liverpool when Heidsieck left for the United States from Charles-Henri Heidsieck, "Overview of Heidsieck Family," 16; and articles provided by Liverpool museums.

2. Ruinart's voyage to the United States described in "Ruinart in the United States," Maison Ruinart Archives, Reims, France.

3. Difficulties in understanding American market from Archimiste Equipe, *Les cahiers d'archimiste*.

4. Problems penetrating U.S. market described by Veuve Clicquot, Krug, Ruinart and Perrier-Jouët outlined in reports by those houses.

5. Erie Canal trip described by Abbot, *Marco Paul's Travels*, 44–47, 75–80.

6. French lottery for the Gold Rush in article by Kamiya, "Lottery Enabled France." See also Krebs, "The Société des Lingots d'Or."

7. Description of Concord Coach by Bentz, "Surprising Start."

## 4. Reading the Stars

1. Accounts of the Second Empire and Napoléon III from Musée d'Orsay, "Spectacular Second Empire."

2. Declining fortunes of Champagne's red wine from Guy, *When Champagne Became French*, 50–53.

3. Champagne's growing popularity in the nineteenth century described by Bonal, *Le livre d'or du Champagne*.

4. Heidsieck's legal troubles with Piper-Heidsieck, Charles-Henri Heidsieck, "Overview of Heidsieck Family," 16.

5. Urban renewal in Reims described in Taquet de Caffarelli's article "L'industrie textile à Reims." Also in Tomes, *Champagne Country*.

## 5. The Panic

1. Panic of 1857 and tumult in New York City described by Potter, *Impending Crisis*.

2. Phony champagne and fraud from Gabler, *Passions*, 107–8, 205–6; and Bonal, *Le livre d'or du Champagne*.

### 6. The Lion of New York

1. Newspapers describe Heidsieck's plans, *Frank Leslie's Illustrated Newspaper*, January 28, 1860.

2. Story of Champagne Charley Townshend from several sources, including "Boston 1775," a blog by J. L. Bell, https://boston1775.blogspot.com/search?q=champagne.

### 7. Southern Comfort

1. Letters from Charles to his wife in Marcel and Patrick Heidsieck, *Vie de Charles Heidsieck*, 63, 67, 70–73.

2. Heidsieck visits a slave auction, Marcel and Patrick Heidsieck, *Vie de Charles Heidsieck*, 27–28.

3. Sale of slaves by Pierce Butler in Baily, *Weeping Time*, 3–11.

4. Heidsieck's description of the bayou, Marcel and Patrick Heidsieck, "Adventures of a Citizen of Rheims," 77–84.

5. His account of Old Billy and camping out from Marcel and Patrick Heidsieck, *Vie de Charles Heidsieck*, 94–99, and their "Adventures of a Citizen of Rheims," 35–39.

6. Heidsieck's view of slavery, Marcel and Patrick Heidsieck, *Vie de Charles Heidsieck*, 89–91, and their "Adventures of a Citizen of Rheims," 24–29.

7. Deslondes slave uprising from Barnes, "America's Largest Slave Revolt."

8. John Brown's rampage, Lapore, *These Truths*, 281–85.

9. Hunting opossums from Stephen Winick, "A Possum Crisp and Brown: The Opossum and American Foodways." August 15, 2019, https://blogs.loc.gov/folklife/2019/08/a-possum-crisp-and-brown-the-opposum-and-american-foodways/.

10. Heidsieck says good-bye to Dora before returning to New York, Marcel and Patrick Heidsieck, "Adventures of a Citizen of Rheims," 22.

### 8. "It's War"

1. Heidsieck's arrival in Boston when war is declared and the confrontation with his sales agent in New York, Marcel and Patrick Heidsieck, *Vie de Charles Heidsieck*, 108, 112–14.

2. Reconstruction of the confrontation and the tensions surrounding it is based on two sources. One of these wrote how Charles "vigorously defended his rights," and the other described the agent's "inelegant behavior."

3. Discussion of erratic weather by Hager, "Weather It All Mattered"; how generals looked to the skies to decide on campaigns from article contributed by Kathryn Shively Meier.

4. All descriptions of guerrilla warfare from Sutherland, *A Savage Conflict*.

5. Efforts to recover his money, letters to his wife, fall of New Orleans, Charles-Henri Heidsieck, "Overview of Heidsieck Family," 17–19; and Marcel and Patrick Heidsieck, *Vie de Charles Heidsieck*, 112–14.

### 9. The Beast

1. Description of New Orleans from www.mardigrasneworleans and various other sources, including the History of New Orleans Museum in New Orleans.

2. Butler as child and lawyer recounted by Hearn, *When the Devil Came Down to Dixie*, 7–22.

3. Butler's treatment of slaves as "contraband of war" in Smith, "The Beast Unleashed," 250.

4. Butler's victory at Cape Hatteras and Lincoln's joy, Hearn, *When the Devil Came Down to Dixie*, 34–36.

5. Butler is one of the most controversial figures of the Civil War, and our information comes from several sources, the most important being West, *Lincoln's Scapegoat General*, and Hearn, *When the Devil Came Down to Dixie*.

6. Warning that Butler's life would be in "utmost danger" if Mumford were executed from Parton, *General Butler in New Orleans*, 346–47.

7. Heidsieck's growing frustration over money, homesickness, Marcel and Patrick Heidsieck, *Vie de Charles Heidsieck*, 123–26.

8. French government warns citizens they could lose their citizenship, *Evenements 1861, Chronologie de la France*, September 28, 1861.

9. Heidsieck's efforts to collect money and his arrest by Butler, from Marcel and Patrick Heidsieck, *Vie de Charles Heidsieck*, 144–50, and their "Adventures of a Citizen of Reims," 54–59.

### 10. Into the Jaws

1. Description of Fort Jackson and Heidsieck's imprisonment, Marcel and Patrick Heidsieck, "Adventures of a Citizen in Reims," 63–69.

2. Kellogg's description of prison camps, article by Johnson, "Sgt. Major Robert H. Kellogg." Suggested further reading, Flavion, "Suffering and Survival," and McGovern, *Abraham Lincoln*.

3. Letter-writing campaign to save Heidsieck, Marcel and Patrick Heidsieck, *Vie de Charles Heidsieck*, 151, 162–65. Also Glatre and Roubinet, *Charles Heidsieck*, 73–74.

4. Butler letter to Halleck explaining why he arrested Heidsieck, *War of the Rebellion: Official Records*, Series 1, vol. 15, pp. 534–35.

5. Uproar in French parliament by Glatre and Roubinet, *Charles Heidsieck*, 76.

6. England building ships for Confederacy from Jones, *Blue & Gray Diplomacy*, 191–201.

7. Halleck letter ordering Butler to change conditions for Heidsieck's freedom, *War of the Rebellion: Official Records*, series 1, vol. 15, p. 674.

### 11. "We Are Not in Venice"

1. Heidsieck's release from prison, Glatre and Roubinet, *Charles Heidsieck*, 177, and Marcel and Patrick Heidsieck, "Adventures of a Citizen of Reims," 67–68.

2. Butler's sale of salt by Hearn, *When the Devil Came Down to Dixie*, 189. More corruption in chapter 10, "The Brothers Butler," 180–97.

3. Butler's war against foreign consuls, Hearn, *When the Devil Came Down to Dixie*, 142–60.

4. Butler's departure from New Orleans, Hearn, *When the Devil Came Down to Dixie*, 214–16, 219, 221–23.

5. Heidsieck meeting with bankruptcy judge, Charles-Henri Heidsieck, "Overview of Heidsieck Family," 22; and Glatre and Roubinet, *Charles Heidsieck*, 77.

6. Report that the emperor is sending a warship to rescue Heidsieck from "The French Emperor and Charles Heidsieck," *The American Gentleman's Newspaper*, December 1862.

7. Attempted assassination of Heidsieck from Marcel and Patrick Heidsieck, *Vie de Charles Heidsieck*, 39. Also from their "Adventures of a Citizen of Reims," 69.

### 12. The Homecoming

1. Heidsieck's return home, Changeux, "Un français en Amérique," 34–35.

2. Czar Alexander's love of champagne, Glatre, *Chronique des vins de Champagne*, 209.

3. Lincoln's second inaugural ball by Megan Gambino in "Document Deep Dive." Also by Bouterie, *Champagne Celebration*.

4. Heidsieck's problems with brother-in-law, Charles-Henri Heidsieck, "Overview of Heidsieck Family," 23.

5. Tomes describes the harvest of 1865 and wines exported to United States in *Champagne Country*, 109–18.

### 13. The Man Who Never Forgot

1. Denver's founding and Thomas Bayaud's arrival, History Colorado Archives (HCA). Quotation "It was as if the angels . . ." from Smiley, *History of Denver*.

2. When Heidsieck met Bayaud, Charles-Henri Heidsieck, "Overview of Heidsieck Family," 25.

3. Bayaud's death, HCA.

### 14. "War Seems to Follow Me"

1. Heidsieck is notified he has inherited land in Denver, Changeux, "Un français en Amérique," 39–41.

2. Napoléon's absolutism, Tomes, *Champagne Country*, 17.

3. Dealings with Mexico and Franco-Prussian War from Jones, *Blue & Gray Diplomacy*, 270.

### 15. The Denver Miracle

1. Winter in Champagne and effect of German occupation, Changeux, "Un français en Amérique," 41.

2. Raverdy's message to Heidsieck described by Heidsieck's daughter Marie in her "Un français en Amérique," 40.

3. Raverdy's history and the problems of buying land in Denver from HCA. Also by Smiley, *History of Denver*.

### Epilogue

1. Heidsieck's resumption of business and family problems, Glatre and Roubinet, *Charles Heidsieck*, 86. Also Charles-Henri Heidsieck, "Overview of Heidsieck Family," 25–28.

2. Study by Perrier-Jouët from documents of that champagne house.

3. Destruction of Heidsieck's grave in World War I, Changeux, "Un français en Amérique," 43–44. Also Glatre and Roubinet, *Charles Heidsieck*, 90.

# BIBLIOGRAPHY

## Manuscripts and Archives

Benjamin Franklin Historical Society, Philadelphia.

Champagne Charles Heidsieck, Reims, France.

Changeux, Marie. "Un français en Amérique pendant la guerre de secession." 1919–20.

Colonial Williamsburg, Williamsburg VA.

Comité Interprofessionnel du Vin de Champagne, Epernay, France.

Doyle, Norman Patrick. "Champagne Charlie and the Beast of New Orleans: The Story of French Champagne Maker Charles-Camille Heidsieck and His Imprisonment in New Orleans in 1862 by General Benjamin Franklin Butler." San Francisco, manuscript for the San Francisco Civil War Roundtable, 2006.

Heidsieck, Charles-Henri. "Overview of Heidsieck Family." Reims, France, n.d.

Heidsieck, Marcel, and Patrick Heidsieck. "The Adventures of a Citizen of Rheims in the United States in 1857, 1860, and 1861, during the American War of Secession." Compiled from Heidsieck Family Papers. Reims, France, 1957.

History Colorado Archives, Denver.

Mount Vernon Ladies Association of the Union, Mount Vernon VA.

Thomas Jefferson Foundation, Charlottesville VA.

## Published Works

Abbott, Jacob. *Marco Paul's Travels on the Erie Canal.* New York: Harper & Bros., 1852.

Ameur, Farid. "'Au nom de la France, restons unis!' Les milices françaises de La Nouvelle-Orleans pendant la guerre de Sécession." *Bulletin de l'Institut Pierre Renouvin*, no. 28 (February 2008): 81–106.

Archimiste Equipe. *Les cahiers d'archimiste: Champagne Perrier-Jouët.* July 2000.

Baily, Anne C. *The Weeping Time: Memory and the Largest Slave Auction in American History.* New York: Cambridge University Press, 2017.

Barnes, Rhae Lynn. "America's Largest Slave Revolt, the German Coast Uprising of 1811."
https://ushistoryscene.com/.

Bentz, Alyssa. "The Surprising Start of Wells Fargo and Company." Wells Fargo History, 1999.

Bonal, François. *Le livre d'or du Champagne*. Paris: Éditions du Grand-Pont, 1984.

Bouterie, Leslie. *A Champagne Celebration*. Washington DC: President Lincoln's Cottage, 2010.

Brenneman, Bill. *Miracle on Cherry Creek*. Denver: World Press, 1973.

Byrne, Janet S. "The Best Laid Plans." *The Metropolitan Museum of Art Bulletin* 17, no. 7 (1959): 183–95.

Catton, Bruce. *A Stillness at Appomattox*. Garden City NY: Doubleday & Company, 1954.

Edwards, H. Sutherland. "The Germans in France." Part of a series of articles by the correspondent during the Franco-Prussian War for *London Times*, 1871.

Egan, Timothy. *The Immortal Irishman: The Irish Revolutionary Who Became an American Hero*. Boston: Houghton Mifflin Harcourt, 2016.

Faith, Nicholas. *The Story of Champagne: The History and Pleasures of the Most Celebrated of Wines*. New York: Facts on File, 1989.

Flavion, Gary. "Suffering and Survival." *American Battlefield Trust*, July 12, 2019.

Forbes, Patrick. *Champagne: The Wine, the Land, the People*. London: Victor Gollancz, 1985.

"The French Emperor and Charles Heidsieck." *The American Gentleman's Newspaper*, December 1862.

Gabler, James M. *Passions: The Wines and Travels of Thomas Jefferson*. Baltimore: Bacchus Press, 1995.

Gambino, Megan. "Document Deep Dive: The Menu from President Lincoln's Second Inaugural Ball." *Smithsonian Magazine*, January 15, 2013.

Genovese, Eugene D. *Roll, Jordan, Roll*. New York: Vintage Books, 1972.

Glatre, Eric. *Chronique des vins de Champagne*. Chassigny: Castor & Pollux, 2001.

Glatre, Eric, and Jacqueline Roubinet. *Charles Heidsieck: Un pionnier et un homme d'honneur*. Paris: Stock, 1995.

Guy, Kolleen M. *When Champagne Became French*. Baltimore: Johns Hopkins University Press, 2003.

Hager, Christopher. "Weather It All Mattered: How the Weather in 1862 Reflected the Broader Social Climate." December, 20, 2012. Commons.Trincoll.edu.

Hearn, Chester G. *When the Devil Came Down to Dixie: Ben Butler in New Orleans*. Baton Rouge: Louisiana State University Press, 1997.

Heidsieck, Marcel, and Patrick Heidsieck. *Vie de Charles Heidsieck*. Reims: Privately published, 1962.

Howe, Daniel Walker. *What Hath God Wrought: The Transformation of America, 1815–1848*, New York: Oxford University Press, 2007.

Johnson, Danielle. "Sgt. Maj. Robert H. Kellogg: 'I wonder if they know of our real condition here.'" Wethersfield CT: Wethersfield Historical Society, 2011.

Jones, Howard. *Blue & Gray Diplomacy: A History of Union and Confederate Foreign Relations*. Chapel Hill: University of North Carolina Press, 2010.

Kamiya, Gary. "Lottery Enabled France to Get Rid of Thousands." *San Francisco Chronicle*, September 4, 2015.

Kielstra, Paul Michael. *The Politics of Slave Trade Suppression in Britain and France, 1814–1848: Diplomacy, Morality, and Economics*. Houndsmills, Basingstoke: Palgrave Macmillan, 2000.

Krebs, Albert. "The Société des Lingots d'Or (1850–1853): Une épisode de la ruée vers l'or des français en Californie." *Revue de Deux Mondes*, July 1, 1967, 43–55.

Lepore, Jill. *These Truths*. New York: Norton, 2018.

Lonn, Ella. *Foreigners in the Confederacy*. Chapel Hill: University of North Carolina Press, 1940.

McGovern, George. *Abraham Lincoln*. New York: Times Book Division, Henry Holt, 2008.

Merriman, John M. *The Margins of City Life*. New York: Oxford University Press, 1991.

Musée d'Orsay. "The Spectacular Second Empire, 1852–1870." www.musee/orsay.fr.

Nye, Russel B. *Society and Culture in America, 1830–1860*. New York: Harper & Row, 1974.

Parton, James. *General Butler in New Orleans*. New York: Mason Brothers, 1864 (Forgotten Books Reprint).

Potter, David M. *The Impending Crisis: America before the Civil War, 1848–1861*. New York: Harper Perennial, 1976.

Rokka, Joonas. "Champagne: Four Founding Myths of a Global Icon." *The Conversation*, January 8, 2018.

Sainlaude, Steve. *France and the American Civil War: A Diplomatic History*. Chapel Hill: University of North Carolina Press, 2019.

Smiley, Jerome C. *History of Denver*. Denver: The Denver Times, 1901.

Smith, Michael T. "The Beast Unleashed: Benjamin F. Butler and Conceptions of Masculinity in the Civil War North." *New England Quarterly* 79, no. 2 (June 2006): 248–76.

Stampp, Kenneth M. *The Peculiar Institution: Slavery in the Ante-bellum South*. New York: Vintage Books, 1956.

Larkin, James E., and Paul L. Hughes, eds. *Stuart Royal Proclamations, Vol. 1: Royal Proclamations King James I, 1603–25*. Oxford: Oxford University Press, 2020.

Sutherland, Daniel E. *A Savage Conflict: The Decisive Role of Guerrillas in the American Civil War*. Chapel Hill: University of North Carolina Press, 2009.

Taquet de Caffarelli, Évelyne. "L'industrie textile à Reims: Une reconversion." *Travaux de l'Institut Géographique de Reims*, no. 4 (1970): 1–83.

Tomes, Robert. *The Champagne Country*. New York: George Routledge & Sons, 1867.

*The War of the Rebellion: A Compilation of the Official Records of the Union and Confederate Armies*. Washington DC: Government Printing Office, 1880–1901.

West, Richard S. *Lincoln's Scapegoat General: A Life of Benjamin F. Butler, 1818–1893*. Boston: Houghton Mifflin, 1965.

# INDEX

Index